Geoffrey Chaucer's *The Canterbury Tales*

A CASEBOOK

CASEBOOKS IN CRITICISM
Recent Titles

William Faulkner's *Absalom, Absalom!* A Casebook
Edited by Fred Hobson

Edith Wharton's *The House of Mirth*: A Casebook
Edited by Carol J. Singley

James Joyce's *Ulysses*: A Casebook
Edited by Derek Attridge

Joseph Conrad's *Heart of Darkness*: A Casebook
Edited by Gene M. Moore

Ralph Ellison's *Invisible Man*: A Casebook
Edited by John F. Callahan

Orson Welles's *Citizen Kane*: A Casebook
Edited by James Naremore

Alfred Hitchcock's *Psycho*: A Casebook
Edited by Robert Kolker

D. H. Lawrence's *Sons and Lovers*: A Casebook
Edited by John Worthen and Andrew Harrison

Cervantes' *Don Quixote*: A Casebook
Edited by Roberto González Echevarria

Fyodor Dostoevsky's *Crime and Punishment*: A Casebook
Edited by Richard Peace

Charlotte Brontë's *Jane Eyre*: A Casebook
Edited by Elsie B. Michie

Jane Austen's *Emma*: A Casebook
Edited by Fiona Stafford

Ezra Pound's *Cantos*: A Casebook
Edited by Peter Makin

William Wordsworth's *The Prelude*: A Casebook
Edited by Stephen Gill

GEOFFREY CHAUCER'S
The Canterbury Tales

◆　◆　◆

A CASEBOOK

Edited by
Lee Patterson

OXFORD
UNIVERSITY PRESS

2007

OXFORD
UNIVERSITY PRESS

Oxford University Press, Inc., publishes works that further
Oxford University's objective of excellence
in research, scholarship, and education.

Oxford   New York
Auckland   Cape Town   Dar es Salaam   Hong Kong   Karachi
Kuala Lumpur   Madrid   Melbourne   Mexico City   Nairobi
New Delhi   Shanghai   Taipei   Toronto

With offices in
Argentina   Austria   Brazil   Chile   Czech Republic   France   Greece
Guatemala   Hungary   Italy   Japan   Poland   Portugal   Singapore
South Korea   Switzerland   Thailand   Turkey   Ukraine   Vietnam

Copyright © 2007 by Oxford University Press, Inc.

Published by Oxford University Press, Inc.
198 Madison Avenue, New York, New York 10016

www.oup.com

Oxford is a registered trademark of Oxford University Press

Library of Congress Cataloging-in-Publication Data
Geoffrey Chaucer's The Canterbury tales : a casebook /
edited by Lee Patterson.
p. cm. — (Casebooks in criticism)
Includes bibliographical references.
ISBN-13 978-0-19-517573-8; 978-0-19-517574-5 (pbk.)
ISBN 0-19-517573-5; 0-19-517574-3 (pbk.)
1. Chaucer, Geoffrey, d. 1400 Canterbury tales.   2. Christian
pilgrims and pilgrimages in literature.   3. Tales, Medieval—
History and criticism.   I. Patterson, Lee.   II. Series.
PR1874G46 2006
821'.1—dc22   2006003074

Preface

The essays in this volume were chosen with one goal in mind: to help readers new to the text and/or the criticism understand those portions of the *Canterbury Tales* that are most frequently taught. This selection does not try to sample every sort of critical work currently being practiced, nor does it seek to present the most recent directions in Chaucer criticism. While other anthologies of essays have that as their goal, this one aims to be helpful to the relative newcomer to Chaucer's poetry. This does not mean, of course, that scholars and critics familiar with Chaucer and Chaucer criticism might not find these essays illuminating. All of the essays provide valuable and trenchant commentaries, and many of the points made here seem sometimes to have gotten lost in the pressure to find something new to say about an old text. Nor are these essays all in agreement on the basic assumptions that underlie the *Canterbury Tales*. Readers will find fruitful areas of disagreement and will have to make up their own minds about a number of fundamental issues. The introduction is meant to introduce not these particular essays but the *Canterbury Tales* as a whole.

In order to provide the reader with a sense of how other critics have dealt with the central issues of the tales under discussion, brief suggestions for further reading have been appended to each of the essays. The amount of criticism on Chaucer is vast, so any suggestions must be a small selection. The same is true of the suggested reading at the end of the volume, which is restricted to materials that are likely to be of special help to students. The Web site of the New Chaucer Society (http://artsci.wustl.edu/~chaucer/) provides access to a searchable bibliography of virtually all Chaucer criticism published since 1980.

In the interest of space, some of the essays in this volume, especially those excerpted from books, have been edited. With the exception of the essay by Professor Wentersdorf, who is deceased, the authors have approved the changes that have been made. I have occasionally added notes to the essays to clarify issues that might not be familiar to the reader. These notes are enclosed in square brackets.

Credits

Berger, Harry, Jr., "Pleasure and Responsibility in the Franklin's Tale," *Chaucer Review* 1 (1967): 135–56. Reprinted by permission of Penn State University Press.

Hanning, Robert W., "'The Struggle between Noble Designs and Chaos': The Literary Tradition of Chaucer's Knight's Tale," *Literary Review* 23 (1980): 519–41. Reprinted with permission from the author.

Kolve, V. A., "Nature, Youth, and Nowell's Flood," from *Chaucer and the Imagery of Narrative: The First Five Tales* (Stanford, Calif.: Stanford University Press, 1984), pp. 158–216. Reprinted by permission of Stanford University Press.

Leicester, H. Marshall, "Of a Fire in the Dark: Public and Private Feminism in the Wife of Bath's Tale," *Women's Studies* 11 (1984): 157–78. Reprinted with permission from the author.

Mann, Jill, "The General Prologue and Estates Literature," from *Chaucer and Medieval Estates Satire* (Cambridge: Cambridge University Press, 1973), pp. 1–16, 187–202. Reprinted by permission of Cambridge University Press.

Patterson, Lee, "The Pardoner's Dilemma," from "Chaucer's Pardoner on the Couch: Psyche and Clio in Medieval Literary Studies," *Speculum* 76 (2001): 638–80. Reprinted by permission of *Speculum*.

Pearsall, Derek, "A Reading of the Nun's Priest's Tale," from *A Variorum Edition of the Works of Geoffrey Chaucer:* The Canterbury Tales, vol. 2, pt. 9: *The Nun's Priest's Tale,*

Contents

Geoffrey Chaucer's *The Canterbury Tales*

A CASEBOOK

Introduction

LEE PATTERSON

◆　◆　◆

G EOFFREY CHAUCER WAS born about 1340 and died in October 1400. His poetry was written during a time when English writers were beginning once again to produce works of lasting literary merit. Prior to the Norman conquest of 1066, the most extensive and sophisticated vernacular literature in Europe was composed in England. Written in the language we now designate as Old English or Anglo-Saxon, this literature produced both poetic masterpieces—*Beowulf* is still the best known, but there are other epic and especially lyric poems of great skill and interest—and a large body of prose, some of it devotional, much of it dealing with more worldly topics such as history and the natural world. But with the coming of the Normans and the cultural dominance of French (or Anglo-Norman, as the French spoken and written in England is called), the number of original works in English diminished dramatically. But then, in the latter half of the fourteenth century, we witness a sudden efflorescence of great literature. Some of it harks back, by routes of transmission that are not fully understood, to the alliterative verse of Anglo-Saxon England. Examples include the great works *Pearl* and *Sir Gawain and the Green Knight*, composed by a single, anonymous poet, who also wrote two and perhaps three other astonishingly elegant poems. In addition to this anonymous poet, there are numerous others who produced alliterative poems, including many romances, that range from the mediocre to the brilliant. In addition, William Langland, a priest about whom we know little, composed and then continuously revised his massive and powerful *Piers Plowman*—also written in alliterative verse—sometime during the last forty years of the century. John Gower (d. 1408)—a friend of Chaucer's—wrote three major works: two didactic and hortatory poems in French (the *Mirour de l'Omme*, or *Mirror of Man*) and in Latin (*Vox clamantis*, or *The Voice of One Calling* [in the wilderness]), and then a long English poem called *Confessio amantis* (*The Lover's Confession*), which is essentially a collection of tales. In the first part of the fifteenth century, this expansive literary activity continued. The monk John Lydgate (d. ca. 1450) produced a massive body of work, much of it of high quality, too much of it not. And Thomas Hoccleve (d. 1424), an eccentric and fascinating poet who claimed to have known Chaucer personally, wrote a number of intriguing and distinctive works. This is as well the time when the biblical dramas known as "mystery plays"—so named because each was staged by a separate trade, or "mystery"—first made their appearance.

The reasons for this sudden explosion of literary activity are not easy to specify. Certainly, one cause was the disappearance of French as a spoken language among the aristocratic classes, with the possible exception of the royal court. Another was the spread of English literacy, plus the financial capacity to buy books, among upper- and especially middle-strata people—itself an effect of striking economic changes (to be discussed more fully later) that followed the plague of 1349–1350. But whatever the reasons, Chaucer must be seen not as a single poetic voice in an otherwise unenlightened land but as part of a large and highly sophisticated literary movement. Nonetheless, he stands head and shoulders above his contemporaries, and he is the only medieval English poet who is still widely read.

In 1700, the poet, playwright, and critic John Dryden endowed Chaucer with an epithet that had previously been occasionally applied but that has now become definitive: "the father of English poetry."[1] Dryden's epithet is accurate. Fifteenth-century poetry had been dominated by Lydgate, but by the sixteenth century he had become an example of all that was medieval and was therefore rejected by the modernists of the Renaissance. He was already on the way to becoming what Joseph Ritson was to call him in 1802, a "voluminous, prosaick and driveling monk."[2] Gower remained a name to be reckoned with, as his odd role as a kind of narrator in Shakespeare's *Pericles* shows. But the very peculiarity, and rarity, of that appearance testifies to the fitfulness of his influence. Langland was read as a proto-Protestant in the sixteenth century, and so enjoyed a brief revival, with two editions in 1550. But then he disappeared completely until a new edition of his poem was produced at the end of the nineteenth century. The alliterative poems were, so far as we know, unread until the mid- and late nineteenth century. The mystery plays were outlawed with the coming of the Reformation. Only Chaucer remained a living presence for his successors. Spenser designated him the source of the native English tradition in the *Shepherd's Calendar*, began and ended the *Faerie Queene* with allusions to the *Parliament of Fowls*, and presented its book 4 as a continuation of, oddly enough, the unfinished Squire's Tale. Shakespeare drew on Chaucer extensively. His reliance is most explicit in *Troilus and Cressida*, *A Midsummer Night's Dream*, and *Two Noble Kinsmen*, but throughout the plays we hear Chaucerian echoes, especially in *Romeo and Juliet* and *The Tempest*. In *Il Penseroso*, Milton again invoked the Squire's Tale; Pope rewrote *The House of Fame*; Wordsworth translated the Prioress's Tale; and William Morris not only produced his famous Kelmscott edition of *The Canterbury Tales* but modeled his own poem *The Earthly Paradise* on Chaucer's early dream poems. Even the central document of literary modernism, T. S. Eliot's *The Waste Land*, begins by alluding to the opening of *The Canterbury Tales*: behind Eliot's gloomy "April is the cruelest month," we can hear Chaucer's cheerful "Aprile with his showres soote."

That Chaucer is the founding figure of the English literary tradition is not really in doubt. But the interesting question is not *whether* but *why*. What did Chaucer do that other poets, writing at the same time, did not? There are at least two plausible answers to this question. The first is that Chaucer was alone among his contemporaries in believing that England could develop a national literary tradition equivalent to that of the other European countries. He got this idea of a national literature primarily from the Italians, and specifically from the three great writers of the *trecento*, Dante, Petrarch, and Boccaccio. So far as we know, Chaucer was the only person in England, and certainly the only person whose works survive, who actually read the Italian writings of these three men. Others read their Latin writings, but the only evidence we have of the presence of their vernacular works in England are the references to them that are present throughout Chaucer's work. The key works are Dante's *Commedia*, Petrarch's *Rime*, and Boccaccio's Italian imitations of the classical epic, the *Filostrato* and the *Teseida*.[3]

The most important influence on Chaucer of the Italian tradition, however, is not individual works but rather *the idea of tradition itself*. For example, just as Petrarch's *Rime* derives most immediately from Dante's *Vita nuova*, so his classicism is inconceivable apart from Dante's anguished struggle over the role of Virgil—"lo mio maestro e 'l mio autore [my master and my author/authority]"—in a Christian world. Similarly, Boccaccio's *Filostrato*—the source of *Troilus and Criseyde*—and his *Teseida*, the source of the Knight's Tale, are both concerned with defining the relation of the contemporary literature of the Christian present to that of the classical past. For Dante, however inspirational the classical past may be, the absence of Christianity places it under an irrevocable judgment. But for Petrarch and Boccaccio, the classical past has within itself the capacity for at least a secular redemption. In the *Teseida*, the bloody world of Theban violence is redeemed by the philosopher-king Teseo; in the *Filostrato*, the betrayals that disfigure Trojan history can be redeemed by the *pietate*—both the pity and the piety—of the narrator's lady. In both cases, Boccaccio's narratives are shaped in reaction to Dante, just as Petrarch's unfinished Latin epic celebrating Rome, *Africa*, is a challenge to Dante's ultimate dismissal of the greatest epic poet of the classical world, Virgil. And similarly, as Chaucer well knew from reading the letter to Boccaccio with which Petrarch introduced his version of the Griselda story, the two later Italian poets worked with a keen sense of their relationship both to each other and to Dante. Less important than the precise terms of the relationship among these three poets is the very fact of relationship, the fact that one vernacular writer is working in response to another. What these examples provided for Chaucer was a model of how past poetry can be a living force in the present.[4] Oddly, Chaucer shows very limited interest in the English writing that either preceded him or was being contemporaneously produced. The tradition of English romance is visible only twice in the whole of Chaucer's work. Once is in the mockery of the Tale of Sir Thopas, where it is presented as a childish form, valuable only when turned into satire by a poet who stands far above it; the second is when the Parson says he will not use the "rum, ram, ruf " sounds of the alliterative tradition. As for Gower, his *Confessio amantis* appears only by implication in the Man of Law's Prologue, and there it serves as the rejected alternative to the far more innovative and sophisticated *Canterbury Tales*. Langland is a more complicated issue. We know that Langland's survey of English social types at the beginning of *Piers Plowman* influenced Chaucer's General Prologue, and there are signs of Langland's influence scattered throughout *The Canterbury Tales*. And while Langland may indeed have functioned in Chaucer's poetic consciousness as his greatest English rival, Chaucer's response is to turn away from the religious obsessions and political concerns that fill Langland's poem to a far more varied, and far more European, set of themes. The fact is that Chaucer's ambition was to become not a great English but a great *European* writer. The irony is that in accomplishing this ambition he empowered English writers to think of their work in the terms that had made the European literatures great—as part of a living *national* literary tradition.

  The text in which Chaucer deals most directly with the *idea* of literary tradition is *The House of Fame*.[5] But *The Canterbury Tales* provided a *model* for the workings of tradition; there he showed his successors how to use one work as inspiration for another. One way in which he does this is by his own allusions to his European predecessors. Here is one small example.[6] Toward the end of the General Prologue, the narrator has described all of the pilgrims except five, and he introduces this last group with a kind of summary:

> Ther was also a reve, and a millere,
> A somnour, and a pardoner also,
> A maunciple, and myself—ther were namo.
>
> (542–44)

Five plus one: where does this pattern come from? The model closest in time is canto 4 of the *Inferno*. Dante and Virgil there greet the great poets of antiquity in limbo. "Four great shades" (4.83) approach them: Homer, Horace, Ovid, and Lucan. Virgil is of course the fifth, and Dante says—with typical false modesty—"they made me one of their company, so that I was sixth amid so much wisdom" (101–2). Chaucer, however, is the sixth among five rogues—a witty commentary on Dante's immense sense of self-importance. Interestingly, however, Dante was not the first to use this model. In the *Roman de la Rose*, Jean de Meun located *himself* as the sixth among five love poets: Tibullus, Gallus, Catullus, and Ovid from antiquity and his thirteenth-century predecessor Guillaume de Lorris.[7] We have here, then, a fine example of a living literary tradition, as a device created by Jean de Meun is imitated first by Dante and then by Chaucer. And in each case the device is given a significantly different meaning.

The Canterbury Tales is full of this kind of small literary allusion, but also of larger ones as well. The work is a compilation of almost every kind of writing known to the Middle Ages. Epic, romance, fabliau, saint's life, exemplum, sermon, mirror of princes, penitential treatise, tragedy, animal fable, Breton lay, confessional autobiography, Marian miracle—all these and more are present in the *Tales*. Each of the genres of which Chaucer provides an example invokes not just specific writers but a whole lexicon of different *kinds* of writing. As many of the essays presented here show, the tales are more fully understood when they are located within those literary contexts and we can understand how Chaucer is adopting—and adapting—European traditions of writing. But there is another kind of conversation going on within the *Tales*, and that is among themselves. There are twenty-four tales in all. While clearly *The Canterbury Tales* as a total project is unfinished, there are strong arguments to support the claim that Chaucer completed all of the tales (although not all of the links between tales) that he meant to write.[8] A second issue on which scholars disagree is the order in which the tales were meant to be presented. Again, while certainty is impossible, there are even stronger arguments that the so-called Ellesmere order (the order in which they are presented in one of the earliest and most carefully prepared manuscripts) is the one Chaucer intended.[9] But even without these assumptions, every reader recognizes that the twenty-four *Canterbury Tales* are organized according to pairs. This pattern begins with Knight-Miller, Miller-Reeve, Reeve-Cook, but then it moves into the simpler structure of independent pairs: Man of Law–Wife of Bath, Friar-Summoner, Clerk-Merchant, Squire-Franklin, and so on. This is not to say that there are not other patterns at work in the tales. One is the famous marriage group.[10] Another is a repeating pattern of a hagiographical tale followed by a tale of self-revelation or confession: the Man of Law followed by the Wife of Bath, the Clerk followed by the Merchant, the Physician followed by the Pardoner, the Prioress followed by Chaucer's own tales of Sir Thopas and Melibee, and finally the Second Nun followed by the Canon's Yeoman. One can also divide the twenty-four tales into two groups of twelve, with the break coming between the Franklin's Tale and the Pardoner's Tale: the first twelve tales deal primarily with social and literary issues, the last twelve primarily with religious ones, a movement culminating in the Parson's Tale. Or the twenty-four tales can be divided into six groups of four each, following the pattern of the so-called first fragment, composed of the Knight's, Miller's, Reeve's, and Cook's tales, which is then replicated in the second group of four: Man of Law's, Wife of Bath's, Friar's, and Summoner's.[11] Regardless of the details, the primary point is that the tales are conceived as in conversation with each other: they are *themselves* an example of the way literary tradition works. One kind of literary form calls up another, and so on—a living and developing process in which the past provides the basis for the future, and the future casts new light upon the past.

This, then, is the first reason that Chaucer is the father of English poetry. He educated his readers to recognize the way in which literary tradition works and showed his poetic heirs how to use his own work as a foundation for theirs. For the second reason, let us turn back to the essay by John Dryden with which I began. Dryden translated a portion of *The Canterbury Tales* into the language of Restoration England, and wrote a preface to this work. The preface includes a well-known passage, in which Dryden asserts that Chaucer

> has taken into the compass of his *Canterbury Tales* the various manners and humours (as we now call them) of the whole English nation in his age. . . . 'Tis sufficient to say, according to the proverb, that here is God's plenty. We have our forefathers and great-grand-dames all before us, as they were in Chaucer's days: their general *characters* are still remaining in mankind,

and even in England, though they are called by other names than those of Monks, and Friars, and Canons, and Lady Abbesses, and Nuns; for mankind is ever the same, and nothing lost out of nature, though every thing is altered.[12]

Dryden is here drawing our attention to the great innovation of *The Canterbury Tales*, one that has become so much a part of English literary tradition that we almost no longer recognize it. This is Chaucer's emphasis throughout the tales on *character*. The point is not so much that *within* each tale we must attend to questions of character, an interest that varies widely from tale to tale. In the Knight's Tale, there is no significant difference between Arcite and Palamon; Emily is a pallid generalization; and Theseus is nothing other than a type of the good ruler. So too the Miller's Tale is populated with stereotypes. With prologues like the Wife of Bath's and the Pardoner's, we do get a far more focused attention to character, but in both cases their tales do not offer us particularly "rounded" characters, to use E. M. Forster's term.[13] No, the innovation of *The Canterbury Tales* is not within each tale but in the very condition of tale telling. In every instance, we are required to read the tale in the light of the teller. Some contemporary Chaucerians dismiss this idea, but not only the demands of interpretation but the manuscript evidence argue against this. The Ellesmere manuscript was created within five to ten years of Chaucer's death, and in all likelihood with some input from his son, Thomas Chaucer.[14] It provides vividly illuminated portraits of each of the pilgrims, with details that carefully reflect their descriptions in the General Prologue. What is most important is that these portraits do not appear in the General Prologue itself. On the contrary, each pilgrim is painted next to the beginning of his or her tale. In other words, the portraits are there in order to key the tale to the teller, and specifically to the description in the General Prologue.

To read each tale in light of the teller is not only an authentically medieval way of reading, but one that Chaucer continually draws to our attention, as many of the essays in this collection show. The effect is to insist upon the priority of the consciousness that creates the tale—or, to put it better, that the tale itself creates. It is fair to say that none of the tales, with the exception of the Shipman's and Parson's tales—which are exceptions for a number of reasons—can stand alone from its teller. Each tale must be read *as told*, in the light of the consciousness that creates it and that it creates. In a very real sense, the subject of *The Canterbury Tales* is the subject—by which I mean subjectivity itself.[15] There are some precedents for this interest in character, in subjectivity, in earlier medieval literature, but not many. We can find traces of it in the *Roman de la Rose* and a more full-blown interest in the French poets of the fourteenth century who drew on the *Roman*, especially in a work like Machaut's *Voir Dit*. Certainly it is present in Dante. Indeed, if one were to seek a single source for Chaucer's interest in presenting the self through its own words, the monologues of the damned in the *Inferno* are a plausible place to look. But the fact is that Chaucer's innovation is truly innovative. There is nothing like it in Boccaccio's *Decameron*, for instance, where the differences among the tellers are largely inconsequential. Chaucer is an original, and so rightly he became the origin of the English literary tradition. The fact that his originality consists in celebrating the individual fits perfectly with the social and political conditions of England. For, as many historians and sociologists have argued, England—and certainly the United States—have always privileged individualism to an unusual degree. For such societies, Chaucer is the perfect model of what literature ought to be: a narrative that reveals the inner workings of the self, a place where—as Dryden said—we "have our forefathers and great-grand-dames all before us."

You will notice that Dryden's comments are not about the tales but about the pilgrims: he refers to "Monks, and Friars, and Canons, and Lady Abbesses, and Nuns." That he chose to focus on the ecclesiastical pilgrims is probably due to the fact that Dryden was a Catholic: living as he did in an oppressively Protestant society, Dryden no doubt wanted to stress the fact that the father of English poetry was a co-religionist. But the important point is his focus on the pilgrims not the tales. If we want to see Chaucer's interest in subjectivity at work, the most efficient way is to examine one of the portraits in the General Prologue and compare it to a similar portrait provided by one of his contemporaries. As Jill Mann demonstrates in the first essay in this collection, the General Prologue is an estates satire; another example of the genre, and one doubtless known to Chaucer, is John Gower's *Mirour de l'Omme*. If we compare two similar portraits from each of these works, Chaucer's originality will become strikingly visible.[16]

In the *Mirour*, Gower provides a severe critique of the contemporary monk, and most of the abuses he describes are relevant to Chaucer's Monk.[17] For example, Gower tells us, "St. Augustine says in his teaching that a fish lives only in water, so Religion must lead its life according to the rule of the convent, fully obedient and cloistered." Whereas in the past, monks led a life of harsh penance, now "Gluttony guards all the doors so that hunger and thirst do not enter in there to make fat paunches lean." Worst of all, "The monk who has been made guardian or steward of any outside property is not a good cloisterer, for then he needs a horse and saddle to get around the countryside, and he spends lavishly." Rather than wearing old habits, as Jerome recommended, "our monk of today regularly seeks fancy adornment for his body and disfigures his soul. Although he wears the habit of suffering, he also has, in vanity, a coat adorned with fur"—and not just any fur, but "gray squirrel fur, for he disdains fleece." "Nor," adds Gower, "does he forget a silver pendant but gaily displays it hanging from his hood on his breast. . . . And moreover, to entertain himself, he goes along the river with game birds, falcon and molted hawk, with swift greyhounds as well, and fine high-spirited horses." Gower finally concludes with the suggestion that contemporary monks father illegitimate children: "for I have heard about the children that our monk accumulated while he was running around here and there, day after day."

At first glance, Chaucer's Monk seems virtually an embodiment of the criticisms that Gower leveled against the monastic establishment. Indeed, one could argue that Gower's account—written in the late 1370s—was the source for Chaucer's portrait, composed at the earliest in the late 1380s. Gower complains of monks who are stewards of outside property; Chaucer's Monk is precisely that, an "outridere" (166). Gower laments the gluttony that afflicts monasteries; Chaucer's Monk is "a lord ful fat and in good poynt" (200) who loves a fat swan "best of any roost" (206)—hardly a man interested in eating fish on fast days. Gower complains that monks wear coats adorned with fur; Chaucer's Monk has "sleves purfiled at the hond / With grys [squirrel fur], and that the fyneste of a lond" (193–94). Gower complains that monks hunt instead of pray; Chaucer's Monk "lovede venerie" (166) and is proud of his fine horses: "Of prikyng and of huntyng for the hare / Was al his lust, for no cost wolde he spare" (191–92). Even the Monk's "love knotte" (197) that fastens his hood finds a precedent in Gower's description, as does the (traditional) comparison of a monk out of the cloister to a fish out of water. And while Gower's claim that monks scatter the countryside with illegitimate children is less explicit in Chaucer's portrait, no reader can miss the implications of sexual license in words like "venerie" and "prickasour."

Yet for all these parallels—and should we think that they are merely coincidental?—Chaucer's portrait is more remarkable for the differences than the similarities. Most striking is the fact that the narrator not only approves of the Monk's flouting of his monastic rule but in this passage the defense comes in a voice that is most like that of the Monk himself:

> What sholde he studie and make hymselven wood,
> Upon a book in cloystre alwey to poure,
> Or swynken with his handes, and laboure,
> As Austyn bit? how shal the world be served?
> Lat Austyn have his swynk to hym reserved!
> (184–88)

This device, by which the voice of the pilgrim infiltrates itself into the verse, is common throughout the prologue: the Parson explains his commitment to Gospel ideals; the Friar himself defends his power of confession—"as seyde hymself " (219)—and expresses his distaste for "sike lazars": "It is nat honest, it may nat avaunce" (246–47). The prologue is also saturated with the pilgrim's professional jargon: the Merchant's "chevyssaunce," the Sergeant of Law's "terms," and so forth. As Jill Mann has rightly said, "It is the *character himself* who is speaking. . . . The narrator assumes that each pilgrim is an expert and presents him in his own terms, according to his own values, *in his own language.*"[18] In sum, the Monk—like the other pilgrims—is less an object to be seen from outside than a subject caught in the very process of self-construction.

Second, Gower never lets us forget the damage that monastic laxity is causing. Monks are no longer protecting laypeople by praying for them; monks are gobbling up property and leaving others in poverty; monks are behaving uncharitably by providing inheritances for their illegitimate children; above all, monks are bringing this foundational institution of Christendom into disrepute. But in Chaucer's portrait, there is no hint of a victim—again, a characteristic of the prologue as a whole, at least until the latter third or so (this is what Mann calls Chaucer's "omission of the victim"). If the monk is damaging anyone—and there is no sense here that he is—it is only himself. Moreover, the details that Chaucer provides present us with a figure whose immense energy is at once appealing and slightly disturbing. He is "A manly man, to been an abbot able" (167), the alliteration serving as a versified expression of a power that is itself poetically creative. This creativity is visible as well in the brilliant rhyme *cloystre/oystre* (181–82): the Monk's force infuses itself into the very language with which he is described. And yet this force also seems almost explosive:

> His heed was balled, that shoon as any glas,
> And eek his face, as he hadde been enoynt.
> He was a lord ful fat and in good poynt;
> His eyen stepe, and rollynge in his heed,
> That stemed as a forneys of a leed.
>
> (197–202)

The protruding eyes and sweating face reveal a man so powerful as to be barely constrained, possessed by an energy that threatens to overwhelm not merely his monastic vocation but his very physical being. My point is that this energy—this *desire* that can find no adequate outlet—is the true subject of the portrait. The Monk's hunting, with its sexual overtones, is presented as a woefully inadequate expression of the power he possesses. The portrait, in short, is not moral but analytic. We are asked not to condemn the Monk but to understand and even admire him—to see him as a human being struggling with the social role in which he finds himself. This analysis leads to two conclusions. First, Chaucer is much less a moralist, or social reformer, than he is an analyst of the human condition. Second, Chaucer directs our attention not to the social value of the pilgrim but to his inner life.

To sum up, Chaucer is the father of English poetry because he taught poets the meaning of literary tradition and because he bequeathed to his successors the literary interest—character—that would dominate English literature. But if this is true, how are we to understand Chaucer's uniqueness among his contemporaries? Earlier, we saw how Chaucer imitates Dante by enumerating five pilgrims and then including himself as the sixth. Why does he present himself in the company of five rogues? The most likely explanation, I think, is not Chaucer's habitual self-mockery but the one quality these five rogues share. They are all untrustworthy servants. The Miller steals corn from the lord who owns the mill; the Reeve cheats *his* lord by manipulating the accounts; the Manciple steals from the lawyers whose residence he oversees; the Summoner deceives the archdeacon for whom he works; and the Pardoner keeps the money for himself that he is supposed to be collecting for the hospital that has provided him with authorization.

Was Chaucer, Controller of the London Customs and Clerk of the King's Works, also a thief? Nothing in the voluminous records leads us to think so. We should understand his untrustworthiness in more metaphoric, and more literary, ways. Prior to the writing of *The Canterbury Tales*, all of Chaucer's poetry, without exception, can be accurately described as *courtly*. This is not to say that it was written *for* the court, since we really know very little about his audience. But it was certainly written within the ideological and cultural context of the world of the nobility. But this is not true of *The Canterbury Tales*: of the twenty-four tales, the only one that is without question aristocratic is the Knight's Tale. Now what is interesting about the Knight's Tale here is its context. First, by being placed within *The Canterbury Tales* at all it is defined *not* as a work by Geoffrey Chaucer, squire, but explicitly as a tale told *by a knight*. Unlike all his previous poetry, this poem is presented not as Chaucer's view of the world but rather as that of a typical member of the ruling class of fourteenth-century England. Second, the theme of the Knight's Tale is (as the essay by Robert Hanning makes plain) the problem—indeed, the failure—of governance. This is a theme, as we shall see, all too relevant to contemporary England. Moreover, the Knight's view of the world is immediately challenged by a drunken Miller, who is skeptical both of the power of the nobility and of their cultural ideals, and who insists that his more relaxed world view be given a hearing. In short, by beginning *The Canterbury Tales* with the Knight and Miller, Chaucer makes a clear statement that he is writing no longer from within the world in which he had for all his life served. On the contrary, he is now standing outside that world as an independent, and by no means uncritical, observer. He is not an untrustworthy servant—like the Miller, Reeve, Manciple, Summoner, and Pardoner. But his position is even more radical: he is a servant no more.

How did this happen? Historians are in the habit of referring to whatever period in which they are most interested as "a time of crisis." But for late fourteenth-century England, the phrase is unavoidable. There were three aspects of this crisis, one economic and social, one military, and the third political. The most important event that occurred during Chaucer's lifetime happened when he was still a young boy: the plague of 1348–1350. Known as the Black Death or just "the Death," this was the highly infectious disease now known as the bubonic plague. In its first pass through Europe, it killed between one-third and one-half of the population; it returned to England, albeit in much less devastating fashion, twice more in the fourteenth century, and did not finally disappear until after the so-called Great Plague that devastated London in 1665. The demographic effects of the plague were tremendous: England did not return to its pre-plague population level until the seventeenth century. The *cultural* effects of the plague are difficult to determine: there is little in the English artistic or literary production of the second half of the fourteenth century that can be attributed with any confidence to the plague. There seems to have been nothing like the immense psychic disruption that accompanied the great plagues of the twentieth century—the horrors of the First and Second World Wars, of the Holocaust, of Stalin's and Mao's tyranny.

But the *economic* and *social* consequences of the plague were enormous. Prior to 1348, medieval Europe was beginning to suffer from an imbalance between population and food production. There were recurrent famines in the first half of the century, especially in 1314–1320, and there was little land available for new cultivation. The plague shifted the balance of power dramatically and hastened the end of feudalism. Before the plague, land and food were scarce while labor was abundant and demand voracious. After the plague, uncultivated land was available, there were far fewer mouths to feed with a now-plentiful agricultural crop, and landlords suffered from a severe shortage of labor. Landless laborers and tenants could now negotiate with their landlords—the nobility—for better terms, and the landlords found their incomes beginning to diminish.

Their response was to pass restrictive legislation. As early as 1349, Parliament enacted the Ordinance of Laborers, and followed it in 1351 with the Statute of Laborers. This legislation restricted the right of a tenant to leave his manor, compelled him to accept work when it was offered to him, forbade employers from offering wages higher than those in force before the plague, codified the wages of artisans in the towns, and fixed the prices of agricultural goods. Historians are uncertain whether these laws achieved their purpose, but the effort to enforce them exacerbated the social friction that had always marked the relation of landlord to tenant under feudalism. The plague had created bright prospects and rising expectations among the poorer and especially middling members of society; the repressive legislation passed by the ruling classes frustrated those expectations; and the predictable result was an explosion. This explosion occurred in 1381 with the so-called Peasants' Revolt, better known as the Rising of 1381, an extraordinary event that had little lasting political effect but that traumatized the ruling class. The Rising had a short but complex history. Its most intense moments were a march into London by rebels from Essex and Kent; the burning of the London palace of the duke of Lancaster, John of Gaunt; and the beheading of (among others) the archbishop of Canterbury. In a field outside London, the young Richard II met with the rebels and promised to redress their wrongs; after they had dispersed, the promised reforms disappeared.

The events that took place at St. Albans, a huge and prosperous manor just northwest of London owned by a Benedictine abbey, provide a vivid insight into the class tensions that characterized late medieval society. The relations between the monks and the tenants of St. Albans had always been fractious. One of the tenants' most bitter grievances had to do with milling: like all feudal landlords, the abbot of St. Albans required his tenants to have their grain ground at large mills owned by the abbey—and to pay for the privilege. The tenants periodically circumvented this requirement by building their own handmills and hiding them in their houses. At least as early as 1274, there are records of the abbot seizing handmills. About fifty years later, in 1327, the tenants laid siege to the abbey and won the concession to have their own mills. But over the next ten years, this concession was canceled, and the people were forced to surrender their millstones. The abbot then had these millstones cemented into the floor of his parlor—a peculiarly uncharitable way to commemorate his victory.

Another fifty years later, during the Rising of 1381, the tenants again laid siege to the abbey and now broke in. Their subsequent actions were described by the abbey chronicler:

Some ribald people, breaking their way into the Abbey cloisters, took up from the floor of the parlour doorway the millstones which had been put there in the time of Abbot Richard as a remembrance and memorial of the ancient dispute between the Abbey and the townsmen. They took the stones outside and handed them over to the commons, breaking them into little pieces and giving a piece to each person, just as the consecrated bread used to be broken and distributed on Sundays in the parish churches, so that the people, seeing these pieces, would know themselves avenged against the Abbey in that cause.[19]

The peasants created a political ritual that replaced and parodied the central religious ritual—the Mass—enacted by the ecclesiastical establishment that had so oppressed them. The leader of the rebels at St. Albans was a man named William Grindecobbe, a name that implies that he was himself a miller. The chronicler also records Grindecobbe's moving words when he was on trial for his part in the Rising:

Fellow citizens, for whom a little liberty has now relieved the long years of oppression, stand firm while you can and do not be afraid because of my persecution. For if it should happen that I die in the cause of seeking to acquire liberty, I will count myself happy to end my life as such a martyr.[20]

Grindecobbe was indeed executed; as a contemporary verse put it, "The stool was hard, the ax was scharp,/The iiii yere of kyng Richard."[21]

What has this to do with Chaucer? Probably nothing personally: he was living in London at the time and doubtless witnessed the invasion of the city by the rebels—an event to which he refers in the Nun's Priest's Tale in a tone that is pretty much unreadable. But Chaucer's Miller is not only allowed to interrupt a monk without retribution—unlike the martyred William Grindcobbe—but is also allowed to tell a tale that is a scathing and very funny parody of the Knight's Tale. In other words, *The Canterbury Tales* seems to begin with a kind of literary Rising.[22] Before exploring the implications of the intriguing (if doubtless fortuitous) parallel between William Grindcobbe and Chaucer's Robin, we must also consider the political and military dimensions of the crisis of governance that afflicted England in the late fourteenth century. For one thing, England's fortunes in the war with France, the so-called Hundred Years War, were in drastic decline. The war began in 1337 when Edward III asserted a (highly dubious) claim to the throne of France. The early decades of the war went brilliantly for the English: in 1346, Edward won a decisive victory over the French at Crecy; then in 1356 his son Edward, the Black

Prince, won an even more spectacular victory at Poitiers, capturing not only many French nobles but even King John of France himself. The effect of these successes was to provide the nobility with valuable hostages: when King John was finally ransomed by his subjects, it was for the immense sum of 3 million gold crowns.

In its early years, then, the war was an economic success for the ruling class and compensated them for the loss of revenues from their estates due to the shift in economic power accomplished by the plague. But these successes didn't continue. In 1367, Edward the Black Prince invaded Spain and won a victory over the French that was all too costly. The campaign ruined his health, and he fell into a slow decline and died in 1376. Meanwhile his father, Edward III, had fallen into his dotage, and the French took advantage of this lack of leadership to reconquer virtually all of the territory they had originally lost. When Edward III died in 1377, the great victories in France were already long past; and he was succeeded not by his heroic son the Black Prince, who was by then dead, but by his grandson Richard II, a boy of ten years old. A biblical verse that medieval political theorists were fond of quoting is "Woe to the land that has a child as king," and the truth of this warning was demonstrated in England. For four years, the government was controlled by Richard's uncle John of Gaunt, the duke of Lancaster, who was highly unpopular and did nothing to revive English fortunes in the war. Then, when Richard himself took over—right after the Rising, when he was fifteen—he demonstrated even less capacity for the chivalric leadership and military success that were so important to the authority of the medieval monarchy.

We come now to a third aspect of the crisis of governance, and the one that most affected Chaucer personally. This was the struggle that went on from 1384 to 1389 between Richard and the most powerful members of the English nobility. A medieval monarch, especially in England, could not rule without the support of the most powerful magnates of his country. This fact had been vividly demonstrated in England a half century earlier, in 1327, when Edward II had been deposed and murdered. For a variety of reasons, Richard quickly lost the support of the magnates. In 1387, he was virtually deposed from the throne, with a warning that what had happened to his great-grandfather Edward II was about to happen to him. Then, in 1388, several of his servants and supporters—some of them known to Chaucer—were executed. Due to its own ineptness, however, the cabal of nobles who led this revolt fell apart in 1389, and Richard regained power. An uneasy peace was made among the feuding parties, but in 1397 Richard struck back at his old enemies, executing and murdering several of them—with the ultimate result that, in 1399, John of Gaunt's son Henry Bolingbroke deposed and murdered Richard and became Henry IV. These unsavory machinations were immediately relevant to Chaucer.

Chaucer was the son of a vintner, a successful wholesaler of wine in London. Like many wealthy merchants, Chaucer's father sent his son to be brought up in a noble household: Chaucer was first a page in the household of the countess of Ulster, and was then in service to Edward III, John of Gaunt, and finally Richard II. It is not easy to know exactly what Chaucer's social position was, a social undefinability that is itself interesting. He would certainly not have been considered a member of the nobility, although by the end of his life he seems to have had a coat of arms. In 1374, Edward appointed him Controller of the Customs: he had to make sure that the customs duties levied on the export of wool and cloth were accurately computed and honestly collected. But, financially important as the job may have been to the Crown, it was not of a high status: Chaucer was required to keep the records in his own hand, and any form of manual labor was considered demeaning. Prior to Chaucer, all of the holders of this office had been clerics; he was the first layman to hold the job. But it was, as one historian has rather woundingly put it, a "modest office for modest men." Moreover, Chaucer lacked the wealth—especially the landed wealth—to be considered a member of the ruling class. He married one of the queen's ladies-in-waiting, who was a foreigner and brought with her no significant dowry. Finally, the various other tasks he performed for Edward and Richard, while by no means unimportant, were exactly comparable to those provided by other merchants' sons who entered noble service; and his remuneration from the monarch—the various grants and annuities—was also entirely typical for a person of his background. In other words, there is no evidence that Chaucer was particularly close to the centers of power and—more striking—no evidence that he was ever rewarded or even recognized by the king for his literary work. About a hundred documents survive that pertain to Chaucer's official life, but not one of them mentions the fact that he was a poet.

There is, however, one moment when Chaucer's service to Richard was of special importance. This was in 1386, when he was selected to represent the shire of Kent in Parliament. This was a crucial Parliament, in which Richard was trying to head off the magnates conspiring against him. Chaucer was almost certainly present in this Parliament as an agent of the king: Richard was later accused of having tried to pack this Parliament, and Chaucer seems to have been one of the men he shoe-horned in. But Richard's strategy failed: his noble opponents took control of the government and then instituted a purge. It was at this point that Chaucer resigned from the controllership and "retired" to

Kent. Nonetheless, Chaucer continued to engage in diplomatic work for Richard—perhaps even initiating secret peace negotiations with the French, actions that would have made him highly vulnerable to the king's opponents. When Richard regained power in 1389, he soon appointed Chaucer Clerk of the King's Works—again, the first layman to hold the position—where he continued until 1391, when he seems to have simply retired, living on a comfortable annuity provided by the king.

The first conclusion to draw from these facts concerns Chaucer's social position. He was the son of a merchant, lived most of his life in London, and as Controller of Customs dealt with merchants and trade every day. He was also, however, a royal servant, a member of the households of Edward III and Richard II (although he seems never to have lived for any extended period in the household itself), was entrusted with important diplomatic missions, and put himself in danger to serve the king both in Parliament and as a diplomat. Finally, he was a layman who was nonetheless capable of performing tasks usually assigned to clerics: he knew Latin, French, and Italian well and he was widely if not deeply read—in fourteenth-century terms, he would certainly have been considered as learned as many clerks. This is what I mean by Chaucer's *social undefinability*: to specify his social identity—his precise status and role—seems impossible. For the evidence reveals a Chaucer who is on the boundaries among several distinctive social formations. He is not bourgeois, nor noble, nor clerical—yet he participates in all three of these groupings. Perhaps this lack of precise social definition can help us to understand (although it cannot be said to cause) Chaucer's interest in individuality—an interest in what we might call a *socially undetermined subjectivity*. By this I mean a concern with that psychological specificity and inwardness that is everywhere present in his poetry, but an inwardness that exists apart from any very strong sense of social determination.

This brief survey of Chaucer's life and times may also help us to understand why Chaucer turned from exclusively courtly writing not just to the variety displayed in *The Canterbury Tales* but to a work that begins by offering a critical perspective on aristocratic values. The Knight's Tale tells the story of how the Athenian man of reason—Theseus—tries to control and discipline, to govern, two Theban men of blood, Arcite and Palamon. More than this, however, the tale bespeaks a crisis of governance in the way it is told: the Knight is continually anxious about organizing, controlling, structuring, and disciplining—about governing—his own narrative. Both Theseus and the Knight are less than fully successful in their efforts: the tale does not describe a world governed by a benign rationality but one tormented by random accident and malignant vengefulness. And as soon as the Knight tells his tale, he is immediately challenged by the drunken Miller, who insists that his "cherles tale" be given a hearing. Does this mean that the events of the late 1380s turned Chaucer into a political radical? Surely not: the fact that the Miller's Tale opens the door to the embittered and dangerous Reeve and then the scabrous Cook argues against so simple a conclusion. But we can say that the events of the 1380s—both those which Chaucer observed and those in which he was a participant—shook him loose from an aristocratic culture that he was already finding less and less satisfactory as a context both for artistic production and for life. The result was *The Canterbury Tales*. The tales are not a radical political document; they promote no consistent political position, nor do they comment in any direct way on any contemporary problems. Certainly, they are nonaristocratic, but they do not propose any alternative social or political vision to that of the aristocratic world. On the contrary, they escape from politics entirely—and, to some extent, from social meaning—by focusing their attention upon individuals, upon character, upon subjectivity. *The Canterbury Tales*, in short, responds to its time largely by withdrawing from it. Whether this represents political indifference or prudence is an open question. But what cannot be disputed is that Chaucer's response to the material conditions of his life resulted in a work that contemporary readers have found both politically congenial and aesthetically irresistible.

Notes

1. John Dryden, "Preface to Fables Ancient and Modern," in *Of Dramatic Poesy and Other Critical Essays*, 2 vols., edited by George Watson (London, 1962), 2:280.

2. Joseph Ritson, *Bibliographia Poetica* (London, 1802), p. 60.

3. Despite persistent claims to the contrary, my own view is that Chaucer did *not* know Boccaccio's *Decameron*. When Chaucer imitates or even alludes to a work, the connection is quite obvious at the level not just of plot but of verbal surface. There is not a single phrase in *The Canterbury Tales* that can with confidence be traced back to the *Decameron*—which is not the case with Chaucer's use of Boccaccio's other works nor with Dante's *Commedia* or Petrarch's *Rime*, nor, for that matter, with Petrarch's version of the story of Griselda. Indeed, Chaucer's Clerk's Tale shows plenty of verbal echoes of both Petrarch's Latin and the French translation of Petrarch that Chaucer used as a guide to the Latin. But this is not true of Boccaccio's version in the *Decameron*, despite the fact that Chaucer must have known of it from Petrarch's letter to Boccaccio, which accompanied the version of the tale he read, and despite the fact that one of the central themes of Chaucer's own version is translation. And *The Canterbury Tales* is

profoundly unlike the *Decameron* both in conception and in execution. Boccaccio's ten storytellers are all of the same class (nobility) and age (young), as well as all being Florentines, and the relation of tale to teller is rarely anything more than superficially appropriate. Chaucer presents instead a broad conspectus of English society, and for him, as many of the essays in this collection demonstrate, the relation of tale to teller is central to the entire project.

4. Much the same point could be made of the French literary tradition. Just as Petrarch and Boccaccio each responded to Dante and to each other, so did Jean de Meun (ca. 1275) respond to Guillaume de Lorris (ca. 1225) in continuing Guillaume's *Roman de la Rose*, and so did Guillaume Machaut (d. 1377), Eustache Deschamps (d. 1407), and Jean Froissart (d. ca. 1410) respond to the *Roman de la Rose* as a whole. These three writers—especially Froissart, who provided the sources for Chaucer's first major work, the *Book of the Duchess*—are everywhere present in Chaucer's work (Chaucer probably knew Froissart and Deschamps personally), as is their ultimate inspiration, the *Roman*. But the intensity and complexity of the interactions among the French writers is less substantial, and less sophisticated, than among the Italians. The other reason for seeing the Italian writers as central to Chaucer's conception of a literary tradition is that he confronts the issue directly in relation to Dante in an early poem, *The House of Fame*.

5. As suggested in the previous note, *The House of Fame* (written probably in the early 1380s, prior to the completion of *Troilus and Criseyde* and before *The Canterbury Tales* project was begun) deals with the ambitions appropriate to a vernacular poet working within a European tradition dominated by Dante. The tone of the poem is satiric, but the issues are serious indeed.

6. See David Wallace, "Chaucer and the European 'Rose'," *Studies in the Age of Chaucer: Proceedings* 1 (1984), edited by Paul Strohm and Thomas J. Hefferman (Knoxville, Tenn., 1985), pp. 61–67.

7. Daniel Poirion, ed., *Le Roman de la Rose* (Paris, 1973), ll. 10508–26.

8. The evidence that is most often invoked to assert that Chaucer intended to write more tales is the Host's definition of the tale-telling game in the General Prologue as requiring each pilgrim to tell two tales in either direction. But this argument ignores the fact that this is the Host's proposal, not Chaucer's. As a figure of festivity, the Host sees the journey as beginning at his tavern and then returning there, a circular pattern. But the journey is a *pilgrimage*: its goal is not a tavern but a cathedral, and the vast majority of pilgrimage narratives are one way, a linearity that implies change rather than a circularity that implies stasis. For the one-way nature of real-life medieval pilgrimage narratives, see Donald Howard, *The Idea of the Canterbury Tales* (Berkeley, Calif., 1976), pp. 29–30 and *passim*.

9. The debate on this issue is extensive, but useful contributions include E. Talbot Donaldson, "The Ordering of *The Canterbury Tales*," in *Medieval Literature and Folklore Studies:*

Essays in Honor of Francis Lee Utley, edited by Jerome Mandel and Bruce A. Rosenberg (New Brunswick, N.J., 1970), pp. 193–204; Larry D. Benson, "The Order of *The Canterbury Tales*," *Studies in the Age of Chaucer* 3 (1981): 77–120; Ralph Hanna III's introduction to *The Ellesmere Manuscript of Chaucer's "Canterbury Tales": A Working Facsimile* (Rochester, N.Y.: 1989); and Helen Cooper, "The Order of the Tales in the Ellesmere Manuscript," in *The Ellesmere Chaucer: Essays in Interpretation*, edited by Martin Stevens and Daniel Woodward (San Marino, Calif., 1995), pp. 245–61.

10. George Lyman Kittredge, "Chaucer's Discussion of Marriage," *Modern Philology* 9 (1911–1912): 435–67.

11. See Lee Patterson, *Chaucer and the Subject of History* (Madison, Wis., 1991), pp. 280–83, and *Putting the Wife in Her Place* (London, 1995), pp. 1–20.

12. John Dryden. "Preface to Fables Ancient and Modern," 2: 280.

13. E. M. Forster, *Aspects of the Novel* (London, 1927).

14. Alfred David, "The Ownership and Use of the Ellesmere Manuscript," in Stevens and Woodward, *The Ellesmere Chaucer*, pp. 307–26; and Hanna's introduction note 9.

15. For a good presentation of this argument, see H. Marshall Leicester, Jr., "The Art of Impersonation: A General Prologue to *The Canterbury Tales*," *PMLA* 95 (1980): 213–24.

16. I am following Mann's lead in making this comparison (see her *Chaucer and Medieval Estates Satire* [Cambridge, UK, 1973], pp. 34–35), although to a somewhat different end.

17. All the quotations from Gower's *Mirour de l'Omme* are from the translation by Glending Olson in *Geoffrey Chaucer, The Canterbury Tales: Fifteen Tales and the General Prologue*, edited by V. A. Kolve and Glending Olson (New York, 2005), pp. 337–39. The citations from the General Prologue are from *The Riverside Chaucer*, edited by Larry D. Benson (Boston, 1987), and are cited by line number.

18. Mann, *Chaucer and Medieval Estates Satire*, pp. 66 and 194; italics in the original.

19. Thomas Walsingham, *Gesta abbatum monasterii Sancti Albani*, translated by Rosamond Faith in "The Class Struggle in Fourteenth-Century England," in *People's History and Socialist Theory*, edited by Raphael Samuel (London, 1981), p. 59.

20. Thomas Walsingham, *Historia Anglicana* in *The Peasants' Revolt of 1381*, edited and translated by R. B. Dobson (London, 1970), p. 277.

21. Dobson, *Peasants' Revolt*, p. 305.

22. This point was first made by Alfred David, *The Strumpet Muse: Art and Morals in Chaucer's Poetry* (Bloomington, Ind., 1976), p. 92.

The General Prologue
and Estates Literature

JILL MANN

◆   ◆   ◆

THE MEANINGS OF the word "estate" which concern us are defined by the
Middle English Dictionary (MED) as follows: "a class of persons, especially a
social or political class or group; also a member of a particular class or rank,"
and "a person's position in society . . . social class." To these definitions I think
it necessary to add a particular reference to the role played by a person's work
in determining the estate to which he or she belongs. It is true that the estates
included in estates literature are not classified only in terms of what we would
now recognize as their occupation; they can, for example, be distinguished
according to clerical or marital status. But clerical and marital status inevitably include some notion of the particular duties and temptations of the
work that accompanies them.

Estates literature has been defined by Ruth Mohl, who has written the
only book entirely devoted to the genre, in terms of four characteristics. First,
an enumeration of the "estates," or social and occupational classes, whose aim
seems to be completeness. Second, a lament over the shortcomings of the estates; each fails in its duty to the rest. Third, the philosophy of the divine ordi-
nation of the three principal estates, the dependence of the state on all three,
and the necessity of being content with one's station. And last, an attempt to
find remedies, religious or political, for the defects of estates.[1] However, these

characteristics are by no means to be found in every piece of estates writing, and estates material is clearly recognizable in works not strictly belonging to the genre, such as *Piers Plowman*. My working definition of estates satire is therefore less rigid; it comprises any literary treatments of social classes which allow or encourage a generalized application.

For one important purpose, however, it is necessary to distinguish works which have an estates form from those which simply contain estates material. For the form of the estates genre and the form of the Prologue are one and the same. The framework of the Prologue is a list of estates. Chaucer specifically says at the end of the Prologue that he has described the "estaat" of all the pilgrims (716). The Prologue is also a collection of portraits, but this is a secondary consideration; if we had been presented with portraits of the seven deadly sins, for example, we should quickly have recognized that the portrait series was merely a vehicle, while the conceptual framework belonged to the sins tradition. It is important to stress this relationship between the form of the Prologue and estates literature because of the common assumption that society itself, rather than a literary genre, would have been Chaucer's model. This assumption applies both to the question of the comprehensiveness of the Prologue, and to the order in which the characters are placed. Thus Bronson remarked on the "relative scarcity of women in the company," and attributed this to the fact that their presence on a pilgrimage was "realistically" unlikely.[2] It can equally well be attributed to the fact that estates literature rarely listed more than two estates of women—religious and secular.[3] Some estates—especially monk, friar, priest, lawyer, doctor, knight—appear with great regularity in estates literature, but each author exercises considerable freedom in his selection. The estates included in the Prologue correspond well enough to this rather vague norm. Chaucer makes no serious omissions. The higher echelons of both clergy and laity are unrepresented, but in other works much of the material applied to them is identical with that assigned to their less exalted counterparts. Bishops and priests, kings and knights, are on the whole admonished in the same way. On the other hand, the third estate is represented in the Prologue with an unusual richness.

It can only have been with the aim of providing a full version of an estates list that Chaucer chose to introduce as many as thirty pilgrims in the Prologue. Thirty is an unwieldy number for description (and Chaucer evades describing all of them), for dramatic interplay, or for tale telling—is there any other collection of tales with so large a number of narrators? Chaucer was concerned to impose an estates form on the Prologue in order to suggest society as a whole by way of his representative company of individuals. To adapt a phrase of Muscatine's to a different purpose, the estates framework provides "a formal, *a priori* ideal ordering of experience, without which the naturalistic detail would have only the barest sociological significance."[4] On the question of the order in which the estates are presented, two misconceptions seem to prevail. The first is that estates literature always proceeds, in an orderly way, from the top to the bottom of the social scale, in contrast to the fairly haphazard method of the Prologue. Support for this view has been found in Chaucer's apparent admission, at the end of the Prologue, that he is unusual in ignoring social ranking:

> Also I prey yow to foryeve it me,
> Al have I nat set folk in hir degree
> Heere in this tale, as that they sholde stonde.
> (743–45)

This may indeed mean that he is thinking of the more tightly organized works of estates literature, and pointing out the vagaries of his own scheme. But tight organization is not a sine qua non of an estates work, and Chaucer's apology cannot therefore be read as a statement that he is writing something else.

The second misconception is about the exact nature of the order which is being neglected in the Prologue. Modern writers have tended to assume that medieval perceptions of the class hierarchy were the same as our own. On these grounds it is usually assumed, for example, that it is correct for Chaucer to begin with the Knight, that the Prioress is of high status, and that the Wife of Bath is middle class. The estates lists show that it would be more "correct" for the clerical figures to precede the Knight, and that despite the high rank achieved by some women, their estate is placed lower in the list than *all* those of the men. The estates framework is more concerned to distinguish "qualitatively," to separate clergy from laity, men from women, than to arrange an exact hierarchy of rank cutting across these divisions. The estates habit of distinguishing by function rather than by rank determines, for example, the treatment of women according to their marital, rather than their social, status, the undifferentiated treatment of *burgenses*, and the presentation of the lowest ranks of the clergy before the secular emperor. Clearly this literary order did not reflect the actual status of each class in society, and it is possible that social actualities affected the order which Chaucer developed for the Prologue. But if we say that the Prologue neglects a proper order, we must make clear whether we mean a literary order, or actual social ranking. And we must provide empirical evidence for the way in which both were perceived in the fourteenth century.[5]

As for Chaucer's apology for not setting his figures "in hir degree," it may just as well refer to a literary as to a social order, since it occurs at the end of a discussion of literary propriety.[6] He apologizes for the apparent lack of literary decorum that he is about to demonstrate in reporting the ribald tales of some pilgrims, and defends himself with a literary principle: "The wordes moote be cosyn to the dede" (742). He continues this line of thought—"Also I prey yow to foryeve it me"—with an apology for another apparent violation of literary decorum; he has not proceeded in the "right" order. The literary context of this apology strongly encourages the belief that the standard of correctness to which Chaucer is referring is provided by estates literature. Chaucer is consciously producing an example of this genre, and just as consciously refusing to adhere to the one principle of order that usually characterizes it, the separate treatment of clergy and laity.

Chaucer's reasons for imitating the least regular, rather than the most regular estates pieces are not immediately obvious; the attempts that have been made to find conceptual schemes in the order of the portraits are forced, and depend on the development of external concepts as the "key" to each portrait. The likelihood that an order which is haphazard and casual as far as significance is concerned is operating, is surely strengthened by the fact that exactly this casualness of procedure operates *within* the portraits. They have indeed been praised for the "lack of regular order" which was "deliberately planned to produce the effect of spontaneity that creates a sense of intimate acquaintance with each pilgrim."[7] Just as the haphazard order within the portraits does not prevent us from recognizing the form of the *descriptio*, so the vagaries on a larger scale are not sufficient to destroy the recognizable estates form of the Prologue.

However, if we cannot find an abstract significance determining a particular order in the Prologue portraits, perhaps there is an abstract significance in their disorder. The strict order of estates literature is governed by the notion of function, of hierarchy in a model whose working is divinely established. It is precisely this notion of function that Chaucer discards. He shows us a world in which our view of hierarchy depends on our own position in the world, not on an absolute standpoint. For some the Knight is at the apex of "respectability" (in both its modern and etymological senses), for some the Plowman, for others the "gentil" Pardoner. More than once, Chaucer uses the estates concept against itself: the notion of specialized duties, when taken to its limit, destroys the idea of a total society in which all have their allotted place and relation to each other. Chaucer's use of the estates form, that is to say, is not the traditional one of criticizing (even in a less heavy-handed, more amusing way) the failures of social classes in the light of a social ideal.

The form of the Prologue is a reason for looking in estates literature, rather than any other literary genre, for its source. But as regards its content—the features attributed to each of the Canterbury pilgrims—I have still to show why we should look to literature at all, rather than to Chaucer's own experience of life. If estates satire criticizes the failings of social classes, could not Chaucer have observed and recorded these failings for himself?

Underlying this question is an assumption that literary works reflect life in a simple way—to make it overly explicit for a moment—that satirists observing their society are independently forced to the same conclusions on the sensuality of women or the greed of lawyers. It is, of course, generally recognized that satire practices both selection and distortion, and that its relationship with "historical reality" is therefore impossible to define with exactness. But it is also necessary to go beyond this, and say that satire takes on a historical life of its own, perpetuating both specific ways of observing reality and conceptual frameworks within which it can be organized. It is the conceptual frameworks, rather than the historical reality, which are of interest to us here. These frameworks are not indeed peculiar to satirists; they are a condition of all kinds of perception. Estates literature depends on and exploits the frameworks known as "social stereotypes"—the traditional images that make some people eager to observe inscrutability in a particular Chinese or astuteness in a particular Jew, because they believe that the Chinese are inscrutable and the Jews astute. And estates literature does not merely reflect, but can also create, or contribute to, stereotypes; the way in which an individual author writes about monks or women can well influence the way in which his audience henceforth perceives monks or women in real life. Stereotypes of this sort are transmitted by a variety of means of differing degrees of formality, ranging from proverbs and anecdotes to learned treatises. It would be a hard task for people today to say precisely whence they derived their stereotypes of a country policeman or a civil servant; similarly, medieval stereotypes must have received constant reinforcement and embellishment from a multitude of daily experiences.

The social stereotype provides a common ground for estates treatments in literary works of the most diverse kinds. There are certain differences in the literary origins of the traditional material underlying the Prologue portraits. The clerical figures are heavily dependent on Latin estates satire, in which the clergy figures very prominently and the laity are classified by a few blanket terms such as *cives* and *rustici*. The treatment of secular trades is mainly developed in vernacular satire, and some figures derive from a more popular tradition reflected at times in Langland, sermons, and the more detailed confessional manuals, but at other times only to be conjectured from proverbs and occasional indirect hints. These differences in source material, however, do not imply disruption in the texture of the Prologue. The popular stereo-types of the clerical orders must have been nourished and influenced by the commonplaces of Latin estates literature, while vernacular estates literature must have drawn on popular prejudices and ideas when it wished to extend its range to new classes of the laity. The process must always have operated in both directions—from high to popular culture, and vice versa—especially at a time when there was little distinction between formal and informal knowledge, when a learned author would write, "Men say that . . . ," and his readers would avow, "A learned authority says . . . "[8] Literature and popular prejudice supported each other, and the social stereotypes became a means whereby estates satire could be smoothly and neatly expanded, as they were its original basis.

The estates stereotypes also afford an explanation for Chaucer's ability to conceive of his estates representatives in topical situations; they are not fixed types whose features are determined *solely* by their existence in a literary tradi-tion and must be consciously brought up to date. What is traditional about their features reflects not just literary tradition, but also what is traditional about their work and the experiences to which it gives rise; what is topical and of the moment reflects the contemporary role of the social stereotype. This is not just true of Chaucer; each satirist recreates the estates stereotypes afresh, "seeing" for himself the vanity of women or the corruption of the clergy. But while his vision is conditioned by what is traditional, it will also reflect something of the immediate situation which he is analyzing in terms of the old formulae.

A look at the Prologue reveals to us an extraordinary amount of unadul-terated information about the careers and occupations of the characters, which can have no other function than to ensure our sense of the estate. We hear of the Squire riding and singing, jousting, dancing, drawing, and writing poetry. We hear of the Wife's cloth making, of the Merchant's bargains and dealings in exchange. We hear of the Franklin's public offices as sheriff, "con-tour," knight of the shire, justice of the peace. We hear of the Cook roasting, simmering, broiling, and frying, of chicken and marrow bones, "poudre-marchant tart and galyngale," "mortreux," and "blankmanger." We are re-minded of the knowledge and skill that each profession calls for, whether it is the Yeoman's skill in woodcraft; the close watch kept by the Reeve on the weather, the farm animals, and the tricks of his underlings; the Sergeant of Law's memorizing of every statute and all the lawsuits since the Conquest; or the Doctor's grounding in astronomy, the humors, and an astonishing num-ber of medical authorities. We have a sense of professional jargon—whether it is the "fee simple" and "termes" of the lawyer, the Shipman's "lodemenage," or the Merchant's "chevyssaunce." All of this contributes relatively little to our sense of the individual psychology of the pilgrims, but it contributes a great deal to our sense of their working lives.

Chaucer's ostensible purpose in introducing this material is to assure the reader that each pilgrim is superlatively skilled in his trade; its presentation is marked by a casual use of hyperbole. This hyperbole is a natural part of Chaucer's "romance style,"[9] and so we accept it as part and parcel of the Chaucerian idiom. It is clear that the hyperbole cannot be taken at face value; even an author's manipulation of coincidence could hardly account for a random assembly of people all of whom are the best exponents of their craft in the country or out of it. In my view, the apparently redundant eulogies of professional skills are simply a means of enumerating professional duties and qualifications. The naturalness of this sort of expression in a romance style, and its conversational tone, enable us to accept it, but its motivation is to direct our attention to the social and occupational functions, habits, and qualities of the Prologue figures. Chaucer keeps reminding us of "all trades, their gear and tackle and trim"[10]—the world of work in which each character is involved, the special knowledge which he commands and toward which we can adopt only a layman's attitude. Chaucer often underlines such an attitude himself by using the word "his" when referring to professional terms: "his bargaynes . . . his chevyssaunce"; "His stremes, . . . his daungers . . . His herberwe, and his moone, his lodemenage"; "his apothecaries . . . his letuaries." Surely it is this attitude which is provoked in us by the Merchant's obsession with keeping open the sea between Middleborough and Orwell—recognizably a bee in a professional bonnet. Far from expecting us to probe the matter more carefully for information about the Merchant, Chaucer wants us to react as laymen—with amusement at, and at the same time fascination with, the specialized viewpoint; how funny it is that this *is* the kind of thing merchants are interested in!

The range of professional characteristics introduced into the portraits is, however, far wider than this. They can include, for example, abstract and personal qualities. Thus, the virtues which the Knight honors and embodies— "chivalrie, / Trouthe and honour, fredom and curteisie"—and even the phrases in which he is described—"worthy," "wys," "verray," "gentil"—are appropriate to an ideal type of religious chivalry. The same is true of the "personalities" of the pilgrims who are not idealized in this way; the pompousness of the Merchant and Sergeant of Law, the Friar's winning charm, the Shipman's ruthlessness, suggest professional manners as much as individual personalities. The Squire's portrait shows us how the estate can also determine the physical appearance of the characters: his "lokkes crulle," his fashionably short clothing embroidered with "fresshe floures, whyte and reede," which recall the conventional romance springtime, are appropriate for his role as a figure of romantic chivalry, contrasted with the more sober religious aspects of chivalry represented by his father. The Clerk's lean and threadbare look has obvious connections with his calling, for in it we recognize the inseparable nature of poverty and scholarship; more important, so does Chaucer, who writes that the Friar was "nat lyk a cloysterer / With a thredbare cope, *as is a povre scoler*" (259–60). We can therefore refer temperament and physical appearance to estates concepts just as well as to the concept of an individual or an "eternal human type."

It is also worth noting how often in the Prologue we have to do with professional rogues and scoundrels: Friar, Merchant, Manciple, Miller, Reeve, Summoner, Pardoner—all take advantage of the opportunities for chicanery offered by their professions. We frequently find a sort of parody of the testimonies to professional skill, asserting the character's proficiency in the "tricks of the trade" rather than the trade itself. The mark of this parody is usually the employment of the phrases "wel koude he," "wel knew he," which elsewhere characterize the straightforward testimonies of professional skill.

> Wel koude he stelen corn and tollen thries.
> (562)

> His lord wel koude he plesen subtilly,
> To yeve and lene hym of his owene good,
> And have a thank, and yet a cote and hood.
> (610–12)

The same phrases are used to give the character of professional skills to yet other types of behavior.

> Wel koude she carie a morsel and wel kepe
> That no drope ne fille upon hir brest.
> (130–31)

> In felaweshipe wel koude she laughe and carpe.
> Of remedies of love she knew per chaunce,
> For she koude of that art the olde daunce.
> (474–76)

Those sleights of hand and verbal dexterities, those frauds and deceptions, those self-interested ambitions and habits of thought and speech which the practice of a profession permits or even encourages, can thus become linked with the concept of the estate.

An estate can be typified in two ways. Chaucer can evoke the qualities that should go with the profession, the "idealized version"; alternatively, he can evoke the malpractices and frauds which usually go with it in actuality, the "normal version." Despite their differences in character, both the Knight and the Merchant, for example, are types of their estate; each corresponds to a certain mental stereotype of the characteristics of their social class.[11] These two versions can be played off against each other; the information that the Clerk would rather spend money on books than on "robes riche, or fithele, or gay sautrie" (296) implies that it is these that would be the normal preference of other clerks. Whether it is the "good" or "bad" version of an estate we are being given, the other is kept in our minds, so that the estate itself, rather than the individual, is the root idea. And it has been noted before that the profession often determines what we regard as sinful in a character. The Monk's love of hunting and good living would take on a totally different significance in the person of a lord of the manor; it is his estate which makes them out of place and so is basic to our appreciation of the portrait.

But we must note one paradoxical aspect of the Prologue's estates content. The neutral and detailed enumeration of the daily duties of each occupation increases our awareness of the estate, rather than the individual—but this sort of enumeration is rarely found in estates literature itself. Where the satirists use concrete detail, it is not neutral, but illustrative of failings; where they are not criticizing failings, they offer generalized moral advice rather than instruction in a trade. We do gain some acquaintance with the daily activities of some estates in the development (on the whole, late) of satire on different classes of artisans; the outlining of the various ways in which they can default in their craftsmanship or selling techniques gives us some idea of the details of their trades. But there is nothing like Chaucer's continued insistence on the assembly of skills, duties, and jargon that characterizes an estate. This type of information is given only in the Prologue; elsewhere in *The Canterbury Tales* we find plentiful use of estates satire of the traditional sort, but nothing of this sense of daily work. Chaucer's introduction of this apparently "colorless" material points to his intentions. It does not work against the assumption that the Prologue figures are estates types, since the new material helps to realize them in precisely this way. But it shows how Chaucer is concerned to develop certain implications of the estates form—its stress on specialization, on the skills, duties, and habits which separate one class of society from another—rather than to remain content with its traditional aims of moral criticism, whether humorous or solemn.

IT IS A CLICHÉ OF Chaucer criticism that the Canterbury pilgrims are both individuals and types. But this critical unanimity coexists with striking divergences on what constitutes the typical or the individual. I have preferred not to attempt another way of defining or describing the typical and the individual, but to work on lines similar to those suggested by R. M. Lumiansky's terms "the expected and the unexpected."[12] Rather than trying to decide whether a character corresponds to a credible combination of personality traits, rooted in the eternal aspects of human nature, I have tried to consider how far the information given about him accords with the expectations raised by his introduction as "a knight" or "a monk." The results of this consideration have shown that the estates type was the basis for Chaucer's creation of the Canterbury pilgrims. But the accompanying analysis of the style in which Chaucer presents the estates type has also shown that the answer to the question "are the pilgrims individuals or types?" would vary according to whether it was based on source material or the reader's impression.

In the past, there seems to have been an assumption that the effect of the Prologue's material would be identical with the source from which it was drawn: if the portraits were drawn from observations of real individuals, they would suggest these individuals to Chaucer's audience; if they were drawn from social satire, they would convey the impression of moralized types. The same assumption encouraged critics to see the union of type and individual in terms of the combination of well-known features of certain social classes with invented details. Thus Lumiansky goes on to say of the Knight: "As a result of a combination of expected and unexpected traits, he assumes memorable individuality in the mind of the reader." But the qualities Lumiansky finds unexpected in "a professional military man"—the fact that he is "prudent, humble, circumspect in speech, modest in dress, and serious in religious devotion"—would not be at all unexpected in the stereotyped ideal of his estate. It is not the concreteness of invented or unexpected details (where we do find them) which produces individuality, for they are not essentially different from the concrete details that are a traditional part of estates satire. Moreover, invented details are used to extend the typical, just as well as the individual, aspects of a character.

A hint of the means by which Chaucer persuades us that the pilgrims *are* individuals—that they exist as independent people—is however given in Lumiansky's comment that the terminology of "the expected and the unexpected" "has the advantage of placing the emphasis upon the reader's reaction to the technique." This emphasis I believe to be correct; the individuality of the figures in the Prologue lies in the technique whereby Chaucer elicits from us a reaction, whether complicated or individual, similar to the reactions aroused in us by real-life individuals. He calls forth contradictory responses—a positive emotional or sensuous response conflicting with an expectation that moral disapproval is called for—in order to make us feel the complexity of his characters. He makes us uncertain of the "facts" that lie behind their social or professional facades. He uses a sense of past experience, discernible from present appearance, personality, or behavior, to give us the conviction that his characters are not eternal abstractions but are affected by time. And he incorporates an awareness of their point of view—their reactions to the traditional attitudes to their existence, their terminology, and standards of judgment—which also gives us a strong sense of their independent life. Chaucer forces us to feel that we are dealing with real people because we cannot apply to them the absolute responses appropriate to the abstractions of moralistic satire.

We may also make some suggestions about the different functions of the typical and individual aspects of the characters. One reason that Chaucer is at pains to give his characters life as individuals is obviously that they are to act as individuals in the drama of *The Canterbury Tales*; they talk and react to each other as individual human beings would. The individual aspect is therefore vital to the frame of the tales. The typical aspect is, however, equally vital to Chaucer's purpose in the whole work. The most obvious aspect of *The Canterbury Tales*, even in its incomplete state, is its comprehensiveness. It clearly aims at universality, at taking up all the themes and styles of contemporary literature and making one glorious compendium of them. The Prologue in a sense constitutes a kind of sample of what is to follow by its wide range of tone and mood. The serious ideals—chivalric, religious, laboring—which operate in the portraits of Knight, Parson, and Plowman furnish a serious tone in addition to the comic and savage ones on which Chaucer can draw in the main body of his work. But as well as this, the Prologue makes its own contribution to the genres included in *The Canterbury Tales* by the clear reference to estates literature in its form and content. It is especially appropriate that estates literature should perform this introductory function, since it lays claim to a universality of its own and since its subject matter is the whole society, the "raw material" from which the other genres select their own areas of interest. *The Canterbury Tales*, however, is not a compendium of literary genres in any simple sense. The method of the work is not additive, but dialectic; the tales modify and even contradict each other, exploring subjects in a way that emphasizes their different and opposed implications. Sometimes we can follow the development of one theme through various mutations; even where the unifying theme is absent, it is noteworthy that the stimulus for tale telling is the quarrel. The overall effect of this process of exploring tensions and contradictions is to relativize our values until we reach the absolute values of the Parson, who is willing to admit of no compromise or modification—but in assigning these absolute values to a character *within* the *Tales* (and, moreover, not to the narrator), Chaucer in one sense makes these values relative too.

The same refusal to take an absolute standpoint can be found in the Prologue. One important demonstration of this has emerged from a comparison with other estates material—the fact that the persons who suffer from behavior attributed to some of the pilgrims are left out of account—what I have called "omission of the victim."[13] I have already stressed the importance of not letting our awareness of these victims, an awareness for which other satiric works are responsible, lead us into supplying them in the Prologue for the purposes of making a moral judgment, whether on Prioress, Merchant, Lawyer, or Doctor. Chaucer deliberately omits them in order to encourage us to see the behavior of the pilgrims from their own viewpoints and to ignore what they necessarily ignore in following their courses of action. Of course, our blindness differs from theirs in being to some extent voluntary—for the pilgrims' viewpoint is not maintained everywhere in the Prologue—while their blindness is unconscious and a condition of their existence. The manipulation of viewpoint, and ignorance (willful or unconscious), are traditionally taken as features of irony, and the omission of the victim is a functional part of the ironic tone of the Prologue. The tone becomes more forthright and moves away from irony precisely at moments when we are made conscious of the victim, and in particular of the victim's attitude to the pilgrim.[14]

The omission of the victim is part of the Prologue's peculiar social ethic, which extends even to the pilgrims whom Chaucer presents as morally admirable. The Yeoman, for example, is certainly an honest and hard-working member of his profession. Yet fault has been found even with him, on the grounds that "no practical application of his skill is indicated. The description stops short at the means, the end is never indicated. . . . The result is the impression of a peculiarly truncated consciousness."[15] As regards the particular portrait, this interpretation is surely mistaken; there is no criticism of the Yeoman as an individual. The comment may however usefully focus attention on the small part played by social ends in the Prologue. . . . The *effects* of the Knight's campaigning, of the Merchant's "chevyssaunce," of the Sergeant's legal activities, even of the Doctor's medicine are not what Chaucer has in mind when he assures us of their professional excellence. It is by ignoring effects that he can present the expertise of his rogues on the same level as the superlative qualities of his admirable figures. His ultimate purpose in this is not to convey any naive enthusiasm for people, nor comic effect, although the Prologue is of course rich in comedy, nor is it even a connoisseur's appreciation of types, although this attitude characterizes the narrator's ironic pose in presenting the individual estates. The overall effect of this method is rather to sharpen our perceptions of the bases of everyday attitudes to people, of the things we take into account, and of the things we willingly ignore.

We may clarify this by pointing out that the distinction between Langland and Chaucer is not just, as is usually assumed, the distinction between a religious and a secular writer, between didacticism and comedy. It is true that Langland, and most of the army of estates writers before him, have a continual sense of the rewards of heaven and the punishments of hell, which of itself provide a reason for moral behavior, and that this sense is lacking in Chaucer. But it is also true that Langland shows, in passages such as the plowing of Piers's half acre, the practical bases for, and effects of, specific moral injunctions, while Chaucer has no *systematic* platform for moral values, not even an implicit one, in the Prologue.

When we first compare Langland and Chaucer, there is a temptation to conclude, as Manly did, that Chaucer's satire is convincing because "he does not argue, and there is no temptation to refute him. He does not declaim, and there is no opportunity for reply. He merely lets us see his fools and rascals in their native foolishness and rascality, and we necessarily think of them as he would have us think."[16] Undoubtedly it is true that Chaucer not only persuades us that fools and rascals can be very charming people, but is at the same time taking care to make us suspect that they are fools and rascals. If, however, we examine more closely what considerations determine what "he would have us think" of the pilgrims, we find that they are not always moral ones. For example, if we compare the portraits of the Friar and the Summoner, we find that many of the faults we attribute to them are identical: fondness for drink; the parading of pretended knowledge; sexual license and the corruption of young people; the encouragement of sinners to regard money payments as adequate for release from sin. Yet what is our attitude to them? I think it is true to say that our judgment on the Friar is less harsh than our disgust for the Summoner. The reasons for this, in a worldly sense, are perfectly adequate: the Friar's "pleasantness" is continually stressed; he makes life easy for everyone, is a charming companion, has musical talent; he has a white neck and twinkling eyes and good clothes, while the Summoner revolts the senses with his red, spotted face and the reek of garlic and onions.[17] But although adequate to account for our reactions, these considerations are not in any sense moral ones.

It is sometimes said that the physical appearance of the Summoner symbolizes his inner corruption; there is certainly a link between physical ugliness and spiritual ugliness in other, moralizing writers. But Chaucer is, as it were, turning their procedure around in order to point to its origins in our irrational, instinctive reactions. The explicit moralizing attitude to beauty and ugliness—that they are irrelevant beside considerations of moral worth—coexists, paradoxically, with an implicit admission of their relevance in the use of aesthetic imagery to recommend moral values. In the *Ancrene Wisse*, for example, the author associates beautiful scents, jewels, and so on with heavenly values, and stinks and ugliness with the devil; he then finds himself in the difficult position of trying to encourage an ascetic indifference to *real* bad smells.[18] Chaucer makes this tension between moral judgment and instinctive emotional reaction into a central feature of the Prologue partly in order to create the ambiguity and complexity of response which persuades us that the characters are complex individuals, but at the same time to show us, in the Prologue, what *are* the grounds for our like or dislike of our neighbors. Moral factors have a part in our judgment, but on a level with other, less "respectable" considerations. There is no hesitation in admiring the unquestioned moral worth of the Knight or Parson, but this will not prevent us from enjoying the company of rogues with charm, or despising those who have no mitigating graces.

I shall return in a moment to the significance of this lack of systematically expressed values after noting some other means which produce it. The first of these again emerges in contrast to estates material and consists of the simple but vivid similes which run through some of the portraits—head shining like glass, eyes twinkling like stars—and which play a large part in convincing us of the attractiveness of such figures as the Monk and the Friar. The constant use of this sort of comparison creates a tone which is at once relaxed, colloquial, and animated—the kind of style which, as Derek Brewer has pointed out, finds its best counterpart in the English romances and which differs strikingly from the taut, pointed style of learned satire.[19] Another type of simile is neutral or explanatory—"As brood as is a bokeler or a targe"—and occasional examples of this sort may be found in French or Anglo-Norman satire. But the first group, in which the stress on attractiveness runs counter to the critical effect of the satire, would destroy the intention of a moralizing satirist. A writer like Langland deals in occasional vivid imagery, but its effect usually works together with the moral comment.

> And *as a leke hadde yleye • longe in the sonne*
> So loked he with lene chekes • lourynge foule.
> (B.5.82–83)

> And *as a letheren purs • lolled his chekes.*
> (B.5.192)[20]

Occasionally, the imagery works *with* the moral comment in the General Prologue also: the animal imagery in the portraits of the Miller, Pardoner, and Summoner persuades us that we are dealing with crude or unpleasant personalities. In both kinds of usage, the imagery does not reflect moral comment so much as create it; and the contradictory ways in which it is used mean that it is also working to destroy the *systematic* application of moral judgments.

The role of the narrator and the use of irony in the Prologue have received abundant comments, but they can in this connection take on a new light.[21] It is the narrator who constantly identifies himself with the pilgrim's point of view—and that means the point of view of his estate—and encourages us to see the world from this angle. Even when the narrator distinguishes a pilgrim's point of view from his own, this also, paradoxically, makes us sharply aware of the series of insights into estates consciousness that we are given and of the tension between their perspectives and our own, which is implied in the "his" of such phrases as "his bargaynes."

Moreover, the narrator acts as a representative for the rest of society in its relation to each estate. In this role, he shows us how often the rest of society is not allowed to go beyond the professional facade, to know what is the truth, or to apply any absolute values to professional behavior. We are in a world of "experts," where the moral views of the layman become irrelevant. The narrator assumes that each pilgrim is an expert and presents him on his own terms, according to his own values, in his own language.[22] All excellence becomes "tricks of the trade"—and this applies to the Parson's virtues as well as to the Miller's thefts. In the Prologue, we are in a world of means rather than ends.[23] A large part of the narrator's criteria for judging people then becomes their success in social relationships at a *personal* level; they are judged on pleasantness of appearance, charm of manner, social accomplishments. Their social role is reduced to a question of sociability.

These criteria are of course ironically adopted, and we must therefore ask, what is the significance of Chaucer's use of irony in the Prologue? We can take as starting point the definition of "irony" offered by the thirteenth-century rhetorician Buoncompagno da Signa:

> Irony is the bland and sweet use of words to convey disdain and ridicule. . . .
> Hardly anyone can be found who is so foolish that he does not understand
> if he is praised for what he is not. For if you should praise the Ethiopian for
> his whiteness, the thief for his guardianship, the lecher for his chastity, the
> lame for his agility, the blind for his sight, the pauper for his riches, and the
> slave for his liberty, they would be struck dumb with inexpressible grief to

have been. praised, but really vituperated, for it is nothing but vituperation
to commend the evil deeds of someone through their opposite, or to relate
them wittily.[24]

This definition is a useful starting point precisely because it does *not* fit
Chaucer's habitual use of irony. For what he does so often is to commend the
lecher, not for chastity, but for lechery—to enthuse, in fact, over his being
the most lecherous lecher of all.

It is true that at certain moments Chaucer seems to be praising someone's
qualities "through their opposite"; we think of the "gentil Pardoner." But in
making his definition, Buoncompagno assumes that the truth about the person ironically described is always clear to us; we know that an Ethiopian is really black. The baffling feature of the Prologue, as we have seen, is how often it
weakens our grasp of the truth about a character, even while suggesting that it
is somehow at odds with the narrator's enthusiastic praise. We begin to wonder
whether the Ethiopian was not after all born of colonial parents, and white.

The same characteristics of Chaucerian irony are revealed if we analyze it
in terms of a modern definition. Earle Birney suggests that the concept of
irony always implies the creation of the illusion that a real incongruity or
conflict does not exist and that this illusion is so shaped that the bystander
may, immediately or ultimately, see through it, and be thereby surprised into
a more vivid awareness of the very conflict.[25] A large part in the creation and
dispersal of the illusion in this ironic process in the Prologue is played by the
narrator and the shifting attitudes he adopts. The shift can be sharp—
"Nowher so bisy a man as he ther nas, / And yet he semed bisier than he was"
(320–21)—or it can be more subtle, as is the case with Chaucer's constant ex-
ploitation of the different semantic values of words like "worthy," "gentil,"
"fair." To illustrate briefly: the adjective "worthy" is used as the keyword of
the Knight's portrait, where it has a profound and serious significance, indicating not only the Knight's social status, but also the ethical qualities appropriate to it. In the Friar's portrait, the word is ironically used to indicate the
Friar's lack of these ethical qualities—but it can also be read nonironically, as
a reference to social status:

> For unto swich a worthy man as he
> Acorded nat, as by his facultee,
> To have with sike lazars aqueyntaunce.
> It is nat honest; it may nat avaunce,
> For to deelen with no swich poraille.
>
> (243–47)

The reference to social status seems to be the only one in the portrait of the Merchant, who "was a worthy man with alle" (283). By the time we reach the Franklin's portrait, the word is used with a vague heartiness which seems to indicate little beside the narrator's approval: "Was nowher swich a worthy vavasour" (360).[26] This attempt to use words with something of the different emphases and connotations that they have in conversation, rather than precise and consistent meaning, produces an impression of the complexity of the characters, for it too makes it difficult to pass absolute judgment on them. The shifting meaning given to the vocabulary parallels, and indeed helps to produce, the shifting bases from which we approach the characters. And the ambivalence reflects not merely their moral ambiguity but also our own; the shifting semantic values we give to words reveal in us relative, not absolute, standards for judging people. The characters whose own values are absolute are described in absolute terms; the others inhabit a linguistic realm which is more applicable to our everyday unthinking acceptance of different criteria.

The irony in this word-play has a more important role than to serve as a comic cloak for moral criticism. Chaucer uses it to raise some very serious questions. For example, in the Knight's portrait, the word "curteisie" is associated with an absolute ideal to which one may devote one's whole life (46).[27] In the literary genre of the *chanson de geste*, from which the Knight seems to have stepped, this ideal provides the whole sphere of reference for action. The Squire's "curteisie" (99), on the other hand, is linked with other characteristics, such as his devotion to love and his courtly accomplishments, which make it seem not so much an exacting ideal as part of a way of life for someone who occupies a particular social station.[28] The "curteisie" in which the Prioress "set ful muchel hir lest" (132) should be spiritual courtesy, but it has become in her case embarrassingly worldly; instead of striving to please a heavenly spouse by spiritual grace, she has become the female counterpart of the type represented by the Squire. At the same time as another idealistic and religious meaning of "curteisie" is being evoked, the concrete manifestations of "cheere of court" (139–40)—personal adornment and accomplished manners—are shown to be in sharp opposition to it. We are left with a sense of the contradictory values implied by the term. Is it a religious value or a secular one? Is it an absolute value or merely appropriate to a certain social class or age group? Is the refined behavior involved in the conception to be defined as consideration of others or as ritualized manners? The different uses of the word reflect our shifting attitude not only to the characters, but also to the ideal itself.

This I take to be the essence of Chaucer's satire; it does not depend on wit and verbal pyrotechnics, but on an attitude which cannot be pinned down, which is always escaping to another view of things and producing comedy from the disparateness between the two. In some cases, the disparateness is indeed that between truth and illusion:

> And over al, *ther as profit sholde arise,*
> Curteis he was, and lowely of servyse.
>
> (249–50)

> For he hadde power of confessioun,
> *As seyde hymself,* moore than a curat.
>
> (228–29)

The necessity that the illusion should be seen through, should be dispersed, explains why we have the presentation of characters who are by any standards truly admirable, the use of words like "worthy" to indicate moral as well as purely social values, and the use of unpleasant imagery to describe characters who are also morally unpleasant.

But, in other instances, we are not allowed to disperse the illusion, because we have only suspicions to set against it. What "true" appellation are we to oppose to the description of the Franklin as a "worthy vavasour"? Do we *know* that his feasts are selfish ones from which the poor are excluded? Do we feel his pleasant appearance to be belied by his character? And what about the Merchant—"Ther wiste no wight that he was in dette"—and yet we do not know either that his prosperity is a hollow pretense. Or the Reeve—"Ther koude no man brynge him in arrerage"—because he was honest or because he was skilled at covering up his fraud?

I should say that all of these ambiguities, together with the omission of the victim and the confusion of moral and emotional reactions, add up to Chaucer's *consistent removal of the possibility of moral judgment.* In other words, our attention is being drawn to the illusion; its occasional dispersal is to demonstrate that it is an illusion, but the illusion itself is made into the focal point of interest. A comment of Auerbach on the irony of the *Libro de Buen Amor* of the Archpriest Juan Ruiz enables us to express this in other terms:

> What I have in mind is not so much a conscious irony of the poet, though that too is plentiful, as a kind of objective irony implicit in the candid, untroubled coexistence of the most incompatible things.[29]

The General Prologue leads us to discover in ourselves the coexistence of different methods of judging people, the coexistence of different semantic values, each perfectly valid in its own context, and uses this to suggest the way in which the coexistence of the people themselves is achieved. The social cohesion revealed by the Prologue is not the moral or religious one of Langland's ideal, but the ironic one of the "candid, untroubled coexistence of the most incompatible things."

It is remarkable that many of the methods through which Chaucer achieves this significance for the Prologue are also those through which he persuades us of the individuality of the pilgrims. Thus, important for both irony and "characterization" in the Prologue is what may be called the lack of context. In estates satire, the estates are not described in order to inform us about their work, but in order to present moral criticism; the removal of this purpose in the Prologue results, as Rosemary Woolf has noted, in the presentation of class failings as if they were personal idiosyncrasies, and thus gives us a sense of the individuality of the figures.[30] Similarly, the lack of narrative context, which would provide an apparent motive for mentioning many items of description by giving them storial significance,[31] creates the illusion of factual reporting in the Prologue, which has been convincingly related to Boccaccio's use of this technique in the *Decameron*.

> Gratuitous information . . . creates wonderfully the illusion of factual reporting. What other reason could there be for volunteering such a point if not that it actually happened?[32]

And the illusion of factual reporting in turn aids the creation of irony; there is no obligation to place the pilgrims on a moral scale if one is simply reporting on their existence.

Yet the fascination of the actual is not quite the same for Chaucer and Boccaccio. The aim of the Prologue is not to describe human beings in the same spirit as that in which Browning's Fra Lippo Lippi painted people:

> Just as they are, careless of what comes of it
> . . . and count it crime
> To let a truth slip.

The complexity of the Prologue portraits consists much more in our attitude to them than in their own characteristics. Bronson seems to be saying something like this in claiming that we are much more deeply involved with the narrator than with any of the characters in the General Prologue, "for he is almost the only figure in his 'drama' who is fully realised psychologically and who truly matters to us."[33] The center of interest in the Prologue is not in any depiction of human character, in actuality for its own sake; it is in our relationship with the actual, the way in which we perceive it and the attitudes we adopt to it, and the narrator stands here for the ambiguities and complexities that characterize this relationship.

If we draw together the results of this discussion, we find that the ethic we have in the Prologue is an ethic of this world. The constant shifting of viewpoints means that it is relativist; in creating our sense of this ethic, the estates aspect is of fundamental importance, for it means that in each portrait we have the sense of a specialized way of life. A world of specialized skills, experience, terminology, and interests confronts us; we see the world through the eyes of a lazy monk or a successful merchant, and simultaneously realize the latent tension between his view and our own. But the tension is latent, because the superficial agreement and approval offered in the ironic comment have this amount of reality—they really reflect the way in which we get on with our neighbors, by tacit approval of the things we really consider wrong, by admiring techniques more than the ends toward which they work, by regarding unethical behavior as amusing as long as the results are not directly unpleasant for us, by adopting, for social reasons, the viewpoint of the person with whom we are associating and at the same time feeling that his way of life is "not our business." To say that the General Prologue is based on an ethic of this world is not to adopt the older critical position that Chaucer is unconcerned with morality. The adoption of this ethic at this particular point does not constitute a definitive attitude but a piece of observation—and the comic irony ensures that the reader does not identify with this ethic. Chaucer's inquiry is epistemological as well as moral. This is how the world operates, and as the world, it can operate no other way. The contrast with heavenly values is made at the end of *The Canterbury Tales*, as critics have noted, but it is made in such a way that it cannot affect the validity of the initial statement—the world can only operate by the world's values. The "final statement" in the *Tales* comes not from the narrator, but from the Parson, who has not participated as we have in the worlds of the other pilgrims. In rejecting the world of the Miller, for example, he is not rejecting something for which he has felt personal enthusiasm. And *because* the final statement is given to the Parson, the narrator of *The Canterbury Tales* remains an observer who can sympathetically adapt to or report a whole range of experiences and attitudes to them.

The Prologue presents the world in terms of worldly values, which are largely concerned with an assessment of facades, made in the light of half-knowledge and on the basis of subjective criteria. Subjectivity characterizes both the pilgrims' attitude to the world and the world's (or the reader's) attitude to the pilgrims. But at least in their case, it must be repeated that their views of the world are not individual ones, but are attached to their callings—in medieval terms, their estates. The Prologue proves to be a poem about work. The society it evokes is not a collection of individuals or types with an eternal or universal significance, but particularly a society in which work as a social experience conditions personality and the standpoint from which an individual views the world. In the Prologue, as in history, it is specialized work which ushers in a world where relativized values and the individual consciousness are dominant.

Notes

1. *The Three Estates in Medieval and Renaissance Literature* (New York, 1933), pp. 6–7.

2. Bertrand Bronson, *In Search of Chaucer*, 2d ed. (Toronto, 1967), p. 60.

3. Langland is as always the exception; he incidentally portrays female retailers, brewers, and so on (W. W. Skeat, ed., *Piers Plowman*, 2 vols. [Oxford, 1886], 5.215–27). Estates literature sometimes classifies women further according to marital status—maid, wife, widow—but the attributes, as opposed to the duties, of each group are very similar.

4. Charles Muscatine, *Chaucer and the French Tradition* (Berkeley, Calif., 1957), p. 170. Muscatine is referring to the portrait-gallery form.

5. One interesting piece of evidence on this point is the scale for the graduated poll tax of 1379, which indicates the assumed income and social status of each group in fixing the amount of tax that each had to pay. See R. B. Dobson, ed., *The Peasants' Revolt of 1381* (London, 1970), pp. 105–11. This scheme, like that of estates literature, divides the clergy from the laity and works from top to bottom in each group.

6. Chaucer's use of the word "degree" does not invalidate this argument, since it can mean much more than "social rank" *(MED* 4) in Middle English; like "estaat," it also means "condition, state" in a very general sense *(MED* 6; cf. *Canterbury Tales* I.1841, IX.146), and a subordinate sense of its use in this way is "order, position" *(MED* 6d), which could well be the meaning here.

7. W. H. Clawson, "The Framework of *The Canterbury Tales*," in Edward Wagenknecht, ed., *Chaucer: Modern Essays in Criticism* (New York, 1959), p. 14.

8. It is an estates tradition to protest that one is simply writing down what everyone else says; Gower, for example, does this in the *Vox Clamantis*, and Gilles li Muisis throughout his works.

9. For the general idea that Chaucer's individual style, "lively, conversational, emphatic, dramatic, stuffed with doublets and alternatives, asseverations that are mild oaths, expletives and parentheses," derives from the Middle English rhyming romances, see D. S. Brewer's article "The Relationship of Chaucer to the English and European Traditions," in Brewer, ed., *Chaucer and Chaucerians: Critical Studies in Middle English Literature* (London, 1966), pp. 3–16.

10. [From "Pied Beauty," a poem by Gerard Manly Hopkins (1844–1889).]

11. There can be different stereotypes for a social class besides the "ideal" and the "normal." For example, a knight's role can be conceived as part of a national system of justice, or as part of aggressive religious proselytization abroad.

12. R. M. Lumiansky, *Of Sondry Folk: The Dramatic Principle in* The Canterbury Tales (Austin, Tex., 1955), p. 22.

13. [Earlier, in her book *Chaucer and Medieval Estates Satire*, Mann argued that the "omission of the victim" is a central descriptive technique in Chaucer's portraiture:

> The concentration on means rather than ends in Chaucer's descriptions of the professional skills of the pilgrims is clearly illustrated by the portraits of the Sergeant of Law, Doctor of Physic, Merchant, and Guildsmen. These pilgrims receive the narrator's enthusiastic admiration for their professional qualifications and capabilities, but the social effects of their sometimes dubious practices are left out of account. What I shall call the "omission of the victim" is a common feature of their portraits. A concomitant feature is Chaucer's substitution of satire on pompousness and self-importance for the attacks on fraud and malpractice made by other writers. (p. 86)]

14. An exception might seem to be the presence of the victim in the Friar's portrait, in the form of the "sike lazars" he neglects; we come very close to abandoning the Friar's viewpoint here, but do not quite do so because the whole passage is clothed in the Friar's own terminology, not the narrator's, and we see the lepers from the Friar's point of view, not vice versa. In the Reeve's portrait, the situation is reversed; we do see the Reeve from the point of view of the "hynes."

15. M. V. Bovill, "The *Decameron* and *The Canterbury Tales*: A Comparative Study" (unpublished thesis, Oxford University, 1966), p. 60.

16. John M. Manly, *Some New Light on Chaucer* (New York, 1926; rept., Gloucester, Mass., 1959), p. 295.

17. Other comparisons could be made. Are we prepared to accept, for example, that Chaucer thinks it morally worse for the Pardoner to be a homosexual than for the Shipman to be a murderer? Is it worse for the Reeve to terrify his underlings than for the Wife of Bath to be sexually promiscuous? The impossibility of answering these questions indicates that there is no systematic moral scale determining our likes and dislikes in the General Prologue.

18. This paradoxical situation characterizes the whole work: see J. R. R. Tolkien, ed., *Ancrene Wisse*, EETS o.s. 249 (London, 1962), pp. 45 and 55. [The *Ancrene Wisse*, or *Ancrene Riwle*, is an early thirteenth-century spiritual guide written for anchoresses, women who lead an enclosed life.]

19. See n. 9 above.

20. *Piers the Plowman*, 1.134, 146.

21. See especially E. T. Donaldson's article "Chaucer the Pilgrim," reprinted in Donaldson, *Speaking of Chaucer* (London, 1970), pp. 1–12.

22. [In the course of her discussion of the individual portraits, Mann stresses the degree to which many of the pilgrims "have absorbed the stereotypes of their own estates and can play them back in their own language" (personal communication). For instance, in discussing lines 496–506 in the Parson's portrait, she comments:

> As we look at the long passage in which Chaucer describes these characteristics, we realize that once again, it is the *character himself* who is speaking. It is not the moralist commentator who quotes from the Gospel and adds the "figure" about rusting gold; it is the Parson himself. And in the lines following, Chaucer is playing a favorite trick; he has merged his own voice with that of the pilgrim, so that we are unsure if it is reported speech, or the narrator's own comment, that is contained in the lines which energetically point out the priest's duty to set an example (501–6). Envisaging the Parson as someone who, like the Monk, is *aware* of the criticism of his class suggests to us his response to the world around him, and thus his actual existence. But a further effect is a little disquieting. This narrator can so easily adopt "false" values that his identification with the "true" values of the Parson also seems to become a temporary thing— a matter of sympathy, although certainly stronger than usual, with a point of view adopted only during association with the person who holds to it. The suggestion is of the subtlest, and is not raised by the rest of the portrait, where the narrator describes the Parson from the "outside." (p. 66)

See also her discussion of the way in which Chaucer, unlike other satirists, does not use the traditional proverb "a monk out of his cloister is like a fish out of water" to criticize the Monk, but instead has the Monk criticize the proverb. (pp. 29–31).]

23. The concentration on means rather than ends has been held by sociologists to be characteristic of the social ethic of societies dominated by economic markets, and particularly of capitalism. See Max Weber, *Economy and Society: An Outline of Interpretive Sociology*, edited by Guenther Roth and Claus Wittich, translated by Ephraim Fischoff, 3 vols. (New York, 1968), especially 3.1188: "under capitalism . . . a person can practice *caritas* and brotherhood only outside his vocational life." The ideology of capitalism has taken as its starting point the division of labor and implicitly assumed that the sum of each group's activities will be the social good. Therefore it has not considered it necessary to analyze the nature of this good or the way in which it was to be achieved. This raises the question of whether Chaucer felt the need to alter estates literature in order to express his consciousness that market relationships were assuming a new importance in his society, although the ironic tone which characterizes the Prologue suggests that Chaucer is not *encouraging* the adoption of a capitalist ethic. Similar social characteristics have been especially associated

with the city in a classic article by Louis Wirth ("Urbanism as a Way of Life," *American Journal of Sociology* 44 [1938]: 1–24):

> Our acquaintances [in the city] tend to stand in a relationship of utility to us in the sense that the role which each one plays in our life is overwhelmingly regarded as a means for the achievement of our own ends. . . . The segmental character and utilitarian accent of interpersonal relations in the city find their institutional expression in the proliferation of specialized tasks which we see in their most developed form in the professions. The operations of the pecuniary nexus lead to predatory relationships, which tend to obstruct the efficient functioning of the social order unless checked by professional codes and occupational etiquette.

Some further comments of Wirth's on the city also have striking resemblances with the world conjured up by the General Prologue:

> The city . . . tends to resemble a mosaic of social worlds in which the transition from one to the other is abrupt. The juxtaposition of divergent personalities and modes of life tends to produce a relativistic perspective and a sense of toleration of difference.

Chaucer may equally well, therefore, be recording a response to the kind of social relationships which were increasingly dominating the growing city of London.

24. Quoted by J. F. Benton, "Clio and Venus: An Historical View of Medieval Love," in F. X. Newman, ed., *The Meaning of Courtly Love* (Albany, N.Y., 1968), p. 37. The quotation is taken from Buoncompagno's *Rhetorica Antiqua*, which was written about 1215.

25. "English Irony before Chaucer," *UTQ* 6 (1937): 538–57.

26. For these senses see *OED* 2: "Of persons: Distinguished by good qualities, entitled to honor or respect on this account; estimable," and 3: "Of persons: Holding a prominent place in the community; of rank or standing."

27. *MED* (2) (perhaps too narrow a definition): "Refinement of manners: gentlemanly or courteous conduct; courtesy, politeness, etiquette." A. C. Cawley's gloss, "gracious and considerate conduct," is better (see his edition of *The Canterbury Tales* [London, 1958], p. 2, n. to line 46).

28. "Curteis" in this passage is glossed as "respectful, deferential, meek" by *MED* (3). It is important that the Squire "proves" his "curteisie" through his dexterous carving; this is an action which still has connotations of service to others, but to call this "curteis" is halfway to applying the word to the refined table manners of the Prioress.

29. *Literary Language and Its Public in Late Latin Antiquity and in the Middle Ages*, translated by R. Manheim (Princeton, N.J., 1965), p. 322.

30. Rosemary Woolf, "Chaucer as a Satirist in the General Prologue to *The Canterbury Tales*," *Critical Quarterly* 1 (1959): 152.

31. I owe this comment to Dr. L. P. Johnson of Pembroke College, Cambridge.

32. Bovill, "The Decameron and *The Canterbury Tales,*" p. 48. See also p. 55ff. on Chaucer.

33. Bronson, *In Search of Chaucer*, p. 67.

Further Reading

Although many critics accept Mann's account of the way Chaucer withholds judgment in the General Prologue, others disagree: see, for example, Rosemary Woolf, "Chaucer as Satirist in the General Prologue to *The Canterbury Tales,*" in her *Art and Doctrine* (London, 1986), pp. 77–84; and Gerald Morgan, "The Design of the General Prologue to *The Canterbury Tales,*" *English Studies* 59 (1978): 481–98. A commentary on this issue is provided by Malcolm Andrew, "Context and Judgment in the General Prologue," *Chaucer Review* 23 (1989): 316–37. The issue of social hierarchy in Chaucer's England has been well dealt with by Paul Strohm, *Social Chaucer* (Cambridge, 1989), pp. 1–23. A discussion that focuses on social meanings in the Prologue is by Stephen Knight, "Chaucer: *The Canterbury Tales,*" in *Literature in Context,* edited by Rick Rylance and Judy Simons (New York, 2001), pp. 1–14. The problem of the number of the pilgrims in the General Prologue is discussed by Caroline D. Eckhardt, "The Number of Chaucer's Pilgrims: A Review and Reappraisal," *Yearbook of English Studies* 5 (1975): 1–18. A full commentary on each pilgrim, with bibliography, can be found in the Variorum Chaucer edition, Malcolm Andrew, Charles Moorman, and Daniel J. Ransom, eds., *The General Prologue*, 2 vols. (Norman, Okla., 1993); see also Laura C. Lambdin and Robert T. Lambdin, eds., *Chaucer's Pilgrims: An Historical Guide to the Pilgrims in* The Canterbury Tales (Westport, Conn., 1996).

"The Struggle between Noble Designs and Chaos"

The Literary Tradition of Chaucer's Knight's Tale

ROBERT W. HANNING

✦ ✦ ✦

THERE IS PERHAPS no better illustration of the processes of continuity and change in medieval literature than the relationship between Geoffrey Chaucer's Knight's Tale (1386?), first of *The Canterbury Tales*, and its literary antecedents, both proximate—Giovanni Boccaccio's *Teseida delle nozze d'Emilia* (ca. 1340)—and remote—the *Thebaid* of Statius (ca. 92 A.D.). Moreover, a comparison of Chaucer's poem with Statius's epic and Boccaccio's epic romance offers important clues to the meaning of one of the most problematic tales in the Canterbury collection.

To Boccaccio and Chaucer, and to medieval authors generally, Statius was *the* authority on the fall of Thebes, one of the most traumatic events of classical legend. Charles Muscatine, in the most influential and perhaps the finest recent assessment of the Knight's Tale, states, "the history of Thebes had perpetual interest for Chaucer as an example of the struggle between noble designs and chaos," a struggle which Muscatine finds at the heart of the tale (*Chaucer and the French Tradition*, p. 190). According to Muscatine, "the noble life . . . is itself the subject of the poem and the object of its philosophic questions" (p. 187), and the manifestations of that life, "its dignity and richness, its regard for law and decorum, are all bulwarks against the ever-threatening forces of chaos, and in constant collision with them" (p. 189). In this reading, the significance of the Knight's Tale lies in Theseus's "perception of the order beyond chaos," revealed in his final speech urging a distraught Palamon and Emelye to marry, despite their grief at the death of Arcite, and thus to conform to the scheme of the universe's "Firste Moevere." As Muscatine puts it, "when the earthly designs suddenly crumble, true nobility is faith in the ultimate order of all things" (p. 190).

The present essay responds to Muscatine's analysis of the Knight's Tale in two ways. First, it examines two main sources of Chaucer's attitude toward Thebes, in order to confirm the contention that the English poet found in Boccaccio and Statius models for "the struggle between noble designs and chaos"—found, that is, a tradition of concern with the tense relationship between the human capacity to control and order life and the forces, internal and external, that resist or negate order. But if Chaucer is profoundly traditional in composing the Knight's Tale, he is also profoundly original in telling it not *in propria voce*, but as the utterance of "a worthy man" and "a verray parfit gentil knyght"—an exponent of the "noble life" of chivalry as Chaucer and his age knew it. By putting the Knight between us and the world of Theseus, Palamon, Arcite, and Emelye, Chaucer invites us to see the conflict of order and disorder as a reflection of the Knight's particular perspective on life. The Knight's Tale thus becomes simultaneously a comment on the possibilities for order in human life and a comment on the tensions Chaucer perceived within the system of late medieval chivalry. Further, since the Knight makes us painfully aware of his difficulties as an amateur storyteller, Chaucer innovates again in inviting us to equate Theseus's problems in seeking to control the realm of experience with his pilgrim-creator's trials in seeking to control the realm of art. The coincidence of problems faced by duke, "gentil" knight, and poet makes the Knight's Tale an even more complex and original poem than its most perceptive critics have noticed. Accordingly, an assessment of the tension among the tale's levels of meaning will constitute my second, more revisionist response to Muscatine's thesis.

I

The *Thebaid* recounts the fratricidal war between Oedipus's sons, Polynices and Eteocles, for the throne of Thebes. Its twelfth and last book contains the germ of Boccaccio's *Teseida*, and thus of the Knight's Tale. In the twelfth book, after the brothers have destroyed each other in a final, emblematic single combat, Creon, their uncle and now ruler of Thebes, forbids burial rites for Polynices and the Greek warriors who beseiged the city with him. The grief-stricken widows of the unburied, outraged at the sacrilegious edict but powerless to contest it, are advised by a Theban soldier to turn to Theseus, ruler of Athens, for succor. The greater part of book twelve comprises a double action attendant upon Creon's prohibition and the widows' response. Spurred on by desperation, Argia, the Greek widow of Polynices, and Antigone, Polynices' sister, attempt to perform funeral rites for the slain prince, defying the edict. They find the body and put it on a pyre with another, half-consumed corpse who turns out to be none other than Eteocles. Implacable foes in death as in life, the brothers resist the joint immolation; the fire divides into warring tongues of flame while the women watch in helpless terror. The posthumous struggle shakes the pyre, and the noise arouses Creon's guards, who apprehend Argia and Antigone and bring them before Creon to be executed—victims, it would seem, of yet another grotesque manifestation of the curse on the house of Cadmus.[1] Meanwhile, the rest of the widows journey to Athens, where, under Juno's tutelage, they win the sympathy of the Athenians and encounter Theseus as he returns in triumph from Scythia, victor over the Amazons and lord of Hippolyta. He learns the cause of the widows' sorrow and, his army swollen by recruits enraged at Creon's behavior, sets out for Thebes. Creon learns of Theseus's arrival as he prepares to punish Argia and Antigone; despite his speech of defiance, his troops are no match for Theseus, who seeks out and dispatches the Theban tyrant. The epic ends on a muted note of grief and resignation as the widows perform the obsequies for their men.

The *Thebaid* offers a dark view of life, shaped as it is by a legend that stresses the inescapable destiny which destroys a family and leads to fratricidal wrath between its protagonists. Yet the last act of the epic incorporates a movement back from the abyss of rage and destruction, and toward a reestablishment of civilized control over the darker impulses that have reigned throughout. Theseus, whose intervention saves Argia and Antigone and allows the fallen warriors to have the funeral rites owed them by heroic society, represents the belated, partial, but real triumph of civilization over passion, both at Thebes and in Scythia. The image of Hippolyta, brought back to Athens in triumph by Theseus, sums up his achievement and his function in the epic's economy: "Hippolyta too drew all toward her, friendly now in look and patient of the marriage-bond. With hushed whispers and sidelong gaze the Attic dames marvel that she has broken her country's austere laws, that her locks are trim, and all her bosom hidden beneath her robe, that though a barbarian she mingles with mighty Athens, and comes to bear offspring to her foeman-lord" (12.533–39). Every detail of this striking portrait testifies to the subduing of wildness by its opposite. The Amazon queen, sworn to enmity toward men, accustomed to flaunting her freedom from male (and social) restraint by her flowing hair, her dress with its one exposed breast (an affront to canons of feminine modesty), and her fierce demeanor, has become a neat, proper, smiling wife and mother-to-be. And as Theseus has tamed the savage Amazon, so will he tame the sacrilegious Creon, rescue Argia and Antigone from being punished for wishing to perform the rituals by which civilization imposes order even on death, and permit the comfort of those rituals to all the bereaved.

Of course, Theseus paradoxically quells rage and violence by unleashing his own, righteous wrath. In his speech to his soldiers as they set out for Thebes, he declares that they fight in a just cause, and against the Furies, emblems of primal chaos; then he hurls his spear and dashes forth on the road to the rage-torn city (12.642–49). This is no statesmanship of sweetness and light, but the sanctioned unleashing of irresistible energy to assure the triumph of "terrarum leges et mundi foedera"—the laws of nations and the covenants of the world (12.642). A similar ambivalence hovers over Theseus's shield, on which is portrayed the hero binding the Minotaur on Crete, yet another emblem of terrifying force subjugated by a greater and more licit violence (12.665–76). All of these deeds of conquest take place away from home—in Scythia, at Thebes, on Crete; Athens, like the Rome of Virgil and Statius, remains the peaceful center of civilization, where mourning women are instructed by Juno in the proper decorum of grief (12.464–70), and where there is a temple dedicated to Clementia, the spirit of mildness and forgiveness.

Despite Theseus's authority and easy victory over Creon, there is still no erasing the terrible memory of the death and destruction which fate and the gods have rained down on Thebes throughout the epic, nor can any image of rage subdued by civilization—not even the domesticated Hippolyta—match for sheer evocative power the horror of that moment when the charred remains of Polynices and Eteocles continue in death the fratricidal fury that ruined their lives. Statius's vision of the noble life offers as its highest realization the double-tongued flame and trembling pyre and the hysterical pleas of Argia and Antigone that the rage cease before it compels them to leap into the flames to separate the brothers (12.429–46). It was to such a pessimistic vision that Boccaccio, and later Chaucer, responded in taking up the poetic challenge of the *Thebaid*.

II

Writing more than twelve hundred years after Statius, Giovanni Boccaccio undertook in the *Teseida* to compose the first martial epic in Italian (12.84). He placed epic formulae of invocation at the beginning of the poem and equally conventional addresses to his book and to the Muses at its conclusion; he imitated epic structure (the *Teseida*, like the *Aeneid* and the *Thebaid*, has twelve books) and diction, reinforcing the latter by some nearly verbatim translations from Statius. But if, in all these ways, Boccaccio self-consciously donned the epic mantle, he also brought to his encounter with Statius literary sensibilities formed by medieval courtly romance and lyric, and thereby created in the *Teseida* a new, hybrid version of the noble life. Boccaccio's eclecticism declares itself at the poem's beginning; he will tell of "the deeds of Arcita and of Palemone the good, born of royal blood, as it seems, and both Thebans; and although kinsmen, they came into conflict by their excessive love for Emilia, the beautiful Amazon" (1.5). The fate of a love affair, not a city, provides a suitably elevated subject. (Even the full title of the work is eclectic: *The Thesiad* [epic] *of Emily's Nuptials* [romance].)

The first book of the *Teseida* cleverly splices Boccaccio's story into Statius's epic world by recounting Teseo's war against the Amazons (mentioned but not described by the Roman poet) and his marriage to Ipolita. Early in the second book, Boccaccio links up with the *Thebaid's* account of the last stages of the Theban war and moves quickly to Teseo's encounter with the Greek widows at his triumphant homecoming from Scythia (2.25). The bulk of book two recounts Teseo's triumph over Creon (whom he kills, as in Statius) and the funeral observances for the Greek warriors. Neither Argia, Antigone, nor the pyre with the twin-tongued flames appear; Teseo is at stage center throughout. Then, as a coda to the action at Thebes, the Greeks who are searching the battlefield for their dead and wounded find two young men, badly wounded and calling for death, whose demeanor and dress proclaim them to be of royal blood. The princes are taken to Teseo, who treats them with respect and holds them in comfortable detention in Athens as book two ends. Thenceforth Palemone and Arcita, the young Thebans, usurp the plot from Teseo, thanks to their love for Emilia, Ipolita's sister (and a character unknown to Statius), which transforms their friendship into a near-mortal rivalry.

The first two books of the *Teseida* abound with self-conscious references to Boccaccio's appropriation of the epic heritage for his own uses. The most obvious emblem of poetic metamorphosis is the discovery and "resurrection" of the half-dead Palemone and Arcita from the field of corpses that constitutes the end of the Theban war and the end of Statius's epic about it. In the *Thebaid*, Polynices and Eteocles "overcome" death by the sheer force of their mutual hatred, becoming, through the image of the warring flames, a symbol of destructive destiny's extension beyond the limits of any single life. Boccaccio replaces the pyre scene with the discovery scene, substituting a new beginning for epic closure, and his own heroes for Statius's. Moreover, Teseo responds to the new protagonists in a courteous, refined manner that distinguishes him from the spirit of the epic universe. When Palemone and Arcita are brought before him, he hears the *sdegno real* (royal disdain) in their voices (2.89), but doesn't respond to such *ira* as it deserves. Instead he is *pio* (compassionate), heals them, and, despite their danger to his rule, refuses to kill them, as that would be a great sin (2.98); as book two ends, he installs them in his palace, to be served "at their pleasure" (2.99).

One more emblem of the transformation the Italian poet has wrought on his Roman master's view of the noble life deserves special mention. After Teseo defeats Ipolita in battle, he falls in love with her, and his sudden subjection to Cupid (1.129–31) is accompanied by an equally unexpected collective metamorphosis of all of Ipolita's Amazon followers: as soon as they put down their arms, they revert to being paragons of beauty and grace; their stern battle cries become pleasant jests and sweet songs, and even their steps, which were great strides when they fought, are dainty once again (1.132). Boccaccio was inspired to this felicitous passage by Statius's image of the domesticated Hippolyta, arriving in Athens as Theseus's captive and wife. But here a whole society of wild Scythian women spontaneously suffers a sea change of beautifying refinement, manifesting precisely the transformation that *courtoisie* as a behavioral ideal imposed on the ruder manners of European feudal society in the centuries just prior to Boccaccio's own, and that the courtly romance and lyric imposed on the martial style of the classical and feudal epic.

In deflecting the *Thebaid* from epic into a new, mixed genre, the *Teseida* comes to grips with the epic theme of order versus chaos in new ways, such as the emphasis on control and refinement implicit in Teseo's courteous treatment of Palemone and Arcita when they are first brought to him as captives and the metamorphosis of Ipolita's warriors after their defeat. Control also manifests itself in other elements of the poem. Boccaccio's mastery of epic conventions—those already mentioned, plus personified prayers flying to heaven (7), catalogs of heroes arriving for battle (6), descriptions of funeral obsequies and games (11)—is a self-conscious exercise of poetic control, and the summit of literary self-consciousness is the temple Palemone builds to honor Arcita's memory: it is decorated with pictures that recapitulate the entire story of the *Teseida* (except Arcita's mortal fall from his horse!), and the narrator characterizes it as "a perfect work by one who knew how to execute it superbly" (11.70)—that is, by Boccaccio himself. The fact, however, that the "perfect work" omits the one detail of its protagonist's story—his death—that has called the temple and its pictures into being suggests that perfect control in art (and life?) is an illusion, created by overlooking those situations in which chaos erupts.

A similar cynicism about control underlies the manipulative gamesmanship used from time to time by Boccaccio's characters in dealing with persons and events. Emilia, having realized that Palemone and Arcita are watching her from their prison when she plays in her garden, encourages their ardor by flirtatious behavior—but out of vanity, not love (3.8–30). Arcita, having been released from prison by Peritoo's intercession with Teseo, speaks ambiguously to his benefactors and lies outright to his kinsman Palemone, the better to hide his passion and his plans to assuage it (3.56–76). Nor is desire the only nurse of deceit; in book nine, after Palemone and Arcita, with one hundred followers each, have fought a tournament with Emilia as the prize, Teseo consoles those on the losing side with diplomatic words, blaming the defeat on the will of Providence and complimenting them as the best warriors he has ever seen (9.51–60). The beneficiaries of Teseo's game of diplomacy are pleased, even though they don't believe all they have heard (9.61)!

The *Teseida*'s ironic view of strategies for controlling life and art ripens at times into open recognition of how attempts to defeat chaos falter when faced by its irresistible forces. When Arcita, having encountered Palemone in the woods outside Athens, attempts to dissuade him from a fight to the finish over Emilia, he recalls the wrath of the gods against the Theban lineage to which they both belong; he points out that they are victims of Fortune, and says that in any case the winner of such a battle still will not have Emilia—and then, having marshaled all these sound arguments against strife, ends with the thumping non sequitur that since Palemone wishes the battle, he shall indeed have it (5.49–60). Dominated by love's passion, Arcita can see (and speak) the truth, but cannot act on it. Later, at the climax of the story, the gods whose wrath Arcita has invoked as a reason for not fighting, intervene decisively (but not on epic grounds) when the young kinsmen commit themselves to battle for Emilia under Teseo's aegis. Arcita, who has prayed to Mars for victory, wins the tournament, only to be thrown from his horse and fatally wounded as he rides about the arena in triumph; Venus sends a Fury to startle the horse, so that she can award Emilia to Palemone, her votary. Emilia, denied her desire to remain chaste and marry neither Theban, can only blame Love for her sorry state (8.96).

To the extent that the poem's characters can control their fates by manipulation, their strategies of control and deceit make them figures of irony. But when they become prisoners of larger forces, they (and the poem's rhetoric about them) become pathetic and sentimentalized. This polarity of responses between ironic comedy, when characters act artfully, and pathetic melodrama, when they suffer victimization, differs markedly from our responses to the struggle between order and chaos in book twelve of the *Thebaid*. There Theseus's

championship of civilized values is intended to provoke admiration, not cynical amusement, and the furious excesses of Polynices, Eteocles, and Creon
elicit horrified repugnance, not sentimental involvement. Sometimes, in the
Teseida, sentiment and irony seem to pervade a scene simultaneously, especially
a scene conceived in terms of the literary conventions of courtly love. The hot
sighs of Palemone and Arcita in prison, as they debate whether Emilia is a goddess or a woman, and then languish and grow pale with love-sickness
(3.12–38), conform so completely to those conventions as to invite us to smile
at the predictability of it all, even as we sympathize with the helplessness of
the imprisoned lovers. Elsewhere, our compassionate response to the affection the young men frequently express for each other must battle with our
sense of the absurdity implicit in the repeated spectacle of the two dear
friends trying to beat each other's brains out to win Emilia.

Much more than the *Thebaid*, then, the *Teseida* moves toward an interpretive impasse, resulting from the tense equilibrium between activity and pas-
sivity, irony and pathos, in its portrayal of the issues at stake in the noble life.
Only Teseo's commanding presence seems to offer a way out of this labyrinth.
Except for the brief period in book one where he suffers from love-sickness for
the vanquished Ipolita, Teseo is the active principle throughout the poem. He
lacks the symbolic integrity of Statius's Theseus, the agent of civilization in a
world driven mad with rage; rather, he functions as an emblem of controlled
variousness in a world where variety of response and perception continually
leads to situations of collision between and within selves. For example, when
Teseo addresses the Greek widows who have sought his aid against Creon, he
moves within a single stanza from being "wounded in his heart by profound
pity" to speaking "in a loud voice kindled by rage" (2.43). Unlike Palemone or
Arcita, Teseo is not hindered by such extremes. He acts with complete martial
authority, killing Creon and capturing Thebes, then responds to the wrath of
the distraught, newly captured Theban princes when they are brought before
him by a show of magnanimity beyond their deserts (2.89); or, finding them
later fighting in the woods, he not only grants them the amnesty they request for having broken his laws, but rewards them richly (5.105). He presides
gravely over Arcita's obsequies and then, in a triumphant show of authority,
convinces Palemone and Emilia to marry, despite their deeply felt unwillingness to sully the memory of the departed prince (12.4–43).

Teseo, in short, makes everything look easy, and in so doing, he seems less
to reflect a large view of the noble life as the triumph of order over chaos than
to represent within the poem the virtuosity of its creator in assimilating and
combining epic and courtly romance conventions, and thus the triumph of
ingenuity over disparateness. The *Teseida's* major concerns are finally aesthetic

rather than moral or philosophical; its ultimate referent is literature, not experience.

III

When Geoffrey Chaucer undertook to adapt the *Teseida* for his Knight's Tale, he performed an impressive feat of truncation, shortening Boccaccio's nearly 10,000 lines to 2,250 and compressing twelve books into four. Chaucer's omissions, and the way he has the Knight call attention to them, affect the meaning as well as the length of his revision of the *Teseida*. The change most immediately noticeable to a reader of both texts is Chaucer's wholesale jettisoning of Boccaccio's self-consciously literary epic trappings—invocations, glosses, catalogs of warriors—so that the story, as told by the Knight, sounds much less like a virtuoso performance, much more like the effort of an amateur—a soldier, not a poet—who, far from taking pride like Boccaccio in his poetic achievement, wishes primarily to finish his task as quickly as possible. (The one exception to the Knight's attitude of self-abnegation, his description of the tournament lists constructed by Theseus, will be discussed shortly.) The Knight shares his creator's desire to abridge his "auctor," although, unlike other, more learned or artistic Chaucerian narrators, he never alludes to his source either by real name (as in the reference to "Petrark" in the Clerk's Tale) or pseudonymously (the "Lollius," alias Boccaccio, of *Troilus and Criseyde*). The rhetorical device by which the Knight (and behind him, Chaucer) calls attention to the process of abridgment is *occupatio*, the deliberate refusal to amplify (or describe completely) some aspect of the narrative. The Knight's first use of *occupatio* comes only fifteen lines into his tale:

> And certes, if it nere to long to heere,
> I wolde have toold yow fully the manere
> How wonnen was the regne of Femenye
> By Theseus and by his chivalrye;
> And of the grete bataile for the nones
> Bitwixen Atthenes and Amazones;
> And how asseged was Ypolita,
> The faire, hardy queene of Scithia;
> And of the feste that was at hir weddynge,
> And of the tempest at hir hoom-comynge;
> But al that thyng I moot as now forbere.
> (875–85)

Chaucer here digests the first book and beginning of the second of the *Teseida* by having the Knight, in effect, tell us what he won't tell us. Chaucer included these details of his omission, not because the story as he tells it needs them, but in order to dramatize the fact that storytelling requires the constant exercise of control in selecting material from a potentially much greater reservoir—ultimately, in fact, from all experience and all antecedent literature. *Occupatio* is an emblem of the hard choices and discipline of art: what do I leave out? And the Knight, as an amateur, is particularly troubled by this aspect of his task, given the scope of his chosen story and his lack of skill. As he puts it:

> I have, God, woot, a large feeld to ere,
> And wayke been the oxen in my plough.
> The remenant of the tale is long enough.
>
> (885–88)

Although the Knight's reference to his limited powers is a traditional *captatio benevolentiae*, it strikes a very different note from Boccaccio's self-confident epic invocations. The image of the oxen and plow is homely and unpretentious, and the idea it conjures up of the rest of the tale stretching before its teller like a great untilled field conveys some of the nervous discomfort felt by the amateur who sets out to tell a story without fully controlling it, knowing that in any case his best hope is to shorten it where he can.

The Knight's difficulties in discharging his unaccustomed artistic responsibilities surface most spectacularly in his description of Arcite's funeral rites. He recounts in some detail the procession of mourners from Athens to the place of immolation (the same grove where Palamon and Arcite first fought for Emelye), and then launches into an *occupatio* forty-seven lines long (2919–66), in which he describes the rest of the obsequies (including funeral games) while protesting that he will not do so! The distension of a curtailing device to a size that completely defeats its rhetorical intent is a masterful comic stroke on Chaucer's part, but also a strategy designed to drive home the impression of the amateur poet unable to control his material.

Precariousness of control in fact constitutes a main theme of the Knight's Tale, linking the Knight's ad hoc artistic activities with the political, and finally philosophical, program of Theseus by which the Athenian duke attempts to solve the potentially disruptive problem of Palamon and Arcite. And behind Theseus lies yet a deeper level of unresolved tension: the ambivalence of the Knight about life's meaning, as revealed in his treatment of his characters. At this last, most profound level, Chaucer confronts the paradoxes inherent in chivalry and thereby transforms Boccaccio's literary tour de force into a troubling anatomy of an archaic but, in his day, still influential ideal of the noble life.

The theme of precarious control finds emblematic embodiment in a detail included by the Knight in his description (absent in Boccaccio) of the preparations for the tournament battle between Palamon and Arcite. Amid the bustle of knights, squires, blacksmiths, musicians, and expert spectators sizing up the combatants, he directs our attention to "the fomy stedes on the golden brydel / Gnawynge" (2506–7)—a superb image of animal passion at its most elemental, restrained by the civilizing force of the (symbolic, we feel) golden bridle, but clearly anxious to throw off restraint and liberate energy.

The golden bridle is a microcosm of the entire artifice of civilization—the officially sanctioned tournament and the lists in which it is held—with which Theseus seeks to enclose and control the love-inspired martial energy of Palamon and Arcite. The lists deserve attention as a focal point of the Knight's Tale that illustrates with special clarity Chaucer's intent in transforming the *Teseida.* Chaucer has Theseus build them especially for this battle (in Boccaccio, the *teatro* where the tournament is held preexists the rivalry of Palemone and Arcita); they are thus an emblem of his authority and wisdom in dealing with the young Thebans who threaten him politically and who wish to marry his ward. Furthermore, the description of the lists constitutes the sole instance when the Knight, abandoning *occupatio*, waxes eloquent and self-confidently poetic. The lists, therefore, fuse the high point of the Knight's art of language and Theseus's art of government.

Theseus orders the lists to be built after he interrupts Palamon and Arcite fighting viciously, up to their ankles in blood, in the woods outside Athens to decide who will have Emelye. The tournament which the lists will house, and of which Theseus will be the "evene juge . . . and trewe" (1864), represents a revision of his first intention, which was to kill the young combatants when he accidentally came upon them—one a fugitive from his prison, the other under sentence of perpetual exile from Athens—fighting on his territory without his permission: "Ye shal be deed, by myghty Mars the rede!" (1747). This second, less furious response of Theseus to the love-inspired violence of his former prisoners is also a second, more legal chance for Palamon and Arcite to fight over Emelye. Theseus controls himself, and thus controls the lovers' behavior. And since the lists are built on the very spot where Theseus found Palamon and Arcite in battle (1862), the imposition of the constructed edifice on the hitherto wild grove provides yet another image of civilized control, this time over nature.

The significance of the lists grows as we learn that Theseus calls together all the master craftsmen and artists of his realm to perform the work of construction (1895–1901); indeed, in the light of these facts and of the extended description of the finished product (1887–2088), we are justified in hearing echoes of Genesis (echoes that emphasize Theseus's powers of control) in the Knight's comment ending his account: "Theseus, / That at his grete cost arrayed thus / The temples and the theatre every deel / Whan it was doon, hym lyked wonder weel" (2089–92). But if Theseus is the deity behind this work of art and government, he must share the honors of godhead with the Knight, who not only uses the same verb, "devyse," to denominate the activities of those who made the lists (1901) and his own activity in describing it (1914), but also (with artistic ineptitude but, for Chaucer, thematic significance) destroys the distance between his reality and that of his tale by describing, as if he had seen them, the insides of the temples built at three compass points atop the round enclosure of the lists ("Ther saugh I . . ."; 1995, 2062, 2065, etc.). Although the Knight clearly admires Theseus more than any other character throughout his tale, nowhere does he identify himself so directly with his surrogate as here, where both are constructing a universal image of their willed authority over their respective poetic and political worlds.

In the *Teseida*, we hear of the "teatro eminente," where the tournament will be held, at the beginning of book seven, but no details of its construction are given until stanzas 108–10, and then a mere twenty-four lines suffice (as opposed to Chaucer's two hundred). In between, various activities and speeches reduce the *teatro* to the periphery of our attention. Chaucer, instead, moves directly from Theseus's decision to build the lists to the elaborate description of them. He also includes in the description (and the structure) the temples to Mars, Venus, and Diana, which in the *Teseida* are not earthly but celestial edifices to which the prayers of Palemone, Arcita, and Emilia ascend. The cumulative effect of Chaucer's compression and redistribution of Boccaccian detail is to make of the lists the poem's dominant image, and a true *theatrum mundi*: an image of the universe, with men below and gods above (the temples are located above the gates or in a turret; 1903–9), and Theseus in the middle, imposing order and public legitimacy on the private passions of Palamon and Arcite.

Seen in this light, the lists are also a concrete, palpable version and foreshadowing of the cosmic order, held together by Jupiter's "cheyne of love" (2988), which Theseus invokes in his last act of control, his proposal and arrangement of a marriage between Palamon and Emelye some years after Arcite's death. And, because of the self-consciousness of the Knight about his artistry, the lists also claim a place in the cosmic order for poetry—not Boccaccio's epic-revival art, with its purely literary and aesthetic triumphalism, but a socially useful poetry that reflects and promotes cosmic order in a manner analogous to the deeds of a good governor. The close relationship between the enterprises of Theseus and the Knight is suggested by the direct juxtaposition of the passage expressing the duke's godlike satisfaction in his creation and this other judgment on the quality of the painting (i.e., of the poetic description) in the temples: "Wel koude he peynten lifly that it wroghte; / With many a floryn he the hewes boghte" (2087–88).

The mention of the costs attendant upon the artist's triumph provides a transition to the larger costs of the ordering activities undertaken by Theseus. First of all, the gods Mars, Venus, and Diana are presented by Chaucer as much more threatening to human happiness than their Boccaccian equivalents, thanks to the later poet's insertion into the temple ecphrases of an accumulation of details illustrating catastrophic divine intervention in human life (1995–2023, 2056–72, etc.). More crucially, Chaucer invents the figure of Saturn, grandfather of Venus and Mars and presiding deity over the greatest human disasters, who undertakes to solve the problem created by his grandchildren's respective partisanship for Palamon and Arcite: Venus has promised to answer Palamon's prayer for Emelye, Mars Arcite's for victory. Theseus, acting as patron of the Theban princes, calls the lists into being, but the last word belongs to Saturn, who undertakes to use Theseus's creation to assert his own patronage over the celestial counterparts of Palamon and Arcite. Hence the question arises: has Theseus's activity, culminating in the building of the lists, really imposed order on potentially disruptive passions of love and prowess, or has it merely provided a compact and intensified "inner circle" within which the passions—and the uncontrollable divine destiny that sponsors them—can operate to intensify human misery?

This is a sobering question, and not, I believe, one that can easily be answered positively or negatively from the data given us by the Knight's Tale, albeit many critics have tried, over the years, to argue for Chaucer's philosophical optimism (or more rarely, pessimism) on the basis of the tale. It seems to me more useful to search out the source of *this deep ambivalence about human happiness*—about whether the golden bridle and the lists control human violence or merely license and intensify it—and thereby to understand more clearly the poet's intent in creating the Knight's Tale. And here, in my view, is where the fact that the tale is told by a professional warrior becomes extremely important.

Chaucer establishes the Knight's professional perspective on the tale he tells—and on life itself—in several passages too frequently ignored by critics, describing events and feelings directly related to the career of a practitioner of martial chivalry. One such passage I have already mentioned: the powerfully mimetic description of the preparations for the tournament (2491–2522), rich with the closely observed sights and sounds of the stable, the grounds, and even the palace, where would-be experts, like bettors at a race track, choose their favorites in the coming contest:

> Somme helden with hym with the blake berd,
> Somme with the balled, some with the thikke herd;
> Somme seyde, he looked grymme, and he wolde fighte.
>
> (2517–19)

In another passage, the Knight describes the various choices of weaponry made by the participants, and ends his catalog with the purely professional, almost bored comment: "Ther is no newe gyse [of weapon] that it nas old" (2125).

The Knight's treatment of the aftermath of the tournament is as professional (almost disturbingly so) in its tone as it is amateurish in its distortion of the narrative line of his tale. When Arcite is thrown from his horse while parading around the lists in apparent triumph, the Knight immediately declares (as Boccaccio's narrator does not) that this is a critical wound; Arcite is borne to bed, "alwey criynge after Emelye" (2699). The picture is infinitely pathetic: the tournament's victor pleads, as if to the gods, for the prize he should now be enjoying, were it not for their intervention to deny it to him just when it seemed in his grasp. At this point, the Knight abruptly forsakes his wounded protagonist (and the story line) to describe in detail how Theseus entertained the rest of the tournament contestants, minimizing Arcite's injury—"he nolde noght disconforten hem alle" (2704)—and assuring them that there have been no real losers on this occasion: after all, "fallyng [as Arcite did] nys nat but an aventure," and to be captured (as Palamon was) by twenty men cannot be accounted cowardice or "vileynye" (2722–30). Theseus seeks to head off "alle rancour and envye" that might lead to posttournament disruptions of the peace (2731–34), of a kind that the Knight would have seen often enough at tournaments in his day: the duke calms the feelings of the warriors and holds a feast for them, then leads them out of town. The Knight reports Theseus's diplomacy here with the quiet approval of one who has himself been so entertained after numerous melees, and therefore recognizes how the duke has effectively defused a potentially dangerous situation—yet another instance of his ability to control life. (By contrast, the purely rhetorical performance of Teseo at the analogous point in the *Teseida* [9.51–60] is, as we have seen, greeted with some skepticism by its recipients; moreover, Boccaccio's version entirely lacks the verisimilar, "locker room" details of the combatants treating their

wounds and talking about the fight after it is over—details that underscore
the Knight's familiarity with the scene he is describing [2705–14].)

The Knight's professional perspective also endows the tournament fighting with a dimension of mimetic power foreign to Boccaccio. The alliterative
vigor with which the combat unfolds (2601–16) and the brilliant description
of Palamon's capture, despite the fury of his resistance, owing to sheer force of
numbers (2636–51), convince us that a soldier is letting us see the martial life
through his eyes, not (as in the *Teseida*) through the eyes of a poet steeped in
epic conventions. But our deepest penetration into the Knight's vocational
psyche comes, not in the lists, but when Palamon and Arcite are preparing to
fight in the woods for the right to woo Emelye. Arcite, who has gone to
Athens for two suits of armor, returns:

> And on his horse, allone as he was born,
> He carieth all the harneys him biforn.
> And in the grove, at tyme and place yset,
> This Arcite and this Palamon ben met.
> Tho chaungen gan the colour in hir face,
> Right as the hunters in the regne of Trace,
> That stondeth at the gappe with a spere,
> Whan hunted is the leon or the bere,
> And hereth hym come russhyng in the greves,
> And breketh both the bowes and the leves,
> And thynketh, "Heere cometh my mortal enemy!
> Withoute faille, he moot be deed, or I;
> For outher I moot sleen hym at the gappe,
> Or he moot sleen me, if that me myshappe";
> So ferden they in chaunging of hir hewe.
>
> (1633–47)

The Knight evokes a Hemingwayesque moment of truth to describe what it
feels like to be about to undertake a "mortal bataille"—an experience the
General Prologue of *The Canterbury Tales* tells us he has had fifteen times. The
loneliness of the moment of truth is stressed at the beginning of this passage,
and the role of Fortune ("myshappe") at its conclusion. The chilling insight
and particular details of this passage are entirely the Knight's (and Chaucer's),
yet it has a Boccaccian point of departure, comparison with which makes
Chaucer's skill and his interests even more obvious. In *Teseida* 7, when Palemone and Arcita arrive at the *teatro* on the day of the tournament, each with
his hundred followers, Boccaccio sums up the feelings on hearing each

other's party and the roar of the crowd by using the simile of the hunter wait-ing for the lion. But the effect is deflating, not exalting: the hunter is so afraid, he wishes he had not spread his snares; as he waits, he wavers between being more and less terrified (7.105–7). So the young princes, facting their moment of truth, think better of their daring: "within their hearts they suddenly felt their desire become less heated" (7.107). From this cynical, comic moment, Chaucer fabricates a perception of the teeth-gritting readiness for death that the professional warrior must take with him into battle.

With this moment, we plumb the absolute depths of the Knight's vision of life as a deadly, and arbitrary, business. This sense underlies another wonder-fully apt remark he makes just before the escaped Palamon discovers the dis-guised Arcite in the grove outside Athens:

> No thyng ne knew he that it was Arcite;
> God woot he wolde have trowed it ful lite.
> But sooth is seyd, go sithen many yeres,
> That "feeld hath eyen and the wode hath eres."
> It is ful fair a man to bere hym evene,
> For al day meeteth men at unset stevene.
>
> (1519–24)

Fortune, that is, will bring together men without an appointment, and the result may well be, as it is this time, that a fight will result. The warrior must live with one hand on the hilt of his sword; he cannot expect ample warning about when to use it.

This fatalistic sense of life, quite amoral in its recognition of the uncontrol-lable element in human affairs, seems to me to lead the Knight toward two contrary sets of conclusions, reflected in his tale's ambivalence about the pos-sibility of order in the world. First, by stressing the arbitrariness of events, he succeeds in reducing all of his protagonists except Theseus to the level of playthings of large forces they cannot control. Palamon and Arcite are found by *pilours*, pillagers, in a heap of dead bodies on the field outside Thebes. "Out of the taas the pilours han hem torn" (1020), and this wrenching, almost ce-sarean "birth" of the young heroes into the story, so different in tone from the courteous rescue afforded them by Teseo's men at this point in the *Teseida*, gives way inside three lines of verse to Theseus's decision to send them "to Atthenes, to dwellen in prisoun, / Perpetuelly" in a tower (1022–32). The import of this brusque movement from *taas* to *tour*, with all of Boccaccio's intervening civilities ruthlessly extirpated, is inescapable: life is a prison into which we are born as Fortune's minions. From this point of view, the rest of Palamon's and

Arcite's lives is a passage in and out of prison, with the differences between captivity and liberation so blurred that at one point Arcite can call his release from the tower through the intervention of Perotheus a sentence "to dwelle / Noght in purgatorie, but in helle" (1225–26), while prison, instead, is "paradys" (1237). Furthermore, the subsequent enclosures prepared for them by Theseus seem as imprisoning as the tower; even the lists, in this reading, render the young princes helpless before Saturn's whim, which is as arbitrary as Theseus's initial decision to imprison them, but more deadly. When Arcite is thrown from his horse, he is "korven out of his harneys" (2696) and carried off to die— a grim act of release that recalls his being torn out of the *taas* and supports a dark view of life as a succession of equally brutal operations of imprisonment and release performed upon humanity by an indifferent or hostile universe.

The Knight, when he espouses this dark view, becomes practically as heedless of the feelings of his characters as is Saturn. He makes fun of the young lovers and turns their heartfelt, Boethian complaints about the meaning of this cruel life into a *dubbio*, or love-problem game, at the end of part one. He leers at Emelye as she performs her rites of purification before praying to Diana to remain a virgin (a prayer doomed to rejection; 2282–88), and, as we have seen, he leaves the wounded Arcite crying for Emelye while he recapitulates Theseus's diplomatic treatment of the rest of the tournament combatants. We are surely intended by Chaucer to blanch in horror at the grim levity with which the Knight ends his expert description of Arcite's mortal condition:

> Nature hath now no dominacioun,
> And certeinly, ther Nature wol not wirche,
> Fare wel physik! go ber the man to chirche!
> (2758–60)

It is against this strand of professionally inspired pessimism and stoicism that the image of Theseus the bringer of order must be placed—as the mouthpiece of a philosophical optimism that expresses the Knight's pulling back from the edge of the abyss to which his sense of death and fortune leads him. Like Statius so many centuries before him, the Knight needs Theseus, and at the ending of his tale allows Theseus's last diplomatic initiative complete success. Invoking the order of the universe to explain to the still griefstricken Palamon and Emelye why they should no longer mourn for Arcite, Theseus counsels them "to maken vertu of necessitee" and "make of sorwes two / O parfit joye, lastynge everemo" by marrying (3042, 3071–72). The rhetoric here is at least in part Boethian—with, as critics have noted, some odd turns—but the strategy behind it is wholly political. Theseus has been led to propose the marriage by his desire "to have with certeyn countrees alliaunce, / And have fully of Thebans obeisaunce" (2973–74). For him, this is a dynastic alliance, and thus another imposition of political order on human passions (here, grief). Because the Knight has given vent to his darker perceptions elsewhere in his tale, however, we are allowed, nay, intended to take some of Theseus's philosophic justifications for his political initiative *cum grano salis*. We know by now how precarious and potentially ironic the duke's structures of control can be, even if the Knight wishes to forget this. Indeed, even here, the phrases from Theseus's speech about virtue and necessity, sorrow and joy, encourage us to detect someone's desperation—whether Theseus's or the Knight's is not clear—to find an alternative to the dark despair that flooded the poem with Arcite's death. The lingering influence of that despair inheres in Theseus's reference to "this foule prisoun of this lyf " (3061), a phrase ironically recalling the tower to which he condemned Palamon and Arcite early in the story, thus literally making their life a prison.

The secret of Chaucer's recreation of the *Teseida* as the Knight's Tale lies, then, in his vivid and profound comprehension of the tensions that might well exist within the *Weltanschauung* of a late medieval mercenary warrior. Or perhaps he simply appreciated the contradictions in his society's concept of chivalry. The knight of Chaucer's day carried with him a very mixed baggage of Christian idealism, archaic and escapist codes of conduct, aesthetically attractive routines of pageantry, and a special function as the repository of skills and graces appropriate to the training of young aristocrats. In his famous General Prologue portrait, Chaucer's own Knight possesses a high moral character of an archaic (if not totally imaginary) kind: "fro the time that he first began / To riden out, he loved chivalrie, / Trouthe and honour, fredom and curteisie" (44–46). He combines this idealism of outlook and behavior ("he nevere yet no vileynie ne sayde / In al his lyf unto no maner wight" [70–71]) with a thoroughly professional mercenary career that has taken him to most of the places where the noble warrior's virtues and skills could be practiced during Chaucer's day. This synthetic phenomenon, the idealistic killer (he had "foughten for oure feith at Tramyssene / In lystes thries, and ay slayn his foo" [62–63]), embodies in his person some but not all of the main strands of chivalry. His son, the Squire who accompanies him on the pilgrimage, supplements these by personifying the virtuosic and aesthetic side of late medieval chivalry: he sings, dances, loves hotly, and fights very little. Chaucer's splitting of the chivalric complex into two generationally distinct segments allowed him to isolate what seemed to him the real paradox of chivalry—its imposition of moral idealism on a deadly, and therefore potentially nihilistic, profession—for treatment in the Knight's Tale, leaving its decorative aspects to be teased in the harmlessly inept story told (but not completed) by the Squire, himself an unfinished creature, when his turn comes on the road to Canterbury.

The Knight's Tale, reflecting as it does the problematic view of life implicit in a code that seeks to moralize and dignify aggression, looks back across the centuries to enter into dialogue with the last book of Statius's *Thebaid*, as well as with Boccaccio's *Teseida*, on the question of what Charles Muscatine calls "the struggle between noble designs and chaos." Reading Chaucer's chivalric tale with its ancestry in mind heightens our appreciation of both the uniqueness of his art and the continuities of its tradition.

Notes

In preparing this essay I have used the following primary texts: Statius, *Thebaid*, ed. and trans. J. H. Mozley (London and New York, 1928); Giovanni Boccaccio, *Teseida delle nozze d'Emilia*, ed. Aurelio Roncaglia (Bari, 1941); *The Works of Geoffrey Chaucer*, ed. F. N. Robinson, 2d ed. (Boston and London, 1957). Of the enormous literature on the Knight's Tale, the following considerations seem to me most useful: Charles Muscatine, *Chaucer and the French Tradition* (Berkeley and Los Angeles, Calif., 1957), pp. 175–90; E. Talbot Donaldson, ed., *Chaucer's Poetry* (New York, 1958), pp. 901–5 (I am especially indebted to Professor Donaldson for calling my attention to lines 1519–24 of the tale); Donald R. Howard, *The Idea of the Canterbury Tales* (Berkeley and Los Angeles, Calif., 1976), pp. 227–37; Robert M. Jordan, *Chaucer and the Shape of Creation* (Cambridge, Mass., 1967), pp. 152–84; John Halverson, "Aspects of Order in the Knight's Tale," *Studies in Philology* 57 (1960): 606–21; R. Neuse, "The Knight: The First Mover in Chaucer's Human Comedy," *University of Toronto Quarterly* 31 (1962): 299–315; H. M. Cummings, *The Indebtedness of Chaucer's Works to . . . Boccaccio* (Menasha, 1919), ch. vi.

On late medieval chivalry, see Richard Barber, *The Knight and Chivalry* (Ipswich, 1970, 1974); Gervase Mathew, "Ideals of Knighthood in Late Fourteenth-Century England," in *Studies in Medieval History Presented to Frederick Maurice Powicke*, ed. R. W. Hunt, W. A. Pantin, and R. W. Southern (Oxford, 1948), pp. 354–62.

All translations from the *Teseida* are my own. Where line numbers are given in the text, they represent: for the *Thebaid* and the *Teseida*, book and stanza; for the Knight's Tale, line numbers according to the system adopted by Robinson in his edition.

1. [Cadmus is the legendary founder of Thebes. In Greek mythology, the city was a place of repeated acts of internecine violence, culminating in Oedipus's murder of his father and marriage to his mother; his curse upon his sons, Polynices and Eteocles; and the battle between them described in Statius's *Thebaid*.]

Further Reading

Hanning's essay argues that the Knight's Tale cannot be fully understood unless placed in the literary context provided by Statius's *Thebaid* and Boccaccio's *Teseida*; the essay is a model of literary history, showing how Chaucer worked within, and altered for his own purposes, a living literary tradition. Some critics have disagreed with Hanning's argument that both Theseus and the Knight fail in their attempts to bring order out of chaos, seeing the tale as more successful in achieving its intended goals. See, for example, Joerg O. Fichte, "Man's Free Will and the Poet's Choice: The Creation of Artistic Order in Chaucer's Knight's Tale," *Anglia* 93 (1975): 335–60; Derek Brewer, "Chaucer's Knight's Tale and the Problem of Cultural Translatability," in *Corresponding Powers: Studies in Honour of Professor Hisaaki Yamanouchi*, edited by George Hughes (Woodbridge, Suffolk, 1997), pp. 103–12; and John Finlayson, "The Knight's Tale: The Dialogue of Romance, Epic, and Philosophy," *Chaucer Review* 27 (1992): 126–49. The gender politics of the tale have been explored by A. C. Spearing, "Classical Antiquity in Chaucer's Chivalric Romances," in *Chivalry, Knighthood, and War in the Middle Ages*, edited by Susan J. Ridyard (Sewanee, Tenn., 1999), pp. 53–73; Susan Crane, *Gender and Romance in Chaucer's* Canterbury Tales (Princeton, N.J., 1994), pp. 169–85; and Patricia Clare Ingham, "Homosociality and Creative Masculinity in the Knight's Tale," in *Masculinities in Chaucer*, edited by Peter G. Beidler (Cambridge, 1998), pp. 23–35. Full readings of the tale, very different in their emphases, are provided by H. Marshall Leicester, Jr., *The Disenchanted Self: Representing the Subject in* The Canterbury Tales (Berkeley, Calif., 1990), pp. 221–383; and Lee Patterson, *Chaucer and the Subject of History* (Madison, Wis., 1991), pp. 165–230.

Nature, Youth, and Nowell's Flood

V. A. KOLVE

◆　◆　◆

Aｌｔｈｏｕｇｈ ｔｈｅ Mｉｌｌｅｒ sets out to "quite" the Knight's Tale—to offer a countervision of human experience—the fact that the Knight has chosen to address the Christian purpose of the journey only by indirection plays no part whatsoever in bringing the Miller to the fore. The Miller's characters, to be sure, swear many a Christian oath, with even St. Thomas of Kent, toward whose shrine the pilgrims travel, twice pressed into service. But such oaths invite no close attention and enjoy no privileged status within the fiction; they are simply part of the colloquial English speech that Chaucer imitates in this tale with a special felicity and accuracy of ear. When Gerveys the smith greets Absolon:

> What, Absolon! for Cristes sweete tree,
> Why rise ye so rathe? ey, *benedicitee!*
> What eyleth yow? Som gay gerl, God it woot
> (3767–69)

he uses three Christian formulas without intending a single one. They are part of his characteristic sound, no more, and other characters in the tale season their speech in similar ways.[1] We even hear a prayer in the course of the tale, but it is a night spell against elves and "wightes" so hilariously muddled as to end, almost logically, with a question for St. Peter's sister. The Christianity it brings into the tale is that of complacent superstition, imperfect in its forms, deficient in its understanding, but solemnly commended as a plain man's religion. "What! thynk on God, as we doon, men that swynke" (3491).

Christian reference of this sort requires little comment; its function is local and limited. But in addition, the action of the tale moves through two large narrative images which might properly be expected to address Christian truth: the one a ritual of religious adoration, the other a rehearsal of the preparations for Noah's Flood. That they are not meant to bear such weight in this instance seems equally clear. Chaucer warns us in the prologue in his own voice that "gentillesse, / And eek moralitee and hoolynesse" are not to be looked for in this story (3179), and nothing he says in the Miller's voice leads us to expect the contrary. But between this expressed intent and the intrinsic tendency of his chosen material there is a radical disjunction that is not only central to the tale, but to the special challenge I think Chaucer set himself in its making: the witty and difficult business of writing about a second Flood without invoking, to any serious religious end, the meaning of the first. The means by which he sought to disengage this "new image" of the Flood from the moral and doctrinal significance that had accrued to its original text across centuries of exegesis involve matters of genre, imagery, and mode of action. Their complex interplay in relation to this great subject is as brilliant and audacious as anything in Chaucer's poetry and constitutes, on a level far deeper than the mimetic, the distinctive "voice" of the Miller in his tale. Within a tale that recalls in its action the Flood with which God once cleansed the world of sin, and which was understood to prefigure the destruction of the world to come, Chaucer chose to explore the possibility of a purely comic, purely secular narrative art.

When Chaucer warns that what is to follow is a "cherles tale" in which "harlotrie" is "tolden," he raises in his audience certain expectations and dismisses others, addressing their prior literary experience as something he will confirm or revise in the course of the tale. For the sake of convenience I shall call the genre "fabliau," though I do not mean to restrict the term to tales derived solely from the French tradition; many of the Italian *novelle*, especially Boccaccio's, imply a similar set of propositions about human experience, and that set as such is our present concern. In writing his "cherles tales," Chaucer drew upon both French and Italian sources, and for our present purposes we may likewise ignore distinctions of provenance in favor of the assumptions—the vision of life—they share.

Characters in such stories live, for the most part, as though no moral imperatives existed beyond those intrinsic to the moment. They inhabit a world of cause and effect, pragmatic error and pragmatic punishment, that admits no goals beyond self-gratification, revenge, or social laughter—the comedic celebration of any selfishness clever enough to succeed. The exclusions of the genre are as decisive as its preferences, chief among them the fact that no one—not the characters, not the author, not the person whom the reader or auditor is invited to think of himself as being—apprehends the action "under the aspect of eternity," in terms of good and evil, heaven or hell. If religious matters intrude, they are more likely to do so as a comic means of manipulation than as an adumbration of the divine. The end sought is laughter, not meditation on a countertruth. The actions are swift, the stories short, and there is little room for detailed characterization: a person is what he does, and one or two actions tell us all we will ever learn about him; for the rest, there is only his membership, already real or (by the end of the tale) at last begun, in a company of more or less grown-up people. The company is made up of familiar types—avaricious merchants, restless wives, suspicious husbands, bragging cowards, lecherous priests, clever clerks—all of them persons who have traveled a certain distance down life's road, show some dust from the journey, and are able to assimilate a further lesson or two without too serious a loss of social composure. In this world of winner and loser, duper and duped, life is a compromising business; it is no great shock to discover, in the course of the action, yet another way in which a person can use or be used.

The generic introduction to this "cherles tale" is meant to free Chaucer's art from certain demands we elsewhere legitimately make upon it. But, as we soon discover, he means nothing reductive thereby. In every one of his fabliaux—I include in this group the tales of the Miller, Reeve, Shipman, Summoner, and Merchant—Chaucer gives us more than the genre promises, or than most other examples had ever thought to provide. In the case of the Miller's Tale, we are offered not only the essential vision of truth that defines the genre—a fiercely comic respect for things as they are and for the way folly will find its own punishment—but something imaginatively finer besides. Working with three fabliau motifs of a highly volatile kind—two of them coarsely obscene (the misdirected kiss and the arse branding) and a third that verges upon blasphemy (the parodic reenactment of Noah's Flood)—Chaucer manages to create a narrative that is not only funny but also oddly innocent and imaginatively gay. The Miller's Tale represents the fabliau largely denatured of its indecency, brusqueness, and cynicism, although it recounts an action as outrageous as any in the entire corpus of such tales.

That of course is the work of a storyteller who is also a stylist, a rhetorician exploring the furthest possibilities of a genre. Charles Muscatine sees in this tale "fabliau at the stage of richest elaboration"—"in no other naturalistic poem of Chaucer is practical circumstance so closely tended, and practical detail so closely accounted for."[2] Muscatine's assessment of the stylistic consequence of this detail is deservedly well known and will permit us to focus instead on the tale's richness of figurative specification, which I take to be of comparable importance: the series of images from the world of nature used to characterize, in highly specific and preferential ways, the energies that inform its action. They are brief similes, often proverbial, and sometimes arranged in catalog form; yet I think Chaucer meant us to visualize them just as surely as he meant us to "see" certain functional details, like the hole alongside Nicholas's door "ther as the cat was wont in for to crepe" (3441), or the larger scenes that potentially address a higher, extrafictional meaning. It was a commonplace of the rhetoric books, both classical and medieval, that metaphor and simile "set things before the eyes," and if we would respond to this tale in its full richness, we must allow ourselves to visualize both setting and simile; we must see "in our mind's eye" both literal and figurative detail.

Alisoun, as the object of all desires, may be said to stand at the tale's center; the way in which she moves, along with the way in which the others move toward her, decisively establishes its underlying ethos. Although the brief description used to introduce her in relation to her husband would suffice for most fabliaux,

> Of eighteteene yeer she was of age.
> Jalous he was, and heeld hire narwe in cage,
> For she was wylde and yong, and he was old
> (3223–25)

Chaucer soon presents her in a portrait thirty-eight lines long, as finely crafted as any in the General Prologue. He takes the phrase "wylde and yong" and explores its meaning through a series of images drawn from the world of young animals and green, blossoming things—a landscape so attractively and exuberantly alive that the adjective "wylde" loses all moral connotations:

> Fair was this yonge wyf, and therwithal
> As any wezele hir body gent and smal.
> A ceynt she werede, barred al of silk,
> A barmclooth eek as whit as morne milk
> Upon hir lendes, ful of many a goore.
> Whit was hir smok, and broyden al bifoore
> And eek bihynde, on hir coler aboute,
> Of col-blak silk, withinne and eek withoute.

The tapes of hir white voluper
Were of the same suyte of hir coler;
Hir filet brood of silk, and set ful hye.
And sikerly she hadde a likerous ye;
Ful smale ypulled were hire browes two,
And tho were bent and blake as any sloo.
She was ful moore blisful on to see
Than is the newe pere-jonette tree,
And softer than the wolle is of a wether.
And by hir girdel heeng a purs of lether,
Tasseled with silk, and perled with latoun.
In al this world, to seken up and doun,
There nys no man so wys that koude thenche
So gay a popelote or swich a wenche.
Ful brighter was the shynyng of hir hewe
Than in the Tour the noble yforged newe.
But of hir song, it was as loude and yerne
As any swalwe sittynge on a berne.
Therto she koude skippe and make game,
As any kyde or calf folwynge his dame.
Hir mouth was sweete as bragot or the meeth,
Or hoord of apples leyd in hey or heeth.
Wynsynge she was, as is a joly colt,
Long as a mast, and upright as a bolt.
A brooch she baar upon hir lowe coler,
As brood as is the boos of a bokeler.
Hir shoes were laced on hir legges hye.
She was a prymerole, a piggesnye,
For any lord to leggen in his bedde,
Or yet for any good yeman to wedde.

(3233–70)

The passages I have italicized, which liken Alisoun to various animals and birds, trees and blossoms, alternate with passages that detail her specifically human situation. We are shuttled back and forth between similes that suggest an animal nature—free, instinctive, sensual, untamed—and an inventory of the costume that is meant to contain those energies and cover all that beauty. Her clothing is insistently black and white—coal-black and milk-white—and is steadily registered as something that limits and confines: she is belted and girdled, with purse attached, brooch fastened, shoes laced high; her hair is held back by a headband and covered by a cap; a goodwife's apron is spread across her loins. The costume serves both to indicate Alisoun's status as a bourgeois wife and to suggest the constraints of that situation; it becomes an emblem of the narrow cage—less moral than social—within which old John seeks to confine all that is "wylde" within her.

The portrait of Absolon is fully as formal and nearly as long; it too greatly exceeds fabliau convention. As parish clerk, his duties at the Mass would have included chanting the *Kyrie* and *Sanctus*, reading the Epistle, bearing the pax bread about the congregation, swinging the censer, and assisting at the offertory. Some of these duties are noted in the portrait, as is the way he converts them into occasions for casting loving glances at the ladies of the parish. But first we are told what he looks like, in a fashion stylistically related to the portrait of Alisoun:

> Now was ther of that chirche a parissh clerk,
> The which that was ycleped Absolon.
> Crul was his heer, and as the gold it shoon,
> And strouted as a fanne large and brode;
> Ful streight and evene lay his joly shode.
> His rode was reed, his eyen greye as goos.
> With Poules wyndow corven on his shoos,
> In hoses rede he wente fetisly.
> Yclad he was ful smal and proprely
> Al in a kirtel of a lyght waget;
> Ful faire and thikke been the poyntes set.
> And therupon he hadde a gay surplys
> As whit as is the blosme upon the rys.
> A myrie child he was, so God me save.
>
> (3312–25)

His golden hair, combed out like a great "fanne" (possibly a basket for winnowing grain from chaff, more likely the "vane," or quintain, set up as a target for jousting with a lance), recalls that of his namesake, King David's comely son, whose luxuriant hair brought about his death and made him in medieval scriptural exegesis an example of the effeminacy of sin.[3] But then we move to Absolon's face, which is described in an image as homely as certain of those employed for Alisoun: his cheeks were red, his eyes as gray as those of a goose. And just as the black and white of her dress loses all austerity in proximity to her body, so here the window of St. Paul's cathedral is asked to do no more than furnish a design cut into the leather of Absolon's shoes: it allows the red of his stockings to show through. The potentially moral notations are not allowed to signify; they do not become signs. In a similar fashion, we do not learn of the white surplice he wears as parish clerk until after we have focused upon his fashionable shoes and stockings, along with the blue tunic that is elaborately laced and closely fitted to his body. The ecclesiastical surplice covers (imperfectly) the clothing of a gallant; indeed, by means of rhetorical sequence, it is made to seem no more than that costume's elegant completion. Far from invoking some standard of devotion or chastity against which to measure Absolon's character, the white surplice is used to make us see him (in the concluding image) as a flowering branch—as "blosme upon the rys"—a part of the natural world burgeoning in the spring.

Since being parish clerk was only a part-time occupation, none too well paid, Absolon expends his energy and time in other ways as well—as barber-surgeon, legal aide, and tavern musician. But our present concern is with what moves him toward Alisoun, and that is defined in a way by now familiar: "I dar wel seyn, if she hadde been a mous, / And he a cat, he wolde hire hente anon" (3346–47). Absolon himself has a fondness for such comparisons, courting her with food, bird, and animal images borrowed from the Song of Songs—its *sensus spiritualis* the last thing on his mind.[4]

> What do ye, hony-comb, sweete Alisoun,
> My faire bryd, my sweete cynamome? . . .
> No wonder is thogh that I swelte and swete;
> I moorne as dooth a lamb after the tete.
> Ywis, lemman, I have swich love-longynge,
> That lik a turtel trewe is my moornynge.
> (3698–3706)

Such imagery invites us to imagine the action of the tale not only as it occurs literally, in the streets of Oxford and within the rooms of a carpenter's house, but in a second way as well, against a country landscape in which Absolon and Alisoun are seen as young animals—charming, instinctual, untamed—a spring landscape of whose natural growth and issue they are part. Absolon dressed in his "gay surplys / As whit as is the blosme upon the rys" belongs to the same fecund world as Alisoun, softer than a sheep's fleece, her eyebrows black as sloeberries, more delightful to look on than a pear tree newly blossomed or flowers in a meadow.

The formal portrait of Nicholas is likewise lengthy and rich in detail, but its procedures are different and link him with another world. Instead of details concerning his person or his clothing, we are given an extended description of his room: the architectural space and its furnishings become an inventory of his inner "condicioun." He has "lerned art"—grammar, rhetoric, logic—as well as a bit of music and predictive astrology, and his room reflects those interests: along with bed and chest, it contains books, an astrolabe, "augrym stones" for arithmetic, and a psaltery on which he accompanies himself in singing. Nicholas is close and secretive, in every way an indoors man, but even he keeps his room strewn with green grasses and herbs:

> A chambre hadde he in that hostelrye
> Allone, withouten any compaignye,
> Ful fetisly ydight with herbes swoote;
> And he hymself as sweete as is the roote
> Of lycorys, or any cetewale.
>
> (3203–7)

The last comparison gives him a characteristic "taste on the tongue"[5]—like Absolon, who chews "greyn and lycorys" and "trewe-love" in order "to smellen sweete" and be "gracious" (3690–93), and like Alisoun, the most delicious of them all, a honeycomb, a piece of cinnamon, her mouth as sweet as honeyed ale or apples laid up in hay. But it also connects him, in its function as simile, to the metaphoric world of Alisoun and Absolon, fully as much as do the literal wild grasses and herbs that adorn his room. He does not live in the poem's "natural landscape" as fully as they; he is instead a shaper of fictions, a clerk "ful subtile and ful queynte" (3275), with some inclination toward theoretical studies. But Nicholas moves toward Alisoun under the same compulsion as does Absolon, in response to the same sort of instinctive desire, and the grasses in his room confer upon his person some share of their freshness and charm. Though "this sweete clerk," as Chaucer frequently calls him, is more intellectual and cunning than Absolon and Alisoun, he is ranged with them in these details, as well as in one of the central oppositions of the tale, the difference between young and old.

That "youthe and elde is often at debaat" is, of course, one of the fundamental propositions of fabliaux (3230), and the youthfulness of Absolon, Nicholas, and Alisoun outweighs all differences among them when set against her husband, John's, old age. It is important, in our survey of the tale's natural imagery, to notice how Chaucer's rhetoric reinforces that fact. The similes that provide us with all we know of Alisoun's size, her singing, her movement, and her capacity for self-delight are either of very young animals, too young to be strictly applicable to a girl of eighteen, much less one already married—the images, for instance, of a calf or kid still with its mother—or

else refer to animals so small and quick that we do not think of them in terms
of age at all, like a mouse, a weasel, or a swallow. When Nicholas proffers his
love and his roaming hands simultaneously, Alisoun springs back like a colt
in a farrier's frame—"as a colt dooth in the trave" (3282)—an image that defines their common condition, for it concerns an animal only beginning to be
tamed, an animal not yet made conformable to wills other than its own. Absolon, a "myrie child" (3325), is likewise made to seem younger than he is,
weeping after his unfortunate kiss "as dooth a child that is ybete" (3759). His
beauty, like Alisoun's, is compared to new blossoms. And Nicholas, too, for all
his skill at both fiction and lechery, presents a most youthful and innocent appearance. In the formal portrait surveyed above, only one line (out of thirty-
one) is devoted to telling us what he looks like, but it has a corresponding
importance. He is "lyk a mayden meke for to see" (so meek he seems virginal,
like a child [3202]).[6] Chaucer, in short, keeps steadily before us the youthfulness of his young people and, not infrequently, by a gift of rhetoric, makes
them seem even younger than they are. It is another of the ways in which he
extirpates from this fabliau plot the cynicism and harshness latent in its
materials—a potential that can be readily assessed by a look at the tale's closest analogues, in which a seasoned town whore with three impatient clients,
or a promiscuous wife with more than one lover, enact the misplaced kiss and
its revenge. The men usually include a lecherous priest or friar, a blacksmith,
and sometimes a miller, and the plot customarily turns on problems of
scheduling rather than erotic preference, since the woman expects to favor
all her suitors. None of them is young, and their fornication, though comic, is
also coarse, urgent, and graceless. Chaucer's version, in contrast, uses certain
ideas about youth to reinforce the attractiveness of the animal images we
have been examining. Two conditions are set in opposition to a third: "for she
was wylde and yong, and he was old."

The young, of course, do not stay young forever. They grow into a moral
life—into a knowledge of good and evil—and in the medieval tradition that divided the life of man into six ages, this process was understood to occur during
the second age, between the seventh and the fourteenth years. But the condition of youth, more broadly defined, was viewed with a certain indulgence, a
certain freedom from the strictest sorts of moral judgment, that can be demonstrated even in the earliest monastic penitentials and can be traced through
a good deal of later medieval thought and literature.[7] Medieval writers on the
ages of man, like the authors of long allegorical poems on human life, although
they urge upon youth some lessons in caution, courtesy, and religious devotion,
also display a realistic sense of the condition they are addressing. Because youth
is an age in which the rational powers are not fully developed, and the will not

fully under rational control, they tacitly acknowledge that wrong or thoughtless choices will almost certainly be made within it, and emphasize instead the fact that youth will pass and cares succeed it, including the most urgent care of all, the salvation of one's soul. However hedged round by those age-old admonitions that do eventually civilize, regulate, and make conformable the energies of the young, the earlier state was regarded with a degree of tolerance not accorded to man's maturity. By auctorial fiat, Chaucer makes the energies of his young people seem to arise outside of any moral system (the purpose of the images drawn from the world of nature) and in advance of any confident moral expectation (the reason he makes them seem even younger than they are). Out of these two related sets of images the energies that animate the tale's action are born. We are shown a world of the "wylde and yong," through which old John wanders at some risk.

The young people of the Miller's Tale inhabit, in short, a special field of imagery that is responsible for much of the tale's charm and vivacity. I think it commended itself to Chaucer as a way of disarming certain kinds of potential response among his audience, as well as affording him a chance to write about a period of human life in which he took evident delight. Through the power of imagery, we find ourselves disinclined to think of the actions of these young people as immoral (or even, in our modern sense, amoral): the condition is too transitory, and *some* lessons are learned. Their actions become instead simply some things that young people do, which (as Helen Corsa has succinctly noted) no more invite stern moral judgment than do branches for putting forth blossoms, calves and kids and colts for gamboling in meadows, birds for singing, lambs for wanting suck, or cats for playing with mice.[8] In such a world, farting, pissing, and the kissing of nether beards lose their power to offend, and even fornication is transformed into music: "Ther as the carpenter is wont to lye. / Ther was the revel and the melodye" (3651–52). Through a series of highly preferential images, not strictly justified by the facts, Chaucer invites us into a world seen in part as prior to, in part as outside of, morality: a world of creatures young and not wholly tame, whose nature cannot be held "narwe" in any cage at all.

To conclude this part of the analysis, we might note that even old John is once invited to imagine himself a member of this numerous and enfranchised "animal" group. In Nicholas's words:

> Whan that the grete shour is goon away,
> Thanne shaltou swymme as myrie, I undertake,
> As dooth the white doke after hire drake.
>
> (3574–76)

The image is derived from the departure of the animals from the ark, once the Flood is past. It offers old John a vision of himself and Alisoun swimming along together as duck and drake that is relaxing and seductive and fully as important to Nicholas's persuasive strategy as the more daring promise that follows: "thanne shul we be lordes al oure lyf / Of al the world, as Noe and his wyf " (3581). Both images play a part in the carpenter's undoing as a victim of "ymaginacioun" (3612).

The action of the Miller's Tale, in short, is seen in two ways at once: as a series of literal events and in terms of similes drawn from the world of animals, birds, flowers, and trees. Such images may properly be said to celebrate the beauty, plenitude, and particularity of the natural creation, but they are untouched by any other idea and invite no moral or doctrinal meditation. It is as though the idea of Nature (which Chaucer personified in a single commanding image as Dame Nature in *The Parliament of Fowls*) had been exploded into a series of discrete images drawn from nature, a plenitude of the merely "natural." Chaucer uses such imagery to invoke a whole, and wholly attractive, category of life lived outside of morality, in order to locate his young people metaphorically within it: an animal world in which instinct takes the place that reason holds for man, a world in which instinct and necessity are one.

So far we have examined briefly the contribution of genre and the contribution of a special field of imagery to Chaucer's immediate poetic purpose: the construction of a fiction perfectly counter to the Knight's Tale. Let us turn now to a third aspect of the poem, no less important than these—to the mode of its larger actions, as determined by the intentions that shape them. This new subject constitutes yet another link between allegorical versions of Youth and Chaucer's young people in the Miller's Tale. Beyond the shared animal images, quick energies, and wildness lies a community of interest that the *Romaunt of the Rose* incorporates into its own portrait of youth: "For yonge folk, wel witen ye, / Have lytel thought but on her play" (1288–89). For similar reasons, play and game become the governing modes of action in the Miller's Tale. From the very first moment in which "hende Nicholas / Fil with this yonge wyf to rage and pleye" (3272–73), there is about everything they do a certain arbitrary and extravagant quality, as though they could not move directly toward their goal without having first to satisfy the rules of a complex and delightful game in doing so. Every enterprise they initiate is cast in a game form that distances it from, and makes it something other than, a direct expression of desire.

Game governs Absolon's wooing, too—an activity so public, so frequent, so multiple in its address ("sensynge the wyves of the parisshe faste" [3341]) that it runs little risk of success. What earnest trespasser upon a marriage would go sing to the wife at an hour when the husband lies beside her in their bed? Nicholas knows the need for secrecy in such matters, if success is what you're after. For Absolon, the process is its own reward, an excuse for dressing up, combing out his beautiful long hair, and waking when others sleep: "Therfore I wol go slepe an houre or tweye, / And al the nyght thanne wol I wake and pleye" (3685–86). Whatever his actual age, he seems in certain ways the youngest of the three, not least in his attempt to win Alisoun by another sort of game: "Somtyme, to shewe his lightnesse and maistrye, / He pleyeth Herodes upon a scaffold hye" (3383–84). There are, of course, better dramatic roles for a suitor to be seen in than that of a half-crazed, comic-grotesque villain: as Herod says in one mystery play, "I stampe! I stare! I loke all abowtt! / . . . I rent! I rawe! and now run I wode!"[9] But it is all one to Absolon, whose pleasure is in roles as such. Even his tenderest wooing is expressed in the formulas of metrical romance, snatches of popular song, and a magpie raid upon the speeches of the bridegroom to the bride in the Song of Songs.[10] Alisoun seems initially little more to him than an occasion for extending his mastery of the games of courtship to some level comparable to his skill in dancing: "In twenty manere koude he trippe and daunce / After the scole of Oxenforde tho" (3328–29). Whatever he may be up to, sexual desire seems at most tangential to it.

Nicholas likewise proves himself no ordinary lecher. Between the intention and the act must fall the shadow of an elaborate and delightful invention, a game to earn him Alisoun:

> And hende Nicholas and Alisoun
> Acorded been to this conclusioun,
> That Nicholas shal shapen hym a wyle
> This sely jalous housbonde to bigyle;
> And *if so be the game wente aright*,
> She sholde slepen in his arm al nyght,
> For this was his desir and hire also.
>
> (3401–7)

The conditional clause I have italicized above bears the impress of both their personalities. To increase their delight, they erect a barrier to the consummation of their desire—a game as elaborate as the Knight's Tale tournament by which a husband is found for Emelye. Nicholas must prove by his wit that he is worthy to lie with Alisoun, though simpler procedures lie readily to hand. On two separate occasions detailed in the poem (and others are implied), Nicholas has ample opportunity to lie with Alisoun without her husband's knowledge. It is the advantage of a lodger, but he chooses instead to earn her by means of a "queynte cast," a parodic restaging of Noah's preparations for the Flood. The difficult and elaborate game is invented for its own sake. Nicholas's object is as much the witty exploration of an old man's gullibility as the "swyvyng" of the wife that he will earn thereby. Like Alisoun's merriment in inventing the arse kiss as a way of getting rid of an unwelcome suitor ("Now hust, and thou shalt laughen al thy fille" [3722]), it serves to alter our feelings about actions that in outline may seem scabrous in the extreme. We witness a delight in game that is obsessive and pure in ways that young people manage best; and when the playing gets rough, they yowl in pain or "weep as dooth a child that is ybete." The complexity and indirection of their preferred means help to free our sympathy and laughter from notions (otherwise perfectly applicable) of adultery, aggression, and betrayal. All but Alisoun pay a certain price before the tale is over, but that price is not very great—nothing like the cost of the corresponding games of chivalry and *fin amors* in the Knight's Tale. The pervasive mood of game lessens to some degree even the carpenter's humiliation after his fall from the roof beam, for his neighbors refuse to take him seriously, ascribing his foolishness to an overwrought imagination ("fantasye") and discounting anything he tries to say:

> The folk gan laughen at his fantasye;
> Into the roof they kiken and they cape,
> And turned al his harm unto a jape.
>
> (3840–42)

Their laughter is at his expense, to be sure, but it is social laughter—less cruel by far than if they were to "make ernest" of the game, contemplating within it the configurations of sin, charging him with pride or presumption. Though his wife has been "swyved," that is not public knowledge—it is possible he does not realize it himself—and anyone can admit, even before the neighbors, to a spell of foolishness now and then. Some tempered portion of his self-esteem will survive the event, just as surely as his arm will heal.

In contrast to Nicholas, who specializes in "deerne love" and roaming hands, free of idealization, Absolon is experimenting in love "paramours"— love in the French manner, the manner of romance literature—which at its most elevated became a highly self-conscious religion of love. But his experience of women is not entirely posturing and fanciful—he knows the barmaids, the "gaylard tappesteres," of every alehouse in the city, and he knows some ways to delight them. The cat-and-mouse image that Chaucer uses to introduce his infatuation with Alisoun (3346) will be ultimately reaffirmed as the truth that underlies his courtship. But it pleases Absolon to dress up his desire in fashionable forms, to cast himself in the role of the idealized and idealizing lover, in a game as formal and, initially at least, as self-aware as anything Nicholas invents in the tricking of old John. Absolon is at Osney "with compaignye, hym to disporte and pleye" (3660) when he learns by chance that old John hasn't been seen for a while ("and axed upon cas a cloisterer / Ful prively after John the carpenter"). He goes to court Alisoun the same night in a similar mood. But he makes a fatal error in seeking to cast Alisoun as "the lady" in this fanciful courtship: "Now, deere lady, if thy wille be, / I praye yow that ye wole rewe on me" (3361–62). That role, which implies high birth and refined sensibility, is so far from Alisoun's secure sense of her own nature that it earns him a crude correction the next time around— when the love language he affects, and the posture from which he speaks it, become most intolerably elevated and grand. A few pictures will make my meaning clear. Figure 1 shows a man and woman on their knees before the God of Love[11]—a design that draws its power (and implicit blasphemy) from its likeness to another design, in which worshipers or donors kneel before a sacred personage, as in figure 2, in which two monks kneel before Christ on the cross.[12] Figure 3, a fourteenth-century carving in ivory, can bring this tradition closer to the Miller's Tale: it shows a lover on his knees offering his heart to his lady, while she places a garland of flowers on his head, cradling a little dog in her arms.[13]

FIGURE 1. A man and woman kneel before the God of Love. Flemish, early fourteenth century. Cambridge, Trinity Coll. MS. B.11.22, fol. 30.

FIGURE 2. Two monks kneel before the cross. East
Anglian, ca. 1310–25. London, Brit. Lib. MS. Add.
49622, fol. 199.

Such images furnish an appropriate background to our reading because
Absolon first pleads for a kiss in precisely that posture:

> This Absolon doun sette hym on his knees
> And seyde, "I am a lord at alle degrees;
> For after this I hope ther cometh moore.
> Lemman, thy grace, and sweete bryd, thyn oore!"
>
> (3723–26)

What follows is quite possibly Chaucer's own invention, for in none of the
contemporary analogues to the tale does the woman present her buttocks
to be kissed—it is her male companion (most often a priest) who does so both

FIGURE 3. A lover kneels before his lady. Ivory writing tablet, French, first half of fourteenth century. Detroit Institute of Arts (42.136).

times—and in none of them does the other suitor kneel to offer that devotion. Absolon's posture is one of religious adoration—he intends it so—just as the language of his petition is charged with scriptural and liturgical echoes from the Song of Songs. The extended arse that answers his concluding plea for mercy and grace ("Lemman, thy grace, and sweete bryd, thyn oore!") offers, in consequence, more than a comic insult, which is all that its masculine equivalent in the analogues can provide. The poet's purpose is comic exposure, the creation of a hilarious synecdoche in which the part is indeed the whole—the whole object of Absolon's adoration and desire, once the mask of manners and the language of fashionable love longing are stripped away.

Absolon receives, almost exactly, what he didn't know he had been asking for, and it works upon him a change that Chaucer describes through a wonderful triple pun, "His hoote love was coold and al yqueynt" (3754). The primary sense of "yqueynt," "extinguished," alternates with another, "foolish, fantastical," to end in yet a third, the most devastating of all—the slang word for pudendum. Though the fastidious Absolon may (in this new definition of his purpose) have missed his mark by a few millimeters, the real nature of what he sought has been made unmistakably clear to him:

> For fro that tyme that he hadde kist hir ers,
> Of paramours he sette nat a kers;
> For he was heeled of his maladie.
> Ful ofte paramours he gan deffie.
>
> (3755–58)

The hairy kiss restores him to his proper person, ending the make-believe and role playing, breaking the game. To this point he has cast his game as earnest, playing the woebegone lover and half believing it himself; henceforth he casts his earnestness in the form of game:

> "I am thyn Absolon, my deerelyng.
> Of gold," quod he, "I have thee broght a ryng.
> My mooder yaf it me, so God me save;
> Ful fyn it is, and therto wel ygrave.
> This wol I yeve thee, if thou me kisse."
>
> (3793–97)

The red-hot colter is intended for Alisoun, not Nicholas.

To understand in its full richness another of the major narrative images in the Miller's Tale—old John as new Noah, preparing for a second Flood—we shall need to look to the drama cycles that grew up in England around the Feast of Corpus Christi in the 1370s. Like much other religious imagery of the time, they were intended to serve as "a tokene and a book to þe lewyd peple, þat þey moun redyn in ymagerye and peynture þat clerkys redyn in boke."[14] But they were very special, being living images in which speech, music, costume, setting, and impersonation came together so powerfully that some claimed religious painting could offer no comparison: "for þis is a deed bok, þe toþer a quick."[15] Certain images from the plays of Noah's Flood are intricately woven into the trick that Nicholas plays on his carpenter landlord. His invention is based upon what had become in medieval art an iconic action.

"Clerkys" that "redyn in the boke" were of course to be found among Chaucer's first audiences as well, and Nicholas proves himself a member of their fraternity. Knowing that the scriptural Flood was sent to punish sexual sin—as Chaucer will tell us in the Parson's Tale, "by the synne of lecherie God dreynte al the world at the diluge" (839)—and knowing as well an exegetical tradition holding that marital intercourse had been prohibited in the ark while the waters covered the earth, Nicholas creates a witty occasion on which to satisfy his own desire. The second Flood will serve to forward lechery rather than forestall it. Nicholas apparently knows as well the tradition that Noah was an astrologer who learned of the approaching deluge through his science, for astrology is Nicholas's own avocation—he's good at predicting rain—and he reenacts the awesome moment of Noah's astrological discovery in a wonderfully comic way: "This Nicholas sat evere capyng upright, / As he had kiked on the newe moone" (3444–45). All this is part of a scholar's joke, and in its higher frequencies was probably heard only by scholars' ears. But the folly of old John, the material with which Nicholas works most directly, is quite another matter, and it is against an essentially popular understanding of the Flood, as developed by medieval drama, that the carpenter's actions can be best understood and most richly enjoyed.

Chaucer alerts us to the relevance of the cycle drama at several points in the tale, including the only two direct references to that drama to be found anywhere in his works. Absolon's attempt to interest Alisoun by playing Herod "upon a scaffold hye" has already been noted, and to it we may add the prologue's description of the Miller interrupting the Host "in Pilates voys," a reference to the high, shrill, and pretentious voice apparently affected by those who played Pilate on the scaffold stage. But the most important clue that it is the drama's image of the Flood we are meant to hold in mind is spoken by Nicholas when he reminds the carpenter of the marital woes suffered by the last man to survive such waters:

> "Hastou nat herd," quod Nicholas, "also
> The sorwe of Noe with his felaweshipe,
> Er that he myghte gete his wyf to shipe?
> Hym hadde be levere, I dar wel undertake
> At thilke tyme, than alle his wetheres blake
> That she hadde had a ship hirself allone."
>
> (3538–43)

Here the drama offers more than a necessary but isolated gloss: since a recalcitrant Mrs. Noah belongs almost entirely to the stage, it furnishes an essential subtext for the action that follows.

The surviving plays of the Flood differ from each other, of course, and ideally one would refer to local traditions only—in this case to the Oxford plays, in which Absolon is said to have played Herod, and to the London plays, as the cycle best known to Chaucer and his first audiences. But too much has been lost to permit such economy and exactitude. Indeed, the Miller's Tale's allusion to

Herod "upon a scaffold hye" constitutes our only evidence that Oxford had plays in the fourteenth century. Since my purpose is to elucidate Chaucer's tale rather than to attempt a reconstruction of the Oxford or London plays, I shall offer no readings I think not demonstrable from his text alone. But I shall draw my evidence from the treatment of similar themes in the several play texts that do survive, which nondramatic treatments of the Flood either pass over in silence or fail to explore with comparable vigor. I wish to study the ways in which Chaucer prevents Nicholas's Flood game from bringing into the tale anything resembling the moral weight of its original—the Flood as recounted in the Book of Genesis, as understood in patristic commentary upon that text, or as represented (sometimes even in comedy though ultimately toward a serious end) on the medieval pageant stage.

The most obvious means by which Chaucer seeks to prevent our thinking about this fiction from perspectives outside it—perspectives as awesome as doomsday, which the biblical Flood was understood to prefigure—turns upon the comic discordance of the image that Nicholas plants in old John's mind with the traditional image of Noah's Flood. The fit is so bad, the two images so comically out of register, that it is the differences that occupy our attention. This flood is going to be much worse than its original—more than twice as big (3518) and infinitely more swift. Instead of 40 days and nights of rain, after which the ark floated for 150 days before the waters began to abate, this time the world will be drowned in an hour and dry again by breakfast. There will be three arks, instead of the three-tiered ark of the theologians, and, replacing an architecture dictated by God (whose very numbers conceal sublime mysteries), brewing barrels and dough troughs will serve. Haste is everything: unlike the medieval texts in which God instructs Noah to spend 120 years building the ark, so that any who amend may be saved, Nicholas speaks this prophecy to John on a Sunday, one day before the Flood is due. Nicholas's use of the Mrs. Noah tradition is similarly free and improvisational, for unlike the drama's Noah, wedded to someone as old and cantankerous as himself—both he and she have a taste for battle—our carpenter loves his young and winsome wife too much. Finally, though it is no part of his plan, Nicholas in his own person experiences that part of biblical prophecy that old John forgets to remember, the promise that punishment will come by fire next time. Nicholas's game version of the Flood is so comic in its distortions and (as we shall see) old John's performance as "second Noah" so remarkable in its omissions that we should perhaps call it, as old John himself does, "Nowell's Flood." The congruences are erratic and haphazard, emphasizing the witty difference rather than a significant similarity. Let us look at "Nowell's Flood" in some detail.

When old John first learns from Nicholas that "thus shal mankynde drenche, and lese hir lyf " (3521), he can think only of his mate: "This carpenter answerde, 'Alas, my wyf! / And shal she drenche? alas, myn Alisoun!'" The absence of any other concern will in time earn him a fall, but this care for her keeps him attractive and sympathetic as well. Overfondness for one's wife is, in fabliau terms, a mistake, but it is not ugly. His failure to ask any other question, however, ultimately earns him his humiliation and harm. He registers no surprise at all that God's inscrutable will should be communicated through his student lodger. He forgets God's promise never to destroy the world again by water, though he recollects having heard "ful yoore ago" the story of "hou saved was Noe" (3534). He neither asks why the world must be destroyed, nor gives any sign of comprehending God's purpose independent of such a question. Above all, he never wonders why God should have chosen to save *him*— and Nicholas, and Alisoun—from the universal catastrophe. The medieval drama offered a very different version of Noah's response.

In the York play, Noah's first speech in reply to this news recognizes his own unworthiness:

> A! lorde, I lowe þe lowde and still,
> þat vn-to me, wretche vn-worthye,
> þus with thy worde, as is þi will,
> Lykis to appere þus propyrly.[16]

And he shows himself able to comprehend as an act of justice God's destruction of a world "that synne would nouȝt for-sake." The York Noah has a certain advantage over his fabliau counterpart—God appears in his own person to tell him his destiny—but when Mrs. Noah appears (a hundred years later), she views the ark with the sort of suspicion that might have saved old John some painful lessons. Learning for the first time of the deluge to come, and having only her husband's word for it, she declares the probabilities not sufficient. She will not leave "þe harde lande" to climb onto some precarious tower; she thinks, indeed, that Noah has lost his mind:

> Now Noye, in faythe þe fonnes full faste,
> This fare wille I no lenger frayne,
> þou arte nere woode, I am agaste,
> Fare-wele, I wille go home agayne.[17]

The Wakefield play, in turn, begins with a speech of seventy-two lines in which Noah at prayer laments the world's sin, fears God's vengeance, and asks his mercy.[18] The N-Town play (edited under the title *Ludus Coventriae* but now thought to have been written at Bury St. Edmunds) makes a similar point by other means: after a brief description of the world lost in sin, Noah introduces "my wyff and my chyidere here on rowe," each of whom pledges obedience to God in a ritual round of speeches, and then God speaks.[19] In both cycles, Noah's troubled response to the world's wickedness, and his sense that correction must be imminent, precedes God's message that he will send a Flood: the sequence of events serves to establish the righteousness of God's anger and to distinguish the family of Noah, who will be saved, from all the others who will be destroyed. John the carpenter is not as thoughtful as the Noah of this second tradition, nor as self-knowing as the Noah of the first—the Noah who proclaims himself unworthy. In this matter of self-knowledge, the drama and fabliau traditions inevitably meet, for the dramatists' Noah, often with less cause than old John, is able to see within himself a profound likeness to those who will be drowned. In most cycles, he acknowledges his age, his physical weakness, and his ignorance of boat building, and in speaking of man's need for grace exempts no one, not even himself: "god is sore grevyd with oure grett tresspas / þat with wylde watyr þe werd xal be dreynt."[20]

Mrs. Noah, flesh of his flesh, is in some cycles used more boldly to this end. She is a "free" character, without scriptural specification, and her sense of community with all that is flawed and found wanting becomes one of the major ways the drama authenticates the right of these survivors to be saved. In failing to see why God's grace should have fallen so remarkably on them, or to sense any great difference between them and the people who will be drowned, Mrs. Noah as matriarch expresses an important kind of humility, even in the versions that explore it through comedy. In Chester, for instance, she refuses to board the ark unless her gossips can come with her—"They shall not drowne, by sayncte John, / and I may save there life"—and when Noah forbids that, she sits down on the bank with them for a last drink and a merry song before the waters rise.[21] In York, more decorously, she is allowed to ask why her friends and kinsmen cannot be saved, remembers them during the Flood, and asks after them again as the waters recede: "But Noye, where are nowe all oure kynne, / And companye we knewe be-fore."[22] In the comic versions, she brings to the ark an imperfect capacity for obedience, some shrewd common sense, and a special kind of humility no one would ever confuse with meekness. But she too has been chosen by God and is one of those who will be saved—however much her husband might have wished for her a ship alone. Mrs. Noah's contribution to this set of ideas within the English tradition throws no special light upon Alisoun, cast as *uxor Noe* in Nicholas's Flood game. Quite the contrary. Alisoun boards her ship without opposition or delay, simply that she may leave it the sooner: her husband has barely begun to snore before she is down the ladder and making music in the lodger's arms. It is old John himself we will understand better for having "herd" some of these things about "the sorwe of Noe with his felaweshipe."

Chaucer, in short, invokes the popular image of the Flood in order to throw the strongest possible comic light upon old John's presumption. Complacent in his certainty that men "sholde nat knowe of Goddes pryvetee" (3454), he forgets they need some candid sense of their own. Given the prospect of universal destruction, he can think only of sweet Alisoun; invited to imagine their singular salvation, he never questions its probability. Like the first Noah, he is found obedient, but to spurious authority and without self-knowledge. The rest of the world is no more to him than Robyn and Gille, the servants he sends off to London (and, by implication, their death by drowning) "upon his nede . . . for to go" (3632). Nicholas, to be sure, is the source of this "fantasye" of a second Flood, and, as Chaucer takes care to emphasize, the power of such images—mental images—can be enormous. John "sees" the coming Flood so clearly it makes him shake, weep, wail, and sigh:

> Men may dyen of ymaginacioun,
> So depe may impressioun be take.
> This sely carpenter bigynneth quake;
> Hym thynketh verraily that he may see
> Noees flood come walwynge as the see
> To drenchen Alisoun, his hony deere.
> He wepeth, weyleth, maketh sory cheere;
> He siketh with ful many a sory swogh;
> He gooth and geteth hym a knedyng trogh.
> (3612–20)

Nicholas, I repeat, is the source of the image, but the assent to its truth, and the translation of it into action, are entirely the carpenter's own. His weary sleep in the kneading tub on high, snoring away in expectation of a morrow when the three of them shall be "lordes al oure lyf / Of al the world, as Noe and his wyf " (3581), offers a comic image of intolerable presumption and complacency, from which he must be cut down. In keeping with the decorum of fabliaux, it is his own hand, not God's, that lays ax to the rope and punishes his folly: the tale concerns foolishness old and young, not sin.

Chaucer seeks and achieves a perfect equilibrium: he shows us folly and complacency above, wit and carnality below, and relates them by an even more elaborate contrivance, the Flood game, which offers a commentary on the action too rich and many-leveled to be summed up in a quip at the end. Indeed, I suspect that the Flood play or plays that Chaucer knew best created a stage image that used music as part of its expressive means at the point of maximum stillness in the action, the moment when the audience was to imagine the ark afloat upon the waves. The N-Town cycle, for instance, after staging the death of Cain, ordains, "Here . . . Noah enters in the ship singing," though it does not specify his song.[23] The Chester cycle, in contrast, gives some fairly detailed information. After Noah has brought his whole family on board, he notices the boat begin to move, and in four of the extant manuscripts we find the stage direction "Then they singe, and Noe shall speake agayne." That speech briefly introduces the action called for immediately after: "Then shall Noe shutt the windowe of the arke, and for a little space within the bordes hee shal be scylent; and afterwarde openinge the windowe and lookinge rownde about" he thanks God for their salvation. The best of the Chester manuscripts, however, conflates these two actions, creating a moment of utter stillness in which all who will survive from the first world are hidden within the ark, directing their whole attention toward God through song. Its single stage direction reads (in Latin):

> Then Noah will close the window of the ark and for a little while, concealed within, they will sing the psalm "Save me, O God," and [after], opening the window and looking about [Noah will say . . .][24]

This image, iconographic in its power, links the death of one world and the beginning of another, and it has a possible counterpart in the Miller's Tale. Chaucer moves the action to a point of comparable fixity and then invites us to imagine music of three contrasting kinds: the carpenter snoring above, Nicholas and Alisoun fornicating below ("Ther was the revel and the melodye"), and the special music of the Church that marks the early hour of the day, the friars singing Lauds:

> And thus lith Alison and Nicholas,
> In bisynesse of myrthe and of solas,
> Til that the belle of laudes gan to rynge,
> And freres in the chauncel gonne synge.
> (3653–56)

In place of religious judgment, Chaucer provides the logic and laughter intrinsic to the genre he called "cherles tales." The narrative comes full circle: Absolon earns a hairy kiss, Nicholas a burned arse, and old John a broken arm and the derision of his neighbors—the townsfolk whose future deaths by drowning had troubled him not at all. Nicholas's anguished cry for "Water!" brings everything together and everything to an end: his revels with Alisoun, Absolon's revised game of courtship (" 'Of gold,' quod he, 'I have thee broght a ryng' "), and the carpenter's expectations as second Noah. But it is fabliau justice only. The hand of an offended God is nowhere to be seen in this comic catastrophe, nor inferred from it against an idea of Doomsday to come. In the Miller's scheme of things, Absolon, Nicholas, and old John sin against common sense, not the deity, and their punishment is in every case poetically sufficient: exposure is cure, and we are not invited to think beyond it. Though the story has moved through two large narrative images that might have been worked poetically in such a way as to address religious truth—Absolon's ritual of misplaced adoration and old John's rehearsal of the Flood—in the Miller's Tale they are insistently parodic in mode, comically out of register, and by means of genre made to short-circuit their highest kinds of potential meaning. The tale's energy is born of youth and natural instinct; it expresses itself in game; and it flows (so to speak) in a circle—within a self-contained fabliau system—not outward toward a world of transcendental meaning and spiritual destinies.[25]

In this sequel to the Knight's Tale, Chaucer sought a perfectly antithetical vision, a look at life through eyes uncomplicated by transcendent idea or ideal. It required a different artistic style. In contrast to the Knight's Tale version of the world as palace/prison or prison/garden, both ultimately places of the spirit's captivity, the Miller invites us into a world of open streets and (through simile) country farmyards, where man's freedom and accountability are like those of the animals: consequence follows cause, not in eternity, but here and now and in scale with his capacities. There is no cynicism in this vision, and no despair. It finds the physical world enough—its plenitude, its charm, its energy, its rules. Out of the law of gravity, the logic of cause and effect, and a respect for ordinary limits, there is constituted an idea of order sufficient to man's needs. The deepest answers returned in this tale are not cosmic but prudential: "stonde he moste unto his owene harm." In celebrating human and animal likeness, the life of the instincts, and the company of youth and wit, Chaucer celebrates as well the possible sovereignty of comic order within the world of daily life, a world temporarily—by an act of imaginative exclusion—unshadowed by Last Things. The tale moves toward adjustment, not judgment, with an audacity fully the equal of its grace.

Notes

1. For the oaths "by seint Thomas," see 3291, 3461. The Miller's joking promise "to telle a legende and a lyf" (3141) is perhaps an implicit admission of what ought to be expected (construing "legende" to mean a "saint's life").

2. Charles Muscatine, *Chaucer and the French Tradition* (Berkeley, Calif., 1957), p. 224.

3. See Fr. Paul E. Beichner, "Characterization in Chaucer's the Miller's Tale," in Richard J. Schoeck and Jerome Taylor, eds., *Chaucer Criticism: The Canterbury Tales* (Notre Dame, Ind., 1960), pp. 117–29, and Beichner, "Absolon's Hair," *Mediaeval Studies* 12 (1950): 222–33.

4. [The *sensus spiritualis*, or "spiritual meaning," is the allegorical significance that biblical exegetes elicited from passages that to a modern reader seem entirely literal. As a love poem, the Song of Songs was particularly likely to receive this sort of reading: it was usually taken by medieval interpreters as an allegory of the relation of Christ to the Church, or of the Holy Spirit to the Virgin Mary, or of God to the soul.]

5. There is a pun on "lycorys" as well, which embodies the rhetorical sequence dominant in these portraits, a movement from the natural image ("licorice root") to an echo ("lecherous") that is potentially moral.

6. In Middle English, the word "mayden" does not necessarily imply gender. It could mean anyone sexually inexperienced. Chaucer's use of the word here may remind us that students in the late Middle Ages customarily entered university at the age of fourteen.

7. On the full tradition and its varying number of ages, see Samuel C. Chew, *The Pilgrimage of Life* (New Haven, Conn., 1962), pp. 144–73.

8. Helen Storm Corsa, *Chaucer: Poet of Mirth and Morality* (Notre Dame, Ind., 1964), p. 114.

9. H. Craig, ed., *Two Coventry Corpus Christi Plays* (London, 1966), p. 27.

10. E. T. Donaldson, "Idiom of Popular Poetry in the Miller's Tale," in his *Speaking of Chaucer* (New York, 1970), pp. 13–29; R. E. Kaske, "The Canticum Canticorum in the Miller's Tale," *SP* 59 (1962): 479–500.

11. Cambridge, Trinity College, Ms. B.II.22, fol. 30.

12. London, British Library, Ms. Add. 49622, fol. 199.

13. An ivory writing tablet from the Detroit Institute of Arts (42.136); see William R. Levin, *Images of Love and Death in Late Medieval and Renaissance Art* (Ann Arbor, Mich., 1976), p. 112.

14. P. H. Barnum, ed., *Dives and Pauper*, 2 vols. (London, 1976–1980), I.i.82.

15. From "A Tretis of Miraclis Pleyinge," in Anne Hudson, ed., *Selections from English Wycliffite Writings* (Cambridge, 1978), p. 100.

16. Lucy Toulmin Smith, ed., *The York Plays* (Oxford, 1885), p. 41.

17. *Ibid.*, p. 48.

18. A. C. Cawley, ed., *The Wakefield Plays in the Towneley Cycle* (Manchester, England, 1958), pp. 14–16.

19. Katherine S. Block, *Ludus Coventriae; or, The Plaie Called Corpus Christi* 120 (London, 1922), p. 39.

20. Ibid.

21. R. M. Lumiansky and David Mills, eds., *The Chester Mystery Cycle* (London, 1974), pp. 50–51.

22. Smith, *York Plays*, p. 53.

23. Block, *Ludus Coventriae*, p. 41.

24. Lumiansky and Mills, *Chester Mystery Cycle*, p. 53.

25. The progress from "But sith that he was fallen in the snare, / He moste endure, as oother folk, his care" (3231) to "stonde he moste unto his owene harm" (3830) is, of course, no progress at all; the story confirms what it knows from the beginning.

Further Reading

Kolve's essay is part of a book—*Chaucer and the Imagery of Narrative*—that argues that each of the tales is organized around a few visual images; in its original form, the essay is copiously illustrated with medieval images, only three of which are included here. His benign view of the tale has been contested by other critics, some of whom think its religious allusions *are* in fact judgmental, some that the tale is motivated by the Miller's sense of class antagonism, and yet others who explore the gender politics of the tale. For representative examples or commentaries on each of these approaches, see, respectively, Andrew Johnston, "The Exegetics of Laughter: Religious Parody in Chaucer's Miller's Tale," in *A History of English Laughter: Laughter from Beowulf to Beckett and Beyond*, edited by Manfred Pfister (Amsterdam and New York, 2002), pp. 17–33; Lee Patterson, "The Miller's Tale and the Politics of Laughter," in his *Chaucer and the Subject of History* (Madison, Wis., 1991), pp. 244–79; and Karma Lochrie, "Women's 'Pryvetees' and Fabliau Politics in the Miller's Tale," *Exemplaria* 6 (1994): 287–304. For further discussion of medieval attitudes toward youth, see John A. Burrow, *The Ages of Man* (Oxford, 1986). Another account of the role of the mystery plays in the tale is provided by Sandra Pierson Prior, "Parodying Typology and the Mystery Plays in the Miller's Tale," *Journal of Medieval and Renaissance Studies* 16 (1986): 57–73.

Of a Fire in the Dark

Public and Private Feminism
in the Wife of Bath's Tale

H. MARSHALL LEICESTER, JR.

❖ ❖ ❖

THE *WIFE OF BATH'S TALE* is not only a text concerned with the position of women, it is a text whose speaker is a woman and a feminist—at least that is the fiction the text offers—and the body of this essay will concentrate on the Wife herself as the speaker of her tale. While my own prejudices, for better or for worse, will no doubt be evident from what follows, I do not claim here to define feminism or to say what women "are" or ought to do. My interest is in the Wife's feminism as it is evidenced in Chaucer's text, and I attempt to discriminate between two versions of feminism—two possible stances women may, in their own interest, adopt in the world—that the Wife seems to embody in the telling of her tale. The first of these I call "public" and identify with a polemical, reactive, and necessarily "illiberal" position that women may take toward the male world and its institutions. The second, "private" form is less easy to classify in the nature of the case, but at least in Chaucer's practice here it is at once more humanist (in the sense of being interested in what individuals can make, positively, of the culture and institutions that precede and surround them) and more humane—or at any rate "nicer." This second form, because it is always dependent on individual situations, choices, and responses, always remains problematical and open to reinterpretation. It should be clear from the outset, however, that my aim is not, or not merely, to denigrate the first kind of feminism at the expense of the second. I am concerned to show that there is a difference between the two kinds, but also to show that these forms or modes are complementary as well as opposed, that there is a dialectical relationship at work in the Wife's situation and her responses.

Though the method I adopt here is largely a version of the time-honored one of "dramatic" analysis, I am aware that "the Wife of Bath" is a fiction, a construction made from the language of the tale, and that that fiction is a male poet's impersonation of a female speaker. It appears that there is some relation for Chaucer between taking a position on women—about who they are, what they want, and how they should proceed—and taking a woman's position. Though I must insist that we take the fact of impersonation seriously (and therefore refrain from too hasty an ascription to "Chaucer" of features in the tale that properly belong to the narrating Wife), I do not wish to lose sight, as I think Chaucer does not, of the issue of the poet's relation to his character, and if I begin with an examination of the Wife's feminism, I will end with some suggestions about Chaucer's.[1]

In this essay I will concentrate on the Wife's tale of the Loathly Lady, leaving her prologue as far as possible in the background and in the shade. I do so partly for reasons of space, but also because I think the tale deserves better than it usually gets. It often seems to be taken by critics as a mere appendage to the more brilliant prologue, an appendage that restates the prologue's main argument about the value of feminine sovereignty or "maistrye" in marriage in a relatively mechanical form, marred (or enlivened, depending on the critic's taste) by some "characteristic" though irrelevant touches by the Wife, like the Midas exemplum; complicated perhaps by a windy and dull (or moving and serious) pillow lecture on "gentilesse" that does not even sound much like her; but concluding straightforwardly enough with the Q.E.D. of the Knight's submission and the magical transformation at the end.[2]

There is something to be said for an interpretation of this sort. It is not so much wrong as incomplete, a place to start in thinking about the tale rather than the last word. In fact, a version of this interpretation is the place where the Wife of Bath starts, in the sense that it seems to be her advance plan for the tale. We can assume, I think, that the Wife knows before she begins the story what she intends to do with it and that she has already decided on the changes in the plot of the traditional version that will produce the polemical feminist moral she draws at the end. This moral and the feminist ideology that goes with it are what might be called the public meaning of the tale— her word is "apert"—and this public meaning is backed, as public meanings always are, by authority. In this case the authority in question is that of the Wife herself. One way of looking at her prologue—and one way she herself presents it—is to see it as a process whereby the Wife's account of her own experiences in marriage leads to her thesis about marriage in general. In this reading, her experiences allow her to say, "The necessity of feminine 'maistrye' is what my life proves, and so does the story I am about to tell." Such a reading constitutes the Wife's past *as* past, as something that is over and done with and therefore something that can be summed up, generalized from. Her life adds up to a final meaning which the tale merely confirms. This reading is at least in accord with the Wife's explicit or public project in both the prologue and the tale. Not liking the exempla that are offered to her by the male world in the guise of "auctoritee," she turns to her own experience with the intention of becoming an authority herself. Like the Pardoner, she sets out to make an example of herself. Once this is accomplished, she offers the tale as a counterexemplum to set in opposition to those in Janekyn's book of wicked wives and the male misogynist tradition. The tale of the Loathly Lady is itself traditional, which is to say that it is public property, and to tell it is to go public, to move beyond a local and idiosyncratic personal history and take one's place in a larger world.

The public world, the past, and authority are thus the determinants of the "apert" project of the tale, which is conceived by the Wife as a statement of counterideology, that is, a statement in *opposition* to the structures of male domination she has encountered and continues to encounter in her life. The form her counterattack takes is that of appropriating the instruments or institutions of masculine power. Both the public world of storytelling and the story itself are by definition male-dominated, and the Wife, as we know, has strong feelings about that. Combative and competitive as ever, she takes an aggressively feminist public position in structuring the world of the tale and pointing its moral. She may be said to *womanhandle* the traditional story, which, as a chivalric romance, is in its original form an instrument of the dominant ideology and its values, such as loyalty and courtesy, that demonstrate male superiority. E. T. Donaldson's succinct summary of the analogues brings out this ideological bias—and the Wife's subversion of it—clearly:

> In the analogues the story is handled in a different style, its real point being to demonstrate the courtesy of the hero, who weds the hag uncomplainingly and treats her as if she were the fairest lady in the land; in two versions the knight is Sir Gawain, the most courteous of Arthur's followers, who promises to marry her not in order to save his own life but his king's. The lady's transformation is thus a reward of virtue. In Chaucer the polite

knight becomes a convicted rapist who keeps his vow only under duress and in the sulkiest possible manner.[3]

As I have intimated, I take the differences between Chaucer's version of the tale and its analogues as evidence of the speaker's agency, evidence that the Wife knows the traditional version and deliberately alters it in a way that makes the feminist message more pointed and polemical. The fact that only in her version is the knight a rapist means that only in her version is the quest for what women most desire linked specifically and logically to the knight's character and to the question of male-female relations. Clearly this particular knight, as a surrogate for men in general, needs to learn more about women, and the plot becomes a device for forcing him to do so, putting him in a position more familiar to women, who have to cater to male desires, and giving power to women from the beginning of the tale. This is one example of appropriation, of using what are normally masculine forms for feminine ends. Another example is the "gentilesse" speech, a form of argument that aims at breaking down the external hierarchies of power constituted by birth and possessions—"temporal thyng that man may hurte and mayme"—in favor of equality before God and individual responsibility for establishing worth and achieving salvation. This argument is traditionally egalitarian, but scarcely feminist. It is sometimes used to urge the right of lowborn men to love and woo noble ladies, but I do not recall it being used before the Wife to argue that ugly old women are good enough not only to go to the same heaven as knights but to marry them. Since in no other version of the tale does anything like this speech occur, its function as additional feminist propaganda in the altered tale is clear. Finally, of course, the sovereignty argument that is the point of the story, affirmed in open court halfway through and supplying the twist at the conclusion, is obviously a reversal of ordinary male-female power relations and an aggressively polemical appropriation of all those dreary (and nervous?) arguments about the proper hierarchical subordination of women to men in medieval discussions of the subject.

This reading I call the "straw man" version of the tale, both because as a critical interpretation it makes the tale easy to summarize and dismiss, and because I think the phrase describes the Wife's open, public project in telling it.[4] She makes a straw man of the traditional tale and its hero, sets up the knight and the old story as images of masculine pretension in order to knock them over, and obviously she carries out this project. Along the way she takes advantage of the power of her temporary position as narrator or straw-stuffer to enjoy her work. She enjoys, no doubt about it, the satisfaction in fiction and fantasy of dominating the ill-bred knight and all his kind and the pleasure of imagining herself, in the form of her surrogate, the hag, magically young and beautiful again, though these pleasures are clearly marginal and incidental to the public message.

So far, I think, there will be little disagreement about the general character of the tale and its "appropriateness" to the Wife. The problem, obviously, is what to do with the more anomalous features of it that do not seem to fit the public project and that raise questions about the character of the speaker. It is very common to see such features, especially perhaps the "gentilesse" speech, as revealing things about the Wife of which she herself is unaware, and to use these slips or contradictions as a way of pinning down her character.[5] Such a proceeding puts the reader in possession of "facts" about the Wife that allow the assumption of a position superior to her from which she can be fixed and placed, understood and dismissed. We know "who she is" and can proceed to construct from that an account of her past and the probabilities of her future, though it is perhaps a matter for uneasiness that such characterizations and careers range in the literature from sociopathic murderess to tragic heroine to comic embodiment of the Life Force.[6]

It seems to me, however, that if the Wife does have a public feminist agenda in the tale, she may also have conscious attitudes about the role she plays in order to carry it out, and that these attitudes are to be elicited precisely from her voicing of the message, from the ways she comments on, revises, ignores, or otherwise deploys the elements of the tale. The matter of what else the Wife gets out of telling the story, whether fantasies of rejuvenation or of power, begins to touch on a set of themes and ideas that are at work in both the prologue and the tale in dialectical tension with their "apert" public and authoritative ones. I have so far reserved these issues, but it is obvious what they are, since the categories are those of the Wife herself: the private ("privy") world and experience.[7] The straw man version of the tale, with its doctrinaire feminism and oppositional stance, has something a little too static and structural about it, something other critics besides myself have found a little uncomfortable. My real point, however, is that the Wife does too. Her public project does not really do justice to the complex and dynamic character of the *now* of speaking in both prologue and tale, the sense of ongoing life and discovery that cannot be totally reduced to an order or an argument, cannot be shut up in forms or completely subjected to authority, even the Wife's own. In the tale, this set of concerns is registered first by the Wife's relative lack of interest in polemical closure: having set up the straw man, she is oddly dilatory in knocking him over, in getting on with the demonstration. She spends the first 120 lines, a good quarter of the tale, not telling it. Instead, she pursues what we might call her private interests.

The most famous example of this tendency is the Midas exemplum, in which the tale of the Loathly Lady vanishes utterly for thirty lines—more if you count the introductory matter—and we find ourselves in the middle of a completely different story about Midas's ass's ears and his wife's inability to keep them secret. The occasion of this digression is the knight's quest to discover what women most desire, and as the Wife lists the variety of opinions he encounters, we can feel her losing interest in the *quest*—whose outcome is a foregone conclusion—and getting interested in the *question*. The old story and its old-time Arthurian world are simply dropped in favor of matters of more immediate interest. Just as it is more fun for the Wife at the beginning of the tale to take a shot at the Friar's virility in retaliation for his disparagement of her prologue than to linger over the romantic world of "fayerie," here it is more interesting to her to consider the variety of possible answers to the question than to give the "right" one. Her voice moves into the present tense, she includes herself among the women whose opinions are being solicited, she indicates that she finds some of them better than others: "Somme seyde that oure hertes been moost esed / Whan that we been yflatered and yplesed. / He gooth ful ny the sothe, I wol nat lye."[8]

The Midas exemplum itself, though superficially unflattering to women and apparently totally unconnected to the story, is actually a reflection of the Wife's impatience with masculine foolishness, and it has a certain relevance to the development of the romance. It is, after all, not just *any* secret that the wife of Midas finds herself unable to contain, but one that a great many women, including the Wife of Bath, have had occasion to notice: "Myn housbonde hath longe asses erys two!" Pope, who borrowed the Wife's revision of Ovid for the *Epistle to Arbuthnot*, saw quite clearly what the message was:

> Out with it *Dunciad*! let the secret pass,
> That secret to each fool, that he's an ass;
> The truth once told (and wherefore should we lie?)
> The queen of Midas slept, and so may I.

This is a secret women have to conceal all the time, especially about their nearest and dearest. The exemplum focuses strongly on the genuine anguish of Midas's queen. She is a woman bound by ties of trust and affection—ties she herself acknowledges—to a man who loves her, and with whom her own reputation is involved. But he is still a fool:

> He loved hire moost, and trusted hire also;
> He preyede hire that to no creature

She sholde tellen of his disfigure.
She swoor him, "Nay," for al this world to wynne,
She nolde do that vileynye or synne,
To make hir housbonde han so foul a name.
She nolde nat telle it for hir owene shame.
But nathelees, hir thoughte that she dyde,
That she so longe sholde a conseil hyde.

(III.958–66)

This is not the sort of secret the Wife herself is used to concealing, as she points out in her prologue (III.534–42), and we have only to replace Midas's wife with the Wife of Bath, and Midas himself with, say, husband number four, or with Janekyn at a moment when he is grinning at her over the top of his book of wicked wives (III.672), to see how graphically the exemplum records a realistic frustration and tension that the Wife knows well as a daily component of real marriages, even, or especially, good ones.[9] But it is equally interesting to replace the queen of Midas with the queen of Arthur, who has to proceed so tactfully to rescue the young rapist from vengeful masculine justice so she can set him on the right track. The Wife puts great stress on the careful courtesy, a style appropriate to a chivalric setting, with which the queen works to get her way. The line "The queene thanketh the kyng with al hir myght" (III.899), in particular, seems deliberately to overstress her courtesy in order to call attention to it. It seems to me that in the Midas exemplum the Wife evokes the real strains involved in feminine submission to and manipulation of masculine egos that the earlier scene leaves out, while reminding us that she herself is considerably less patient than either queen. She reacts to something she feels is missing in her original and supplies it, but she does so only outside the framework of the story.

Something similar happens with the issue of the quest itself. If the Wife gets involved in the question of what women most desire, and drops the story in order to pursue it, this suggests that the question is hardly settled for her except for polemical purposes. The "right" answer is always hedged. The hag remarks that there is no woman, however proud, "That *dar seye nay* of that I shal thee teche" (III.1019; emphasis added), and when the knight announces the answer, the ladies who judge him are similarly cagey. They do not say he is right; they just don't say he is wrong: "In al the court ne was ther wyf, ne mayde, / Ne wydwe, that *contraried* that he sayde, / But seyden he was worthy han his lyf " (III.1043–45; emphasis added). In fact, the queen gets exactly what she asks for, "An answere suffisant in this mateere" (III.910), that is, an answer that suffices, one that will do rather than one that is definitive.[10] The reason for this is, as the Wife knows and demonstrates by her digressive interest in the "wrong" answer, that the question is an impossible one and the quest for a single answer is a fool's errand anywhere outside a story. In reality—in experience— different women want different things, and the same woman, like the Wife herself, may want different things at different times.

What we are seeing here is a developing tension between the public and authoritative functions of the tale as polemical feminist propaganda and a more complex set of experiential interests that do not seem to fit the public plot very comfortably. The doctrinaire feminist argument of the tale is acceptable as a position for women in general, and the Wife certainly does not disagree with it, but it is not very responsive to the detail and nuance of her own situation, and therefore it does not interest her very much. When she introduces herself into the tale in the figure of the hag, she does so in a way that, while never losing sight of the public message and her status as an authority, focuses increasingly on a set of "privy" and experiential concerns of her own that come to constitute a subtext running underneath and in some tension with the "apert" surface.

The description that accompanies the entrance of the hag into the tale is a compact portrayal of the Wife's sense of her own career as she has developed it in the prologue and makes most sense when it is read in reference to that development:

> And in his wey it happed hym to ryde,
> In al this care, under a forest syde,
> Wher as he saugh upon a daunce go
> Of ladyes foure and twenty, and yet mo;
> Toward the whiche daunce he drow ful yerne,
> In hope that som wysdom sholde he lerne.
> But certeinly, er he cam fully there,
> Vanysshed was this daunce, he nyste where.
> No creature saugh he that bar lyf,
> Save on the grene he saugh sittynge a wyf—
> A fouler wight ther may no man devyse.
>
> (III.989–99)

As I have already suggested, in order to constitute herself as an authority, the Wife has to give her experience a definitive shape and meaning from which she can generalize, and this means that her past is behind her, over and done with. It disappears as experience in a way that makes her feel that her life is finished. Her famous lines on her youth. "But, Lord Christ! whan that it re-membreth me," leading to the reflection "That I have had my world as in my tyme" (III.469–73), are followed immediately by a meditation that conveys her sharp awareness of the sad difference between now and then:

> But age, allas! that al wole envenyme,
> Hath me biraf my beautee and my pith.
> Lat go, farewel! the devel go therwith!
> The flour is goon, ther is namoore to telle;
> The bren, as I best kan, now moste I selle.
>
> (III.474–78)

This pattern, this set of feelings, is recapitulated in the description of the hag. The four-and-twenty dancing ladies are connected with the dance of feminine freedom from the "limitacioun" of friars and other masculine trammels, a freedom associated with the elf queen and her "joly compaignye" at the dawn of time and the beginning of the tale. But they are also associated with the Wife's youth—"How koude I daunce to an harpe smale" (III.457)—and with her richly variegated experience of life and love, the "olde daunce." Her memory swirls and dances with all the women she has been until they vanish away, she knows not where, and leave her all alone as she has become, as she is now. The analogues often spend time having fun with the comically grotesque ugliness of the hag: "Then there as shold haue stood her mouth, / then there was sett her eye,"[11] and so forth. The Wife's more reserved refusal to describe her is also more inward, suggesting not what can be seen but what is felt. I think her words here will bear the inflection: "A fouler wight ther may no *man* devyse," that is, "If you, the men who look at me as I speak, think that I am decayed, what must I feel, who know what I was—no mere description will do justice to that." It is no wonder that the hag tells the knight, "Sire knyght, heer forth ne lith no wey" (III.1001).[12]

Now, in public terms, this is a range of experience with which courtly romance does not deal, and the only answer the form has to the problems of the passing of the "flour," especially in a woman, is magic, that is, fantasy, like the transformation at the end of this story. Those problems are relegated to what happens after stories like this one are over, when, as we know, they lived happily ever after. The Wife does not believe in magic of this sort, any more than she believes that real men deal with the prospect of marrying old and ugly women with the courtesy and equanimity of a Sir Gawain, and part of what she is doing in her description of the wedding and the wedding night is *confronting* a genre that has no room for her and other women in her situation with the *fact of herself*. One can feel the glee with which she appropriates the rhetoric of courtesy, "smylynge everemo" (III.1086), and baits the knight (and the self-congratulatory masculine conventions he stands for so shakily) with a blank-eyed rehearsal of official ideals:

> Is this the lawe of kyng Arthures hous?
> Is every knyght of his so dangerous?
> I am youre owene love and eek youre wyf;
> I am she which that saved hath youre lyf,
> And, certes, yet ne dide I yow nevere unright;
> Why fare ye thus with me this firste nyght?
> Ye faren lyk a man had lost his wit.
> What is my gilt? For Goddes love, tel me it,
> And it shal been amended, if I may.
>
> (III.1089–97)

The knight's heartfelt response shows how much the Wife thinks such chivalric courtesy is worth in the face of real-life decay: " 'Amended?' quod this knyght, 'allas! nay, nay! . . . / Thou art so loothly, and so oold also' " (III.1098–1100).

The hag replies that she *could* amend all this, and in the story she can, since she has magical powers. If that were all the Wife was interested in, the tale might now proceed to its conclusion in the assertion of mastery and the pleasures of fantasy. But because she does not believe in magic, the Wife *refuses* the temptation to fantasy that the tale offers, puts it off to a brief moment at the very end, and proceeds to digress, that is, to *take over* the tale and turn it forcibly toward what I see as a more tough-minded examination of her own situation and its potentialities. The speech on "gentilesse," "poverte," and "elde" is notable for the diminished image of human possibility it presents throughout, for its constant stress on the inadequacy of earthly hopes and earthly power:

> Ful selde up riseth by his branches smale
> Prowesse of man, for God, of his goodnesse,
> Wole that of hym we clayme oure gentillesse;
> For of oure eldres may we no thyng clayme
> But temporel thyng, that man may hurte and mayme.
>
> (III.1128–32)

In the face of all this human weakness, the speech consistently urges a stoic position. Boethius and Seneca are prominent in it. The burden especially of the account of poverty is "stop striving for impossible goals and the fulfillment of petty human desires." "He that coveiteth is a povre wight, / For he wolde han that is nat in his myght" (III.1187–88). Instead, embrace your weakness, understand it, and make of it an occasion of virtue. True "genti-lesse" lies not in human glory but in gentle deeds, and the hateful good of poverty leads a man to know his God. The Wife of Bath uses the mask of the hag, as an image of her own diminished powers and vanished "flour," to try out this rhetoric, to see what the bran is worth. As a version of herself, the hag functions as a kind of worst-case scenario for the Wife: "Suppose I never get married again, suppose I *am* old and ugly and my life *is* essentially over; suppose that the energy of my youth is gone forever and that there is nothing left from now on but the downward slope to death. What resources of self-respect and dignity remain to me?" If all she has left is her wisdom, she can at least use it to guide her into old age, where it may be necessary for her to adopt a more conventional style of life and attend to the needs of her soul.

If it feels like there is something a little disingenuous about this position, and if a less respectful paraphrase of it might be "Well, I can always get religion," this is probably because we know the Wife too well by now to be entirely convinced by the more pious version. My real point, again, is that the same is true of her, and that the inadequacies for her of this passive, static, and renunciatory position are part of what she discovers in the very act of trying it out. The best evidence of this is the emergence of a countermessage in the "gentilesse" digression itself, a "privy" subtext that affirms something very different from its "apert" argument and in fact subverts it. This first shows up in what I call the torchbearer simile, the rhetorical treatment of a formal argument that is in itself clear and easy to make. Boethius does it in a brief sentence: If "gentilesse" were a gift of nature, it would always be the same everywhere, "sicut ignis ubique terrarum numquam tamen calere desistit," as fire is always and everywhere hot.[13] This is the Wife of Bath's version:

> If gentillesse were planted natureely
> Unto a certeyn lynage doun the lyne,
> Pryvee and apert, thanne wolde they nevere fyne
> To doon of gentillesse the faire office;
> They myghte do no vileynye or vice.
> Taak fyr, and ber it in the derkeste hous
> Bitwix this and the mount of Kaukasous,
> And lat men shette the dores and go thenne;
> Yet wole the fyr as faire lye and brenne
> As twenty thousand men myghte it biholde;
> His office natureel ay wol it holde,
> Up peril of my lyf, til that it dye.
> Heere may ye se wel how that genterye

> Is nat annexed to possessioun,
> Sith folk ne doon hir operacioun
> Alwey, as dooth the fyr, lo, in his kynde.
>
> (III.1134–49)

The point to notice here is how the image of the fire is detached from the argument, slightly displaced from logical sequence, and foregrounded in a way that makes the argument itself hard to follow because the image is so detailed and so compelling, so much more developed than what surrounds it (or, I might add, than it is in any of its sources). This foregrounding makes the voice seem fascinated by the image of the fire flaming out in isolation and darkness, and this effect of fascination is independent of the place of the image in the argument. Its bright energy is affirmed over against all the conventional rhetoric of human weakness that surrounds it, and this is one key to its source and meaning.

Another key is the associations that fire has taken on in the Wife's prologue and elsewhere in the tale, which find their way into this image:

> For peril is bothe fyr and tow t'assemble:
> Ye knowe what this ensample may resemble.
>
> (III.89–90)

If fire is initially and fundamentally associated with sexuality for the Wife, it also acquires an aggressive dimension in the intimations of sexual threat that her free use of her sex sometimes takes on:

> He is to greet a nygard that wolde werne
> A man to lighte a candle at his lanterne;
> He shal have never the lasse light, pardee.
> Have thou ynogh, thee thar nat pleyne thee.
>
> (III.333–36)

> Thou liknest [women's love] also to wilde fyr;
> The moore it brenneth, the moore it hath desir
> To consume every thyng that brent wol be.
>
> (III.373–75)

As the second example here suggests, fire comes to be associated with what is *uncontrollable*, especially by masculine limits and standards. It is something that breaks through and consumes the oppressions of male decorum, as in the case of Midas's wife:

> Hir thoughte it swal so soore aboute hir herte
> That nedely som word hire moste asterte;
> And sith she dorste telle it to no man,
> Doun to a mareys faste by she ran—
> Til she cam there, hir herte was a-fyre.
>   (III.967–71)

Fire has, then, for the Wife, far more than conventional connotations of inexhaustible energy, linked not only with sexuality but also with her self-assertion and sense of independence, with everything at the core of her that makes her aware of her own vitality. If that vitality is presented in more negative and destructive terms earlier in the poem, presented more as men see it when they try to smother it, here in its more inward manifestations it takes on a more positive sense as an image of the Wife's freedom even in the midst of constraint. Her private attraction to the image of the torch is an index of her *resistance* to the darkness, to the message of human weakness and decay that surrounds the fire and the woman. What is important about this upsurge of inner fire is that it happens spontaneously, and it happens *now*, in the act of speaking. The Wife rediscovers as she speaks that her resistance, her energy, her fire, is not gone at all and has lasted beyond the decay of her youth and beauty. It is this awareness that lies behind the reservations she expresses when she comes to draw the moral consequences of the "gentilesse" argument:

> Yet may the hye God, and so hope I,
> Grante me grace to lyven vertuously.
> Thanne am I gentil, whan that I bigynne
> To lyven vertuously, and weyve synne.
>   (III.1173–76)

The conditional mood in which this statement is cast calls attention to the fact that the speaker withholds herself from complete identification with the position expressed: "I hope God grants me the grace to live virtuously when I decide to begin" carries the implication that that time is not yet.[14]

There is thus little point to the sort of critical objection that notes how the Wife of Bath cannot qualify as "gentil" under her own definition in the speech and takes this circumstance as an "irony" of which she is unaware, since this is precisely the point the Wife is affirming triumphantly in her handling of the speech.[15] The content or *doctrine* here is neither "out of character" nor in it for the Wife. Rather, it is something that culture (masculine culture) makes available, and which the Wife is *using* for her own purposes—here perhaps as a kind of potential *remedia amoris* or "remedye of love." What the Wife reaps in this section of the tale are the real fruits of her experience. External youth and beauty are and were, she discovers, just as deceptive as the traditional wisdom has always maintained them to be, because they worked to conceal from her the real inner sources of her vitality, the capacity for the enjoyment of life and the indomitable spirit that are still with her now that their conventional physical signs have passed. The external deprivation, the "poverte," is the condition that makes possible the discovery of inner richness. It is indeed a bringer-out of busyness and an amender of sapience, precisely because it "maketh [a man] his God *and eek hymself* to knowe."

By the time she gets to "elde," the hag is speaking out clearly for the Wife, in words we have heard before:

> Now, sire, of elde ye repreve me;
> And certes, sire, *thogh noon auctoritee*
> *Were in no book*, ye gentils of honour
> Seyn that men sholde an oold wight doon favour, . . .
> And auctours shal I fynden, as I gesse.
>
> (III.1207–12; emphasis added)

"Elde" is essentially dismissed, left for the future, because it is not yet time in the Wife's life—and that time may never come—for her to lapse into decorum, piety, and silence. No more than Janekyn with his book can those Church fathers and stoic philosophers—men, every Jack of them—tame her. As she moves into the ending of the tale, the Wife asserts her vitality and her resistance to the deadening pressure of conventional proprieties in her treatment of the conclusion of the story. She does this, for instance, in the riddle, whose form in the analogues is a choice between having the hag fair by day and foul by night or vice versa. The Wife of Bath's version—foul and obedient or fair and take your chances—reaffirms the sense of her own energy, independence, and impenitence that has been growing in her during the latter part of the tale: "I'd do it all again, and I *will* if I get the chance."

> Or elles ye wol han me yong and fair,
> And take youre aventure of the repair
> That shal be to youre hous by cause of me,
> Or in som oother place, may wel be.
>
> (III.1223–26)

The extent to which the concerns and the mood generated in the subtext of the "gentilesse" speech dominate the more conventional aspects of the story is

further pointed up by the Wife's handling of the final lines of th.
she drops the happy ending in the middle of a line and goes out

> And thus they lyve unto hir lyves ende
> In parfit joye; and Jhesu Crist us sende
> Housbondes meeke, yonge, and fressh abedde,
> And grace t'overbyde hem that we wedde;
> And eek I praye Jhesu shorte hir lyves
> That wol nat be governed by hir wyves;
> And olde and angry nygardes of dispence,
> God sende hem soone verray pestilence!
>
> (III.1257–64)

This concluding speech is a return to the public occasion of the tale in the
sense that it presents the Wife in the polemical and oppositional role that is
appropriate to the general feminist message and her original battle plan for
the tale. But that public role, and even that message, are qualified by the private experience of the telling. The shrew of the end of the tale is a straw
woman, a role the Wife plays for tactical reasons that have to do precisely
with the inadequacies of the public situation in which she speaks, with respect
to the complexities of experience. It is clear from both the prologue and the
tale that, for the Wife, "maistrye" is not really a simple mechanical reversal of
male domination. In both cases, once the woman has been granted sovereignty, she refrains from exercising it, and this suggests that it is primarily a
tool for achieving feminine independence *within* marriage so that more satisfactory relations between the sexes can have a chance to develop.[16]

"Maistrye" is a way of making room for the possibility of love in the patri-
archal world by giving women space to be responsible partners in a relationship. As only an "answere suffisaunt," it is where everything that is important
about marriage begins, not where it ends. If anyone knows that "they lived
happily ever after" is no way to talk about the experience of marriage, it is the
Wife. Marriage is where things get harder, though potentially richer and
more satisfying, not easier. But this aspect of marriage, the potential it offers
for private fulfillment, is not really appropriate to the situation in which the
Wife is performing. In the first place, the experience of real relationships is not
something that can be conveyed in a story like this, and the Wife makes no effort to present the knight as someone who really learns something or
changes his mind; he is simply coerced throughout the tale.[17] In the second
place, and more especially, the experience of real relationships is not something that can be or that needs to be conveyed to a casually assembled group
of strangers encountered on a pilgrimage, most of them males, with whom

there is little likelihood of, and little reason for, intimacy. The man-eating monster of the end of the tale and elsewhere may be a caricature of the real Wife of Bath, but as a role it is also a way of making sure that no one will try to take advantage of her—it asserts her independence and keeps it firmly in view, and it is in this sense that "maistrye" and the polemical feminism associated with it are dialectically necessary in the world as a woman finds it, as a precondition for the mutuality she might prefer. The conditions of the male-dominated public world may be said to force this position on the Wife, and its necessity shows just how unsatisfactory the public situation of women is in human terms. To make the male world into a straw man—to be forced to do so in order to fight its ubiquitous and dehumanizing public pressures—is to accept a logic of opposition and appropriation that can only drive one to constitute oneself as a straw woman.[18]

"But lordynges, by youre leve, that am nat I." Beyond and behind the public, necessarily caricatured feminism of the "apert" narration, there is a set of "privy" experiences that constitute, for Chaucer in the person of the Wife, a deeper and more existentially responsible feminism and a more searching critique of male domination. At this level, what the Wife responds to intuitively about the story is less what it includes than what it leaves out. One of the most notably sexist things about this particular story and the courtly romance genre of which it is a part is the assumption that women have no other consequential interests beyond courtship and marriage. Men may do battle and have adventures, but the stories of the women in romances are all love stories. As we have seen, such a story has no way of handling an ugly old woman—or even an attractive but not classically beautiful middle-aged one—except by magic, and no place at all for issues like a woman's experience of age and the prospect of death. Too narrowly feminist a reading of the Wife of Bath's Tale—or perhaps I should say, a reading of the Wife as too narrow, too exclusively polemical a feminist—runs the danger of being itself antifeminist because, like the masculine-conditioned romance, it confines the Wife of Bath too exclusively to issues of gender and sexual relations. These issues are very important to the Wife herself; they have dominated much of her life, and they are fully represented in her tale. But to hold her exclusively to them, or for her to do so herself, does not allow her all the other things in her life and experience, including her personhood before age and death. In fact, in her tale we see the speaker as a woman exercising her "purveyaunce," considering her options in line with her own philosophy: "I holde a mouses herte nat worth a leek / That hath but oon hole for to sterte to" (III.572–73). She may find her way back into marriage and the dance of relationship that has occupied and engaged her for so long, but she may not. In this open situation, she herself remains open. By the end of her tale, she has evoked her own energies in the face of what those energies have to contend with and enacted a variety of possible responses to her situation and her unknown future. What she finds is that her experience has provided her with extensive resources for continuing to *womanhandle* the authorities—with God the father, with the masculine world, and with Old Man Death—and that she need not commit nor confine herself to any particular role or position except as a tactical move in whatever game she may have occasion to play. She does not need to define herself once and for all.

This lack of closure in the Wife's life and personality is, finally, an aspect of Chaucer's feminism, since of course there is no Wife of Bath. What there is is an impersonation, a man's attempt to think himself inside a woman's head and to speak from her point of view and with her voice. While I think from the evidence that Chaucer knew a lot about women, I am not in a position to speak with authority on this topic since, like the poet, I lack certain essential experiences. But I do see that in imagining what it might be like to be a woman, Chaucer felt it important to imagine one who remained in a final sense provisional and a mystery to herself—one who had not settled her own fate, and whose inability to predict for certain what would happen to her and who she might become kept her alive to herself and to him. This is still, no doubt, a masculine projection, since I do not think he knew these things about himself either, but in allowing the Wife of Bath to be as genuinely uncertain about these matters as he was himself, I think Chaucer was trying to sustain her mystery, her possibility, and her independence—I think he was trying to respect her privacy.

Notes

1. For a more extended and theoretical account of some of these issues, see Leicester, "The Art of Impersonation: A General Prologue to *The Canterbury Tales*," *PMLA* 95 (1980): 213–24.

2. See, for example, George Lyman Kittredge, *Chaucer and His Poetry* (Cambridge, Mass., 1915; rpt., 1972), p. 191; R. M. Lumiansky, *Of Sondry Folk: The Dramatic Principle in The Canterbury Tales* (Austin, Tex., 1955), pp. 117–29; Bernard F. Huppé, *A Reading of The Canterbury Tales*, rev. ed. (Albany, N.Y., 1967), pp. 107–35 (Huppé actually uses the phrase "Q.E.D." p. 134); Trevor Whitlock, *A Reading of The Canterbury Tales* (Cambridge, 1968), pp. 118–68.

3. *Chaucer's Poetry: An Anthology for the Modern Reader*, 2d ed. (New York, 1975), p. 1077. On the Wife's changes in the traditional story, see also Meredith Cary, "Sovereignty and the Old Wife," *Papers on Language and Literature* 5 (1969): 375–80.

4. This point has not been altogether lost on critics, though they seldom seem to give the Wife much credit for seeing it too. John P. McCall, *Chaucer among the Gods* (University Park, Pa., 1979), uses the phrase "straw men" of the Wife's exempla, p. 139. Ellen Schauber and Ellen Spolsky, "The Consolation of Alison: The Speech Acts of the Wife of Bath," *Centrum* 5 (1977): 20–34, have shown how the basis of all four of what they identify as the Wife's most common speech acts is the setting up of a proposition which is subsequently denied.

5. See, e.g., Lumiansky, *Sondry Folk*, pp. 126–29.

6. For the murderess and sociopath, see Beryl Rowland, "On the Timely Death of the Wife of Bath's Fourth Husband," *Archiv für das Studium der Neueren Sprachen und Literaturen* 209 (1972): 273–82; Doris Palorno, "The Fate of the Wife of Bath's 'Bad Husbands,' " *ChauR* 9 (1975): 303–19; and Donald B. Sands. "The Non-Comic, Non-Tragic Wife: Chaucer's Dame Alys as Sociopath," *ChauR* 12 (1978): 171–82. For intimations of tragedy, see, among others, F. M. Salter, "The Tragic Figure of the Wife of Bath," *Transactions of the Royal Society of Canada* 48, ser. 3 (1954): 1–13. For the life force, see Rose A. Zimbardo, "Unity and Duality in the *Wife of Bath's Prologue and Tale*," *TSL* 11 (1966): 11–18.

7. So far as I can tell, the distinction between the public and private functions of the tale was first made in Charles A. Owen's pioneering and still fundamental study, "The Crucial Passages in Five of the *Canterbury Tales*: A Study in Irony and Symbol," *JEGP* 52 (1953): 294–311, rpt. in Edward Wagenknecht, ed., *Chaucer: Modern Essays in Criticism* (New York, 1959), p. 260. Owen is also one of the first to identify the element of fantasy or wish fulfillment in the tale, a perception that has become so common in discussions of it as to make specific citation pointless.

8. *Canterbury Tales*, III.929–31. Line references are to F. N. Robinson, ed., *The Works of Geoffrey Chaucer,* 2d ed. (Boston, 1957).

9. Since I do not have space or occasion here for an analysis of the Wife's prologue, I ought perhaps to say that I consider her fifth marriage a good one. The Wife's remark "And yet in bacon hadde I nevere delit" (III.418) refers not only to her dislike of old meat in a sexual sense but also to the fact that she is not much interested in conventional marital harmony of the sort for which the Dunmow Flitch was awarded (see III. 217–23). From this point of view, Janekyn and the Wife are a remarkably compatible couple: they both like to talk, they both like to fight, and they both like to make love.

10. See R. E. Kaske, "Chaucer's Marriage Group," in Jerome Mitchell and William Provost, eds., *Chaucer the Love Poet* (Athens, Ga., 1973), p. 52.

11. *The Marriage of Sir Gawaine,* in Bartlett J. Whiting, "The Wife of Bath's Tale," in W. F. Bryan and Germaine Dempster, eds., *Sources and Analogues of Chaucer's Canterbury Tales* (rpt., New York, 1958), p. 237.

12. See P. Verdonk, " 'Sire Knyght, Heer Forth Ne Lith No Wey': A Reading of Chaucer's *The Wife of Bath's Tale*," *Neophilologus* 60 (1976): 305–7.

13. *Consolatio Philosophiae,* III pr. 4.

14. Dorothy Colmer sees this: "Character and Class in the *Wife of Bath's Tale*," *JEGP* 72 (1973): 335.

15. E.g., Lumiansky, *Sondry Folk*, J. F. Ropollo, "The Converted Knight in Chaucer's Wife of Bath's Tale," *CE* 12 (1951): 263–69; W. P. Albrecht, "The Sermon on 'Gentilesse,'" *CE* 12 (1951): 459; Tony Slade, "Irony in the Wife of Bath's Tale," *MLR* 64 (1969): 241–47.

16. Once again a number of commentators have recognized the provisional and preliminary—what I would call the public—character of the idea of "maistrye," though once again the Wife herself has not been given much credit for understanding it. Owen, "Crucial Passages," was the first to note the importance of the hag's refusal to exercise domination. Of the several critics who have developed this perception and seen that what the Wife wants—what women want—is some form of mutuality in relationships, particularly fine accounts are given by Donald R. Howard, *The Idea of the Canterbury Tales* (Berkeley, Calif., 1976), pp. 254–55; and T. L. Burton, "The Wife of Bath's Fourth and Fifth Husbands and Her Ideal Sixth: The Growth of a Marital Philosophy," *ChauR* 13 (1978): 34–50, esp. 46–47.

17. See Colmer, "Character and Class," p. 336; and Verdonk, "Sire Knyght," pp. 305 and 307.

18. David Aers, *Chaucer, Langland and the Creative Imagination* (London, 1980), ch. 6, "Chaucer: Love, Sex and Marriage," pp. 143–73, sees this point as "Chaucer's" message in the poem. See also Alfred David, *The Strumpet Muse* (Bloomington, Ind., 1976), pp. 135–58.

Further Reading

Few pilgrims have attracted as much critical attention as the Wife of Bath. For the misogynist tradition against which Alisoun rebels, see Alcuin Blamires, ed., *Women Defamed and Women Defended: An Anthology of Medieval Texts* (Oxford, 1992). An argument that Chaucer's representation of the Wife is complicit with this misogyny is presented by Elaine Tuttle Hansen, *Chaucer and the Fictions of Gender* (Berkeley, Calif., 1992), pp. 26–57. Other notable interpretations are provided by Mary J. Carruthers, "The Wife of Bath and the Painting of Lions," *PMLA* 94 (1979): 209–22; Arthur Lindley, " 'Vanysshed Was This Daunce, He Nyste Where': Alisoun's Absence in the Wife of Bath's Prologue and Tale," *ELH* 59 (1992): 1–21; and Jill Mann, *Feminizing Chaucer* (Woodbridge, Suffolk, 2002). A variety of interpretations from different critical points of view appears in Peter G. Beidler, ed., *Geoffrey Chaucer: The Wife of Bath* (Boston, 1996), and an annotated bibliography of the criticism can be found in Peter G. Beidler and Elizabeth M. Biebel, *Chaucer's Wife of Bath's Prologue and Tale: An Annotated Bibliography, 1900 to 1995* (Toronto, 1998).

Imagery, Structure, and Theme in Chaucer's Merchant's Tale

KARL WENTERSDORF

✦ ✦ ✦

T
HE MERCHANT'S TALE of January and May is by common consent one
of the finest examples of Chaucer's narrative art. Structurally, the story
falls into two carefully balanced and slightly overlapping parts. In the first
part (1245–1865),[1] we are introduced in detail to the character and marital intentions of the elderly knight, January; the introduction is followed by a debate between his two brethren over the advisability of his plan to marry a
young woman: Placebo encourages him, Justinus warns against the marriage.
January decides to take young May as his wife; he makes preparations for the
wedding, and the first half of the story culminates in a description of the
bridal festivities and the subsequent consummation of the marriage. The second part of the tale (1768–2418), beginning just before the Merchant has completed his account of the wedding, starts with a description of the old knight's
young squire, Damian, who is lovesick for May from the moment he sets eyes
on her; May decides to take Damian as her lover as soon as the opportunity
arises. In January's walled garden, where the lovers' first rendezvous is to take
place, there is a debate—this time supernatural—over May's intention of
cuckolding her husband, in the course of which Pluto announces his opposition to the adultery and his young wife, Proserpine, decides to take May's
part. The tale ends with the consummation of the illicit affair, with January's

discovery of his wife's infidelity, and with the old man's naive acceptance of May's ingenious excuse for the betrayal.

It is a commonplace of Chaucerian studies that this tale abounds in irony—some would say savage irony.[2] It fascinates, partly because it is one of Chaucer's darker, more complex, yet still comical commentaries on the foibles of humanity, and partly because it transcends the traditional medieval criticism of women for their seductive powers and inconstancy in love; equally important is the tale's demonstration of the reprehensible folly and lechery of men. Thus the lust and folly of January, as depicted in the first half of the tale (A), counterpoise the lust and infidelity of May in the second half (B). More important, the story of Adam and Eve (A), whose Fall (though this is not mentioned) introduced into the world death, suffering, and the changing of the seasons, is paralleled by reference to the "fall" in classical mythology, a fall resulting from the ravishing of Proserpine by Pluto (B); it was this rape that led to the death of nature (through the anger of Ceres at the crime against her daughter) and subsequently to the introduction of the seasonal variations. The biblical story, traditionally interpreted as indicating the prime responsibility of a woman for "the los of al mankynde" (III. 720), is balanced by the implications of the classical fall, for which not a disobedient young woman but a lecherous elderly god was responsible.

The two-part structure provides the basis for the most powerful effect of the tale—the striking contrast between the "Heigh fantasye" (1577) or the sweet dream of marriage, as conceived by January in spite of the cogent warnings of Justinus (A), and the bitter realities that arise almost inevitably after the ill-advised wedding (B). That contrast, spelled out step by step in the parallel developments in the first and second halves of the story, is underscored in various ways. Chaucer embellishes his basic folklore materials with literary images in A which foreshadow, sometimes ironically, the situations and events in B. He uses pairs of simple images (metaphors, similes, and proverbial expressions), one of each pair occurring in A and its counterpart in B; and some of the paired images employed are traditional symbols for the motifs of love and lust.

THE MERCHANT'S TALE contains numerous literary references and allusions evoking complex images, sometimes singly and sometimes in series, from stories found in both biblical and mythological sources. As Charles Muscatine has put it, "Chaucer has become so sure of his materials that he can play with them, and in this play he often gives up patient and safe elaboration for the fireworks of rapid allusion."[3] What is noteworthy about this imagery is, firstly, the dichotomy between the favorable tone of the references or allusions and the unfavorable implications when their original contexts are considered and, second, the reflection of the literary imagery of A in the literal situations and incidents of B.

Near the beginning of the tale, January thinks of his future wedded bliss by conjuring up a vision of the joys experienced by Adam and Eve in Paradise before the Fall (1323–32); but in view of the concentration by medieval theologians and preachers on the sinfulness of the guilty pair, on their shame and pain after the Fall, and especially on the role played by Eve in their mutual lapse from grace, hardly anyone in the Merchant's or in Chaucer's audience would have been unaware of January's shortsightedness in overlooking what was widely regarded as the primary significance of the story of Paradise. Furthermore, the innocent though doomed happiness of Adam as recalled in A is mirrored sardonically in the naive and short-lived joys of January in B.

A similar relationship exists between the superficially positive but subtextually negative or ambiguous aspects of the other biblical and mythological motifs in the first part of the Merchant's Tale and the comparable literal situations that develop in the second part. When the Merchant holds forth in A on the supposed felicities of married life, he buttresses his arguments regarding the wisdom and integrity of women with a series of biblical examples:

> Lo, how that Jacob, as thise clerkes rede,
> By good conseil of his mooder Rebekke,
> Boond the kydes skyn aboute his nekke,
> For which his fadres benyson he wan.
> Lo Judith, as the storie eek telle kan,
> By wys conseil she Goddes peple kepte,
> And slow hym Olofernus, whil he slepte.
> Lo Abigayl, by good conseil, how she
> Saved hir housbonde Nabal, whan that he
> Sholde han be slayn; and looke, Ester also
> By good conseil delyvered out of wo
> The peple of God, and made hym Mardochee
> Of Assuere enhaunced for to be.
> Ther nys no thyng in gree superlatyf,
> As seith Senek, above an humble wyf.
>
> (1362–76)

The ostensible purpose of this fireworks display is to exemplify womanly virtue, but the deeds involved have some contradictory connotations.

The references in this passage must be in some sense ironical. As J. S. P. Tatlock put it half a century ago, the four biblical women mentioned by the Merchant were all "deceivers of their men."[4] Even as the Merchant is praising Rebecca for her sagacity in securing the ceremonial blessing of her husband for their younger son, Jacob, he undoubtedly expects his audience to recall the inescapable circumstance that Isaac, who was then old and blind, intended to give his paternal blessing to his older son, Esau, and that the blessing was obtained by Jacob through the use of disguise and lies, in which he was prompted and abetted by Rebecca (Gen. 27:1–40). The Merchant then recalls that Judith was praiseworthy for saving the Israelites from destruction at the hands of the Assyrian general Holofernes; to achieve this end, however, she used her physical attractions to gain access to Holofernes as his willing handmaid, pretended to be ready to betray the defense secrets of the Israelites, and, when he had fallen asleep after feasting privately with her, she hacked off his head and so saved her people (Jth. 7:1–13:31). It was the accomplishment of Abigail, through clever diplomacy, to save her husband, Nabal, from execution: Nabal, who was wealthy but churlish, had refused to receive King David's servants hospitably (in spite of the king's earlier hospitality to Nabal's servants), and David had angrily decided to kill him. Then Abigail, without the knowledge of the husband whom she despised, secretly visited David with peace offerings and thus appeased the king's wrath; after Nabal's death, she quickly became one of David's wives (I Samuel; I Kings 25:1–42). Esther, the fourth of the sagacious women, was another Jewish heroine: when King Ahasuerus of Persia decided to take a new wife, the beautiful Esther, who concealed her nationality on the advice of her uncle Mordecai, entered the harem of Ahasuerus and later became his consort, even though she abhorred him. Because she dissembled, however, she became a great favorite of the king and was able to scheme successfully not only to save the life of Mordecai when he was in danger but also to prevent the planned annihilation of her people (Esther 2–15). . . .

The traditional interpretation of the biblical women's deeds as reprehensible does not, however, take us quite far enough. All four of the Israelite heroines practiced deception for what the biblical writers regarded as being proper and even divinely ordained goals. For this reason, as Emerson Brown has demonstrated, the four women were regarded by Christian exegetes throughout the Middle Ages as virtuous heroines, to be interpreted "allegorically as figures of moral strength and typologically as figures of the Church and the Blessed Virgin"; and this exegesis is reflected abundantly in theological writings, in popular literature, and in art.[5] Thus Chaucer probably intended the Merchant's biblical references in A to convey the motif of deception that is directed toward a good end. May's guile in B, on the other hand, albeit prompted by understandable abhorrence of her husband, is practiced in pursuit of a selfish and ignoble goal.

Chaucer's use of biblical materials is not restricted to stories about less than perfect women; and in his references to one of the greatest of Old Testament kings, Solomon, the poet does not leave it entirely to his audience to detect his irony. Praise for Solomon's wisdom is implicit in one of the statements made in the course of the debate over January's proposed marriage by that sycophantic trimmer Placebo (A):

> This word seyde he [Salomon] unto us everychon:
> "Wirk alle thyng by conseil," thus seyde he,
> "And thanne shaltow nat repente thee."
>
> (1484–86)

Once again we hear that ambiguous word *conseil*. More explicit praise for Solomon comes, not surprisingly, from the elderly and self-important god of the underworld, Pluto, in the course of the debate with his much younger consort, Proserpine, over his intended intervention if May carries out her plan to betray her blind husband with Damian (B):

> O Salomon, wys, and richest of richesse,
> Fulfild of sapience and of worldly glorie,
> Ful worthy been thy wordes to memorie
> To every wight that wit and reson kan.
> Thus preiseth he yet the bountee of man:
> "Amonges a thousand men yet foond I oon,
> But of wommen alle foond I noon."
> Thus seith the kyng that knoweth youre wikkednesse.
>
> (2242–49)

Proserpine, however, swiftly takes the wind out of Pluto's sails:

> Ey! for verray God, that nys but oon,
> What make ye so muche of Salomon?
> What though he made a temple, Goddes hous?
> What though he were riche and glorious?
> So made he eek a temple of false goddis.
> How myghte he do a thyng that moore forbode is?
> Pardee, as faire as ye his name emplastre,
> He was a lecchour and an ydolastre,
> And in his elde he verray God forsook;
> And if that God ne hadde, as seith the book,
> Yspared him for his fadres sake, he sholde
> Have lost his regne rather than he wolde.
>
> (2291–2302)

Proserpine's point is well taken: all of Solomon's heroism and wisdom did not save him in his old age from the sins of lechery and literal idolatry (1 Kings; 3 Kings II:1–10). Similarly, January's wisdom—and we recall that it is not Justinus but the flatterer Placebo who credits him with "sapience" and "heighe prudence" (1481–82)—does not save him from the typical sins and embarrassing fate of the *senex amans*.[6]

Chaucer makes comparably striking use of several mythological references. When January is attempting to persuade his two brethren that his determination to take a young wife is the correct decision for him even though he is advanced in years, he supports his disparaging arguments against older women with what seems at first sight to be a somewhat odd analogy (A):

> I wol no womman thritty yeer of age;
> It is but bene-straw and greet forage.
> And eek thise olde wydwes, God it woot,
> They konne so muchel craft on Wades boot,
> So muchel broken harm, what that hem leste,
> That with hem sholde I nevere lyve in reste.
>
> (1421–26)

In Germanic mythology, Wade is a remarkably clever and courageous warrior (like Beowulf, he overcomes a dragon), who builds an unusual boat, a Nordic equivalent to the wooden horse of the Greeks, designed so as to conceal a band of warriors in order to facilitate the capture of a beautiful Irish princess; the lady is desired as wife by Wade's lord, a king of the Hegelings in Friesland; the Irish king is hoodwinked as to the real purpose of Wade's mission, the plan is successful, and a war of revenge follows.[7] Whatever the truth regarding January's assumption that elderly widows possess the kind of cunning displayed by Wade in his famous exploit, the old knight is certainly egregiously wrong in assuming that no young woman could be endowed with the kind of cunning that May reveals in B.

While January is sitting at his wedding feast (A), he is said to be "ravysshed in a traunce" (1750) as he impatiently awaits the approaching bedding of his bride; and

> . . . in his herte he gan hire to manace
> That he that nyght in armes wolde hire streyne
> Harder than evere Parys dide Eleyne.
>
> (1752–54)

That the Merchant should recall the ardors of the young Trojan prince as an ironic image for the lechery of old January is comical enough. More mordantly ironical is the circumstance that the rape or seduction of Helen by Paris as mentioned in A is paralleled in the seduction of May by the young squire, Damian, in B.

Not only is the motif of rape introduced twice, if only obliquely, in the first half of the Merchant's Tale; it also appears twice in the second half. On its first occurrence in B, the motif is again presented indirectly. In speaking of the beauty of the knight's garden, the Merchant declares it to be such that not even the author of the *Roman de la Rose* could have described it. He then adds that Priapus, too, "ne myghte nat suffise,/Though he be god of gardyns, for to telle/The beautee of the gardyn" (2034–36). Priapus, the ithyphallic god of gardens and fertility, was widely popular with the Romans; furthermore, as Ovid tells in the *Fasti* (1:391–440), he once attempted to rape the maiden Lotis, but was frustrated in the nick of time by the braying of Silenus's ass. Chaucer refers specifically to this well-known story in an earlier work (*Parliament of Fowls*, 253–56), and he is surely alluding to it again in the Merchant's Tale.

The second occurrence of the motif of rape in B is explicit, and it occurs when the narrator tells how Pluto appears in January's walled garden, accompanying his young wife:

> Pluto, that is kyng of Fayerye,
> And many a lady in his compaignye,
> Folwynge his wyf, the queene Proserpyna,
> Which that he ravysshed out of Ethna
> Whil that she gadered floures in the mede—
> In Claudyan ye may the stories rede,
> How in his grisely carte he hire fette.
>
> (2227–33)

The fourfold allusion to rape in the Merchant's Tale makes it obvious that beneath the outward impression of a potentially happy marriage between an entranced groom and his modestly silent bride, there is the harsh truth of an unnatural union between a naive and libidinous dotard and a lusty wench who apparently has been pressured (the hope of financial benefits probably also played a role in her calculations) into a marriage that disgusts her physically and in her eyes merits revenge.

There are two further allusions to the world of classical mythology near the end of A, both of them in the Merchant's account of January's wedding feast. One occurs when the marriage is given, as it were, the seal of approval by the pagan deities who grace the festivities with their presence. Bacchus serves the wine (1722), at once an age-old adjunct to a genuinely joyous occasion and a reputed stimulant to the performance of "Venus werkes" (1971). It is not surprising that the goddess of love herself is present: she "laugheth upon every wight" and "Daunceth biforn the bryde" (1723, 1728). Venus, of course, is the goddess who betrayed her unattractive and crippled husband, Vulcan, by taking as her lover the handsome and virile war god, Mars (Ovid, *Metamorphoses* 4:169–89). So, too, in B, the beautiful and amorous May betrays her unattractive elderly husband with the young and lustful squire.

The other and equally ironic mythological reference in the description of the hymeneal festivities in A appears when the Merchant apostrophizes the fifth-century poet Martianus Capella, asserting that he was not talented enough to compose a proper description of January's celebrations:

> Hoold thou thy pees, thou poete Marcian,
> That writest us that ilke weddyng murie
> Of hire Philologie and hym Mercurie,
> And of the songes that the Muses songe!
> To smal is bothe thy penne, and eek thy tonge,
> For to descryven of this mariage.
>
> (1732–37)

The symbolic wedding of Mercury, the young god of learning, with the wise and modest virgin Philologia, as described in Martianus's treatise on the seven liberal arts, is a properly chaste affair: as the virtuous girl rises toward the heavens to be welcomed by Juno, Martianus notes that Cupid did not dare to be present. Furthermore, even as Philologia is supplicating Venus "as much as was appropriate," Martianus leaves no doubt as to the disparity in character between the modest bride and the voluptuous goddess: Philologia notices that Venus, though undeniably fair, has forelocks curled about with snakes and permits her hair to flow freely, sure signs of wanton inclinations.[8] As the Wife of Bath observes earlier in the Canterbury pilgrimage, those people born under the influence "of Mercurie and of Venus/Been in hir wirkyng ful contrarius," because "Venus loveth ryot and dispence" whereas "Mercurie loveth wisdam and science" (697–700). The union initiated by the wedding of Mercury and Philologia was virtuous and hence dramatically different from the relationship that develops in B between those wanton "children" of Venus, the lecherous January and his disgusted but lustful wife.

THE IMPORTANCE OF the ironic relationship between the literary references and allusions in the first part of the Merchant's story and the parallel literal happenings in the second is enhanced by the effect of the poet's duplication in the second half of the tale of a series of simple images occurring in the first half. Thus January's proverbial statement in A, made after decades of personal sexual license, that life without a spouse is not "worth a bene" (1263), is echoed by May's private feeling later in B, after her husband's eager consummation of the marriage, that "his pleyyng" was not "worth a bene" (1854). To describe the endemic unhappiness of bachelors, the Merchant employs in A a biblical image:

> On brotel ground they buylde, and brotelnesse
> They fynde, whan they wene sikernesse.
>
> (1279–80)

But the anticipated happiness of January's married life turns out in B to be a "brotil joye" (2061, with a probable pun on *brothel*, "a prostitute"), and his union is only one of many in which women are said to have revealed their "brotilnesse" (2241). As a gourmet thinking of marriage, January observes in A that he enjoys "Oold fissh and yong flessh," adding:

> Bet is . . . a pyk than a pykerel,
> And bet than old boef is the tendre veel.
>
> (1418–20)

In his opinion, age is to be preferred in husbands, while youth is better in their wives. The fish image crops up again in B, and this time in a derogatory sense, when the Merchant is describing May's feelings of repugnance toward her husband: as a woman "tendre of age" desiring young love, she finds January's love making to be revolting because, among other things, his newly shaven bristly face is "Lyk to the skyn of houndfyssh" (1825). There may also be an echo here of the common use of *hound* as an image for lechery, as when Chaucer's Parson, later in the Canterbury pilgrimage, asserts that "thise olde dotardes holours [lechers] . . . been lyk to houndes" (X.856–57).

   The most interesting feature of the numerous image pairs is that a metaphor or allusion in A is frequently echoed by a literal image in B. Thus the biblical image of the Garden of Paradise (1325–34) is reflected literally in the specially created walled garden where January disports himself with May (2028–54) and where May's infidelity is consummated.[9] Adam and Eve in their state of innocence are pictured as "belynaked" (1326), as also is May when she is embraced by Damian in the pear tree (2352–53, 2393–95). In A, the Merchant describes the "yong wyf" who is the object of her husband's desire as "the fruyt" of his treasure (1270–71); and treasure, to Chaucer's audience, was something best kept under lock and key. In B, where January's human treasure, May, is literally locked up with him in his garden, and where the young man who is the object of *her* desire is already ensconced in a pear tree, she thinks of him in terms of the tree's fruit, as she tells her husband that she has a great craving for the as-yet-green pears (2330–33), brazenly hinting that she is pregnant:

> I telle yow wel, a womman in my plit
> May han to fruyt so greet an appetit
> That she may dyen, but she of it have.
>
> (2335–37)

When January wishes to express his conviction that an old man can easily maintain control over a young wife (A), he employs a commonplace simile:

> But certeynly, a yong thyng may men gye,
> Right as men may warm wex with handes plye.
>
> (1429–30)

In B, May demonstrates how dubious this assumption is, by literally using a piece of wax to circumvent January's plan to safeguard the privacy of his walled garden and keep out unwanted visitors by means of its locked gate:

> This fresshe May, that I spak of so yoore,
> In warm wex hath emprented the clyket
> That Januarie bar of the smale wyket,
> By which into his gardyn ofte he wente:
> And Damyan, that knew al hire entente,
> The cliket countrefeted pryvely.
>
> (2116–21)

The introduction of the wax motif, together with the traditionally sexual imagery of the key and the lock,[10] is typical of the improvements made by Chaucer in the process of transforming the original story. As Dempster points out, the literal use to which the warm wax is put in B is not only one of the poet's "[M]ost subtle twists of dramatic irony" but also one for which "neither the finest fabliaux nor the rest of Chaucer's probable or possible reading offers the slightest parallel."[11]

As January is endeavoring in A to persuade his brethren that he is still capable, notwithstanding his advanced age, of playing the normal sexual role of a married man, he speaks of himself symbolically in terms of a tree:

> For, God be thanked! I dar make avaunt,
> I feele my lymes stark and suffisaunt
> To do al that a man bilongeth to;
> I woot myselven best what I may do.
> Though I be hoor, I fare as dooth a tree
> That blosmeth er that fruyt ywoxen bee;
> And blosmy tree nys neither drye ne deed.
>
> (1457–63)

When May escapes from the unwelcome clutches of her repulsive husband to the welcome embraces of a much younger man, the place to which she repairs for the infidelity (B) is literally a fruit tree (2324–53). January also likens himself fatuously, during the conversations with his brethren in A, to the evergreen laurel, a shrub sacred to the handsome, young sun god, Apollo:

> Myn herte and alle my lymes been as grene
> As laurer thurgh the yeer is for to sene.
>
> (1465–66)

A laurel figures in January's walled retreat not only literally (B), since there is a well in the garden located "under a laurer alwey grene" (2037), but also symbolically, because of the concealed presence there of May's youthful lover.

With reference to January's choice of May from among several potential brides, the Merchant observes sarcastically, if proverbially (A), "love is blynd alday, and may nat see" (1598); and not long after his marriage, January literally and most inopportunely (B) "Is woxen blynd, and that al sodeynly" (2071). Even as he rejoices in the sexual freedom he believes himself to have achieved legitimately through marriage, he nevertheless realizes that his love making—his "trespace"—cannot fail "greetly" to offend his wife (1828–30). The justification he offers is unconvincing:

> It is no fors how longe that we pleye;
> In trewe wedlok coupled be we tweye;
> And blessed be the yok that we been inne,
> For in oure actes we mowe do no synne.
> A man may do no synne with his wyf,
> Ne hurte hymselven with his owene knyf;
> For we han leve to pleye us by the lawe.
>
> (1835–41)

The dangerousness of January's views on this matter (A) is clarified later in *The Canterbury Tales* by Chaucer's Parson, in his denunciation of lechery and particularly the lust of old dotards. He uses the same simile of the proverbial knife:

> And for that many man weneth that he may nat synne, for no likerous-nesse that he dooth with his wyf, certes, that opinion is fals. God woot, a man may sleen hymself with his owene knyf, and make hymselve dronken of his owene tonne. (X.858–61)

The idea that a married man like January might kill himself spiritually through mortally sinful (because excessive) sexual gratification is strictly in accord with the teaching of the medieval Church. As Richard Rolle (d. 1349) put it, marriage as a social institution is good in itself; but when men marry to satisfy their lust, they transform the marital relationship into something evil.[12] The image of the dangerous knife recurs in the Merchant's Tale in B, this time literally, when January seeks to assure May that he is more con-:erned for her personal feelings than for the possibility of his own death by stabbing: "Levere ich hadde to dyen on a knyf, / Than thee offende" (2163–64). That he can envision the possibility of physical death, whether from another man's knife or from his own, but not the serious danger of spiritual death (the knife, as a secret weapon, is here a phallic symbol) is typical of his obtuseness.

It is the Merchant telling the tale who makes the lyrical but ironic comment on the marriage (A):

> Whan tendre youthe hath wedded stoupyng age,
> Ther is swich myrthe that it may nat be writen.
>
> (1738–39)

The mirth or solace that January enjoys is certainly not shared by May, who is determined to experience her own youthful pleasure with Damian. Since January believes that her alleged desire for green pears is reasonable (B), he agrees to help her: he "stoupeth down" (2348), thus enabling her to stand upon his back and so climb into the arms of Damian for the solace he provides amid the branches of the tree.

A clue to the thematic significance of the parallelism of the imagery in A and B is provided by the (nonparalleled) simile of the mirror, when January is ruminating on the various candidates for the honor of marrying him:

> Many fair shap and many a fair visage
> Ther passeth thurgh his herte nyght by nyght,
> As whoso tooke a mirour, polisshed bryght,

> And sette it in a commune market-place,
> Thanne sholde he se ful many a figure pace
> By his mirour; and in the same wyse
> Gan Januarie inwith his thoght devyse
> Of maydens whiche that dwelten hym bisyde.
> He wiste nat wher that he myghte abyde.
>
> (1580–88)

Just as the mirror in the marketplace would simply reflect images showing the external features of the people passing by, so January's nocturnal imagination offers a vision of eminently nubile maidens with winning faces and lissome bodies; and since he unthinkingly accepts the Platonic notion that physical beauty is evidence of a virtuous disposition, he is not at all concerned regarding his future spouse's personality traits. The artist's mirroring of life, on the other hand, reveals, directly or obliquely, the discrepancies that often (and, in the story of January, certainly) exist between the favorable surface appearance of things and the unedifying deeper reality. Thus the images in A—mostly metaphors, similes, and literary allusions—have a more profound significance or resonance than is apparent at the time of their initial occurrence, a significance that first becomes fully evident when they recur in B, often as literal images or actions. . . .

AS HAS ALREADY BEEN NOTED, the reference to the biblical Garden of Paradise near the beginning of A finds its literal parallel in the walled garden of B, the pleasance where January and May can roam in strict seclusion "aboute the aleyes" (2324) and perform those amorous works "that were nat doon abedde" (2051). Among the many such literary gardens, the prime example of the topos is the great walled garden in the *Romance of the Rose*, described at length in the opening segment of the poem as translated by Chaucer (*Romaunt*, 479–1634). That garden is presided over by "Venus sone, daun Cupido," or Eros, whose nets are set to trap not birds but "damoysels and bachelers" (1616–23). Within its walls are flowery lawns, trees of every kind, birds, squirrels, and rabbits, streams and wells, especially the Well of Love. January's *hortus conclusus* is less pretentious than that in the *Romaunt*, though the Merchant hyperbolically implies that it is more beautiful; the poet could assume that the audience would take many of the details for granted (lawns, flowers, birds), and he confines himself to mentioning the well under the laurel and (later) the all-important pear tree. There is no mention of the young god of love in connection with this garden; instead we are told that it is haunted by the elderly ravisher Pluto, together with his wife and erstwhile victim, Proserpine. Of course the garden (as already noted) would have met with the approval even of the lustful Priapus; and since it is there that not only January but also May and Damian satisfy their sexual desires, it is diametrically opposed to the vision of innocence conjured up by the prelapsarian Garden of Paradise.

The image of a tree, like other popular symbols, could have both a favorable and an unfavorable meaning; which of the two the author intends is generally indicated by the context. Tropologically, the fruit tree, deriving ultimately from the tree of the knowledge of good and evil in Paradise, could be thought of either as rooted in grace, with its branches representing the various virtues, or else as rooted in evil, in which case the branches stood for vices. D. W. Robertson, Jr., draws attention to an example of this usage in a late twelfth-century treatise attributed to Hugh of St. Victor, *De fructibus carnis et spiritus*. There, the good tree, symbolizing a man or a woman in the state of grace, is rooted in *humilitas*, produces branches and fruits of the spirit, and bears as its crowning fruit spiritual love. The tree of evil, on the other hand, symbolizing a sinful man or woman, is rooted in *superbia*, or pride; it bears as its branches and fruits the various sins, and its crowning product is *luxuria*, or lechery.[13] Chaucer uses the symbol with a *significatio in malo* in A when January confides in his brethren and implies his determination to "kepe hym fro the synnes sevene, / And eek from every branche of thilke tree" (1640–41). In B, by way of contrast, January symbolically embraces the tree of evil, rooted as it is in *superbia* (the pride behind his egoism) and having such branches as *scientia* (worldly wisdom leading to a false sense of security), *idolatria* (the false worship of pleasure), *invidia* ("the fyr of jalousie . . . brente his herte" [2073–75], and *luxuria* (his unbridled lechery). Furthermore, January literally and ludicrously embraces a real tree in his garden; and as he puts his arms around the trunk, he is as ignorant of the extent of his own fall from grace as he is unaware of the plan to cuckold him.

There remains the question: why does May choose a pear tree . . . as the place where she and Damian will satisfy their amorous desires? . . . Of course, May is going to use her pretended longing for fruit as the pretext for climbing the tree. But why does she feign a yearning for pears, rather than some other fruit?

Part of the answer is to be found in the circumstance that Chaucer found the pear tree in his source or sources. There are numerous medieval erotic tales in which this tree is an important part of the setting.[14] In one folklore category, the "enchanted pear tree" group, a husband perched up in the tree sees his wife making love with his squire on the ground below, but he is then duped into believing that he was mistaken and that something magical about the tree had caused his delusion. This motif is exemplified in the late twelfth-century Latin poem, Matthieu de Vendôme's *Comœdia Lydia,* and in Boccaccio's "Pamfilo's Story," told on the seventh day of the *Decameron*.[15] In the second and more common category, the "miraculous cure" group, an elderly blind husband is duped by his wife into allowing and even helping her to climb up a pear tree, into the arms of her waiting lover; when the husband is miraculously enabled, by supernatural intervention, to see the infidelity, the wife explains that she was merely doing what she had been told was necessary to bring about the cure of his blindness. This motif is found in many forms: in an untitled story which appears in a collection of *novellini* made about 1300, which was probably used by Chaucer as one of his sources; in a collection of Latin fables in verse, written in 1315 by Adolphus of Vienna; in a tale in Latin prose, *De ceco et eius uxore ac rivali*, printed in an appendix to Steinhöwel's edition of *Aesop* (1476–1477); and in a French translation of the Latin prose *D'ung aveugle et de sa femme*, in Julien Macho's *Ésope* (1480).[16]

Undoubtedly, Chaucer specified that the tree was a pear because he found the feature in his source materials. But did he take over this detail uncritically, or did he make it his own because it was a symbolically appropriate motif? Certainly none of the surviving analogues indicates any specific reason for the choice of a pear tree as the place for the adultery, other than the wife's pretended desire for fruit.

There is considerable evidence that the pear was thought of as related— whether sympathetically or allegorically—to human sexuality. . . . In Thibaut's mid-thirteenth-century erotic allegory *Li Romanz de la Poire*, the persona tells how one fine day he was sitting with his lady under a pear tree in a garden when, unnoticed by others who were present, she gave him a pear from which she had taken a bite; he, too, ate from the pear and immediately, as if by magic, was overcome by passion and felt himself drawn irresistibly toward the lady.[17] The anonymous author of the late thirteenth-century romance *Kyng Alisaunder* describes a scene of feasting and raucous merry making, where "Noyse is gret wiþ tabour and pype, / Damoysels playen wiþ peren ripe. / Ribaudes festeþ also wiþ tripe" (B 1573–75).[18] The connotations of *peren* here are highlighted by a parallel passage in the social satire *Mum and the Sothsegger* (ca. 1405): there the persona dreams of a luxuriant landscape crowded with erotic symbols (891–943), where "Peris and plummes and pesecoddes grene, / That ladies lusty loken muche after, / Were gadrid for gomes ere þay gunne ripe" (904–6).[19] The *plummes* and *pesecoddes* imply, like the *peris*, that the games are of an erotic nature. Even the detail that the desired fruits are green and "gadrid . . . ere þay gunne ripe"—those longed for by January's wife are likewise "smale peres grene" (2333)—may be intended to underscore the salacity of the ladies' intentions, since the attractive color green was associated with the deceptive wiles of the Devil and hence with pleasurable sin.[20] . . .

The development of this symbolic significance is probably connected with the circumstance that some pears were thought to resemble female breasts, while others were seen as being shaped like the male genitalia. One pear, known to the Romans as the *Pomponian*, was also called the *pirum mammosum* because it was breast-shaped; and in *The Destruction of Troy* (ca. 1400), the bosom of the beautiful Helen is described as "pleasaund . . . / With two propur pappes, as a peire rounde, / ffetis and faire" (3078–81). As for the phallic symbolism, one kind of pear, the Flemish *Poperin(g)*, was seen as being shaped in such a way as to be appropriate for a sign of the phallus and hence the male lover. There is a strong hint of this connotation in the otherwise obscurely motivated detail in Chaucer's Tale of Sir Thopas: there the ridiculous would-be knightly lover—he says "An elf-queene shal my lemman be" (1978)—is said to have been born "In Flaundres . . . At Poperyng" (1909–10), and the allusion creates a typically Chaucerian irony. The Poperin(g) pear was still a phallic symbol in the England of Shakespeare's day. Thus Mercutio, believing that Romeo is still enamored of Rosaline, cries out, "O Romeo, that she were, O that she were / An open [arse], thou a pop'rin pear!" (*Romeo and Juliet* [2.1.37–38]).[22] This variety of pear functions similarly as a symbol of sexuality in several other Renaissance dramas. . . .

Probably the most striking piece of medieval evidence for the erotic significance of the pear tree is the anonymous fourteenth- or fifteenth-century lyric "Love in the Garden":

> I haue a newe gardyn,
> & newe is be-gunne;
> swych an oþer gardyn
> know I not vnder sunne.
> In þe myddis of my gardyn
> is a peryr set,
> & it wele non per bern
> but a per Ienet.
> þe fayrest mayde of þis toun
> preyid me,
> for to gryffyn her a gryf [graft]
> of myn pery tre.
> quan I hadde hem gryffid
> alle at her wille,
> þe wyn & þe ale
> che dede in fille.
> & I gryffid her
> ry3t vp in her home;
> & be þat day xx wowkes
> it was qwyk in her womb.

> þat day twelfus month,
> þat mayde I mette:
> che seyd it was a per robert
> but non per Ionet![23]

In this poem, the *peryr* is clearly phallic, and *grafting* is a euphemism for swiving. . . .

In view, therefore, of the pear tree's long-standing erotic connotations—morally neutral in classical literature, usually unfavorable in medieval literature—it is evident that it appears in the Merchant's Tale primarily on account of its common tropological significance rather than as a realistic detail introduced specifically to provide a place for the consummation of the adulterous liaison. It is more than simply an image for the multibranched tree of mortal sins: it represents specifically the sin of lust, and its artistic function in the tale is twofold. First, the fact that the infidelity takes place, as planned, amid the branches of a pear tree reinforces the audience's impression of the lechery of May (and, of course, her lover). Second, the picture of January clasping the trunk of the tree in a futile effort to forestall any infidelity on May's part does more than remind the audience of the old man's failure to avoid the seven-branched tree of sinfulness in general: just as he had clasped his bride in his arms at the end of the first part of the tale, so now he embraces the tree that symbolizes his own dominant weakness, lechery.

IT HAS BEEN OBSERVED by Muscatine that in the Merchant's Tale, "the structure of comparisons and relationships is essential to the theme." One purpose of this essay has been to argue that the structural parallelism in characterization and theme between the first and second halves of the story supports the contention that Eve's role in bringing about the Fall in the Garden of Eden prefigures May's role in the tale, and that Pluto's role in the mythological counterpart to the biblical narrative prefigures January's role. Just as the reference to Paradise in the first part of the tale reminds us of Eve's victory over Adam, in persuading him to eat the fruit of the forbidden tree, so events in January's "paradise" in the second part reveal Proserpine's victory over her husband (Pluto says, "I yeve it up!" [2312] during the argument over whether May should be punished for her adultery or should escape scot-free). And as Emerson Brown notes, Pluto's surrender "leads to the surrender of Januarie himself, who, when given sight, refuses to see and subjugates himself completely to the will of his wife."[24]

The "rich backdrop of references" (the phrase is Muscatine's), one of the most striking aspects of the tale, repeatedly demonstrates Chaucer's ability to introduce literary allusions in such a way as to comment obliquely on the difference between the favorable but misleading surface appearance of things and the unpleasant realities beneath the surface. And this aspect of the Merchant's theme is strengthened by the technique in which the metaphorical and mostly positive images in A are paralleled by realistic and negative images—sometimes objects, sometimes actions—in B, thus reinforcing the idea that reality does not always correspond with appearances. As Muscatine rightly points out, the tale "is very much a poem in which the single line and the single image carry enormous weight."[25]

The story of January's marriage and its aftermath is more than just another instance of a very common attitude toward women in medieval literature, an attitude exemplified in Jankyn's "book of wikked wyves" (685). What sets the Merchant's Tale apart from other antifeminist writings of the Middle Ages is the fact that the sexuality of young May, leading swiftly to her infidelity, is offset by the sordid manifestation of old January's sexuality, stimulated as it is by the wines drunk "t'encreesen his corage" (1807–8) and leading to the marital embraces that are surely as revolting to May as any outright rape would have been.

Imagery and action combine with structure to show that responsibility for the breakdown of January's marriage lies only partly with May. It is true that she is all too ready to respond willingly to Damian's approaches, even though her own amorousness vis-à-vis the young squire is at first comically veiled by the Merchant's highly ironic comment on her feelings and motivation: "Lo, pitee renneth soone in gentil herte!" (1986). January is equally culpable because of his insistence on entering into a marriage which bodes ill on account of the great disparity between his age and that of his bride. That this joint responsibility has its basis in the erotic natures of the married couple is emphasized by Chaucer's employment, among the parallel images in A and B, of some notable medieval symbols for sexual passion, symbols applicable equally to January and May.

The ultimate effect of the Merchant's Tale is to place the burden of fault for the woe that prevails in January's marriage squarely on the shoulders of both spouses. Hence the tale suggests that behind the facile assumption, manifested in centuries of misogynistic criticism, that *Mulier est hominis confusio* (it is Chauntecleer in another tale who cites the phrase [VII. 4354]) lies the truth that men are equally accountable for suffering and disaster in the spheres of love and marriage. It would be wrong to suggest that the implications of the Merchant's Tale show Chaucer to be a forerunner of the modern feminist movement, but it is evident that he takes a more balanced view of human sexual relationships and responsibilities than many other writers of his age.

Notes

1. Chaucer is cited from *The Works of Geoffrey Chaucer*, ed. F. N. Robinson, 2d ed. (Boston, 1957).

2. For a discussion of many of the minor ironies in the action of the Merchant's Tale, see Germaine Dempster, *Dramatic Irony in Chaucer* (New York, 1959 [1932]), pp. 46–58.

3. *Chaucer and the French Tradition* (Berkeley, Calif., 1966), p. 231.

4. "Chaucer's Merchant's Tale," *Modern Philology* 33 (1936): 376.

5. Emerson Brown, Jr., "Biblical Women in the Merchant's Tale: Feminism, Antifeminism, and Beyond," *Viator* 5 (1974): 389–98.

6. A further example of ironic biblical allusiveness occurs in B when January, on being urged by May to go with her "to pleye / In his gardyn," agrees:

> Rys up, my wyf, my love, my lady free!
> The turtles voys is herd, my dowve sweete;
> The wynter is goon with alle his reynes weete.
> Com forth now, with thyne eyen columbyn!
> How fairer been thy brestes than is wyn!
> The gardyn is enclosed al aboute;
> Com forth, my white spouse! out of doute
> Thou hast me wounded in myn herte, O wyf!
> No spot of thee ne knew I al my lyf.
>
> (2138–46)

As F. N. Robinson and others have pointed out, these lines contain clear echoes of the imagery of love in the biblical Song of Songs (or Canticle of Canticles):

> "Arise, my love, my fair one, and come away; for lo, the winter is past, the rain is over and gone. The flowers appear on the earth . . . and the voice of the turtle-dove is heard in our land" (Song of Sol., R.S.V. 2:10–12); "Behold, you are beautiful, my love; behold you are beautiful; your eyes are doves" (1:15); "Oh, may your breasts be like clusters of the vine, and the scent of your breath like apples, and your kisses like the best wine" (7:8–9); "You are all fair, my love; there is no flaw in you" (4:7).

Here January is deliberately echoing the sensual biblical phraseology to express his joy and to imply the absolute propriety of his own song of love; but there could hardly be anything more mistaken than his belief that May, like the biblical bride, is spotless.

7. For a detailed account of Wade's boat and his cunning exploit, see Wentersdorf, "Chaucer and the Lost Tale of Wade," *JEGP* 65 (1966): 274–86.

8. *Martianus Capella and the Seven Liberal Arts*, trans. W. H. Stahl et al., 2 vols. (New York, 1977), 2:48–63; 2:141–218.

9. In Paul A. Olson's phrase, it is "a paradise of earthly lust": see his essay "Chaucer's Merchant and January's 'Hevene in Erthe Heere,' " *ELH* 28 (1961): 207.

10. This erotic symbolism goes back at least to Anglo-Saxon times: see *The Exeter Book: Part II*, ed. W. S. Mackie (London, 1958 [1934]), p. 140, riddle 44: while the ostensible solution is *key*, the riddle is ingeniously written so as to suggest *phallus*.

11. Dempster, *Dramatic Irony*, p. 51.

12. *The Fire of Love*, trans. C. Wolters (Bungay, England, 1972), p. 117.

13. See Robertson's essay "The Doctrine of Charity in Medieval Literary Gardens" (1951), rept. in *Essays in Medieval Culture* (Princeton, N.J., 1980), pp. 24–25.

14. See Antti Aarne, *The Types of the Folktale*, trans. and enlarged by Stith Thompson, 2d ed. (Helsinki, 1964), pp. 420–21, no. 1423.

15. *Comœdia Lydiæ*, in *Poésies Inédites du Moyen Age*, ed. Edélestand du Méril (Paris, 1854), pp. 371–73; Giovanni Boccaccio, *The Decameron* (New York, 1940), pp. 351–60 (7:9).

16. See *Sources and Analogues of Chaucer's Canterbury Tales*, ed. W. F. Bryan and Germaine Dempster (Chicago, 1941), pp. 341–56. For an English version of Macho's tale, published in Caxton's *Fables of Aesop* (1484), see *Originals and Analogues of Some of Chaucer's Canterbury Tales*, ed. Frederick J. Furnivall (London, 1888), pp. 181–82.

17. Messire Thibaut, *Li Romanz de la Poire*, ed. Friedrich Stehlich (Halle, 1881), pp. 45–50 (398–624).

18. *Kyng Alisaunder*, ed. G. V. Smithers (London, 1952), p. 89.

19. *Mum and the Sothsegger*, ed. Mabel Day and Robert Steele (London, 1936), pp. 53–54. The romantic scene, with its trees, flowers, songbirds, and a river full of fish, boasts such popular erotic elements as *honysoucles* and *havthorne, conyngz* [conies], and *hares*, as well as *hertz, hyndes*, and *buckes*.

20. Cf. D. W. Robertson, Jr., "Why the Devil Wears Green," *MLN* 69 (1954): 470–72.

21. *Pliny: Natural History*, ed. and trans. H. Rackham (London, 1952), 4.324–27; *The Gest Historiale of the Destruction of Troy*, ed. G. A. Panton and D. Donaldson (London, 1869–1874), 1.100.

22. *The Riverside Shakespeare*, ed. G. Blakemore Evans et al. (Boston, 1974), p. 1067. The editor of the *Riverside* text comments on this passage "*open-arse*, another name for the medlar, with allusion to female pudenda; *pop'rin pear*, Flemish pear of phallic shape." It may be pertinent that in medieval Latin, *pirum* could mean not only "pear" but also "rod, staff, cudgel."

23. R. H. Robbins, *Secular Lyrics of the XIVth and XVth Centuries*, 2d ed. (Oxford, 1968), pp. 15–16.

24. "Biblical Women," pp. 399–402.

25. *French Tradition*, p. 230.

Further Reading

The sense of the Merchant's Tale as unrelievedly cynical has been countered by several critics in a variety of ways: see, for example, J. A. Burrow, "Irony in the Merchant's Tale," *Anglia* 75 (1957): 199–208; Martin Stevens, " 'And Venus Laughteth': An Interpretation of the Merchant's Tale," *Chaucer Review* 7 (1972): 118–31; C. David Benson, *Chaucer's Drama of Style* (Chapel Hill, N.C., 1986), pp. 116–30; Richard Neuse, "Marriage and the Question of Allegory in the Merchant's Tale," *Chaucer Review* 24 (1989): 115–31; and Robert R. Edwards, "Narration and Doctrine in the Merchant's Tale," *Speculum* 66 (1991): 342–67. Allusions in the final scene in the garden have been well explained by Bruce A. Rosenberg, "The 'Cherry-Tree Carol' and the Merchant's Tale," *Chaucer Review* 5 (1971): 264–76; and Kenneth Bleeth, "Joseph's Doubting of Mary and the Conclusion of the Merchant's Tale," *Chaucer Review* 21 (1986): 58–66. The relation of the Merchant's Tale to the Clerk's Tale that precedes it has been well discussed by Jerome Mandel, *Geoffrey Chaucer: Building the Fragments of* The Canterbury Tales (Rutherford, N.J., 1992), pp. 23–49. A fascinating guide to the historical world of merchants in late medieval England is provided by Sylvia Thrupp, *The Merchant Class of Medieval London, 1300–1500* (Ann Arbor, Mich., 1948).

Pleasure and Responsibility
in the Franklin's Tale

HARRY BERGER, JR.

◆ ◆ ◆

THAT THE FRANKLIN narrates a story about a happily married aristocratic couple involved in a courtly situation tells us something about his
preferences and perhaps about his reading habits.[1] The sympathy and warmth
he feels for his chivalric hero and lady are obvious, yet it is equally obvious
that they are but slightly individualized. They exist for him as embodiments
of ideals, and they are presented in soft focus:

> In Armorik, that called is Britayne,
> Ther was a knyght that loved and dide his payne
> To serve a lady in his beste wise;
> And many a labour, many a greet emprise
> He for his lady wroghte, er she were wonne.
> For she was oon the faireste under sonne,
> And eek therto comen of so heigh kynrede
> That wel unnethes dorste this knyght, for drede,
> Telle hire his wo, his peyne, and his distresse.
> But atte laste she, for his worthynesse,
> And namely for his meke obeysaunce,
> Hath swich a pitee caught of his penaunce

> That pryvely she fil of his accord
> To take hym for hir housbonde and hir lord,
> Of swich.lordshipe as men han over hir wyves.
> And for to lede the moore in blisse hir lyves,
> Of his free wyl he swoor hire as a knyght
> That nevere in al his lyf he, day ne nyght,
> Ne sholde upon hym take no maistrie
> Agayn hir wyl, ne kithe hire jalousie,
> But hire obeye, and folwe hir wyl in al,
> As any lovere to his lady shal,
> Save that the name of soveraynetee,
> That wolde he have for shame of his degree.
>
> (729–52)[2]

This has the effect of bringing up and then disposing of the more realistic problems connected with the so-called marriage debate; the Franklin is interested in other matters and another, more literary, form of experience. He admires the virtues Arveragus personifies; he is both charmed and amused by Dorigen, whose ingenuousness he brings to a comic climax in her suicide complaint, which went on "a day or tweye," and is recognized by the Franklin as a healthy piece of therapy. He also recognizes that her childlike inability to cope with the black rocks might cause serious trouble in any world more real than the controlled fiction in which she lives.

The Franklin's method of description similarly reveals both his attraction to what he describes and the control which keeps it from being too real. Like the symbolic garden and prison in the first two parts of the Knight's Tale, the places of the Franklin's world are not concretely visualized beyond the needs of symbolic settings which accompany states of mind or give rise to half-allegorical meditation. Thus after describing Dorigen's excessive grief at Arveragus's absence, and her friends' efforts "awey to dryve hire derke fantasye," the Franklin tells us that her castle stood "faste by the see" (847). This brings on Dorigen's complaint concerning the black rocks (853–93), as a result of which her friends lead her away from the sea to the garden (895–919). A few lines later, the essential qualities of the garden are transformed into the figure of Aurelius:

> Upon this daunce, amonges othere men,
> Daunced a squier biforn Dorigen,
> That fressher was and jolyer of array,
> As to my doom, than is the month of May.
> He syngeth, daunceth, passynge any man
> That is, or was, sith that the world bigan.

> Therwith he was, if men sholde hym discryve,
> Oon of the beste farynge man on lyve;
> Yong, strong, right vertuous, and riche, and wys,
> And wel biloved, and holden in greet prys.
>
> (925–34)

Though the landscape is real enough to provide a stage for action, the soft focus, the careful selection of places and details, point it toward symbolic expressiveness. Dorigen's "derke fantasye" materializes in the black rocks; her castle elevated above yet "faste by" the sea suggests a basic security (her marriage) which may be exposed to life's vicissitudes (the sea, Arveragus's absence) but need not be disturbed. Her main problem is learning how to pass the time, and the Franklin describes the situation so as to make the "philosophical" meditation on black rocks seem like the effect of her having nothing better to do than watch the ocean (857–64). It is almost as if she intensifies her apprehensions in preference to being merely bored; looking "*into* the see" she projects her mood and so converts the scenery to a symbol. Thus when her friends take her from sea to garden, this constitutes a withdrawal from one objectified frame of mind to another, from the symbol of pure pain to the symbol of pure pleasure.

The unruly sea and rocks both cause and express Dorigen's lack of *pacience*; she converts the normal hazards of life and love into a purely negative vision. The Franklin, who would agree with Dorigen's clerks that "al is for the beste" (866) in spite of ire, sickness, separation, and black rocks, impersonates his Job-like heroine smilingly:

> Why han ye wroght this werk unresonable?
> For by this werk, south, north, ne west, ne eest,
> There nys yfostred man, ne bryd, ne beest;
> It dooth no good, to my wit, but anoyeth.
> Se ye nat, Lord, how mankynde it destroyeth?
> An hundred thousand bodyes of mankynde
> Han rokkes slayn, al be they nat in mynde.
>
> (872–78)

What Dorigen needs is *temporary* relief, a change of scene, distraction from care, and the Franklin has her friends lead her by gradual stages to the *locus amoenus*. The garden which the Franklin envisages, and on which he lovingly dwells, differs from literary gardens in one respect: the first thing he notes is that it has a well-stocked larder, and later he remarks in passing that they go to dance and sing "after dyner." Clearly the Franklin, after beginning with a practical, Franklinlike observation, warms up to the paradisaic image as he describes it until its purely ideal aspects break loose from the more realistic context and emerge in the figure of the perfect courtly lover. From the moment the latter's passion is mentioned, however, the Franklin makes Aurelius look a little silly, for the lovelorn squire has reduced life to the single obsessive concern which the courtly garden symbolizes and which he personifies:

> He was despeyred; no thyng dorste he seye,
> Save in his songes somwhat wolde he wreye
> His wo, as in a general compleynyng;
> He seyde he lovede, and was biloved no thyng.
> Of swich matere made he manye layes,
> Songes, compleintes, roundels, virelayes,
> How that he dorste nat his sorwe telle,
> But langwisseth as a furye dooth in helle;
> And dye he moste, he seyde, as dide Ekko
> For Narcisus, that dorste nat telle hir wo.
>
> (943–52)[3]

The Franklin's descriptions of place and behavior are in sharp contrast to those of the Squire in his tale, closer in attitude and control to those of the Knight. The narrative energy is sustained, not dissipated, by the various reflexive devices; unlike the Squire, the Franklin does not get in the way of his story either by frequent interruptions or by descriptions whose detailed literalness reflects the interests of the teller rather than the needs of the tale. The blocks of lyric declamation are neither disproportionately long nor the utterances of puppets speaking for the narrator—in this, the major complaints of Aurelius and Dorigen differ somewhat from those of Palamon and Arcite as well as from the falcon's lament.[4]

The Franklin's feeling about courtly gardens and lovers is best gauged by comparing his description with the following lines from his portrait:

> His breed, his ale, was alweys after oon;
> A bettre envyned man was nowher noon.
> Withoute bake mete was nevere his hous
> Of fissh and flessh, and that so plentevous,
> It snewed in his hous of mete and drynke,
> Of alle deyntees that men koude thynke.
> *After the sondry sesons of the yeer,*
> *So chaunged he his mete and his soper.*
>
> . . . .

> Wo was his cook but if his sauce were
> Poynaunt and sharp, and redy al his geere.
> His table dormant in his halle alway
> Stood redy covered al the longe day.
>
> (341–48, 351–54; italics mine)

It is consistent with the Franklin's attitude toward *pacience* that his appetites and menus accord with the rhythm of the seasons and that his innate tendency to self-indulgence is fitted into the wider frame of social and natural order. As a natural and sensual function, eating is self-directed, but the Franklin has made it the basis of a social or ritual occasion; his cooks and tables stand ready to communicate his pleasures to others, so that Chaucer's emphasis on gourmet refinements suggests something quite different from the curiosity motivated by sybaritic boredom. Eating provides a legitimate excuse for sharing and gathering together, for those moments of relaxation, recreation, or relief so important to the continuance of life and *pacience*. Seasonal change offers a model of the variety in scene, mood, and occupation essential to a balanced state of mind. But seasons and meals suggest also the other side of natural variety, which is the transience of pleasures; *pacience* demands that the withdrawal to such pleasures be justified by the return—or the intention to return—to responsibility. Thus the Franklin's word *vitaille* (904) may be extended to things which are essential to life in the most general sense—to the life of the soul and mind as well as to that of the body. The Franklin's feeling about *vitaille* and *poynaunt* sauces is only one aspect of the total frame of mind they symbolize. And even if we read his careful hospitality as a display of status which may reflect upwardly mobile tendencies, it seems clear that this indulgence is also justified by his generosity. If the Franklin is aware of his weaknesses (supposing them to be weaknesses), he knows how to make the most of them for himself as well as for others.

There is a subtle but real difference between a cosmetic improvement which follows nature and one which vexes nature to art. Dorigen's garden, like any actual or literary retreat, is the selective embodiment of a single season, and this artifice of the mind is heightened by the curious "craft of mannes hand." The *purveiaunce* of God (865) which allows black rocks in the world is improved and in fact countered by the "ordinaunce / Of vitaille and of oother purveiaunce" of manmade gardens. Some of E. T. Donaldson's remarks on rhetoric made with reference to the Nun's Priest's Tale, are directly relevant to the Franklin and his tale:

> It is . . . possible to think of rhetoric . . . as a kind of cosmetic art—that of adorning bare facts. Yet something is lacking here. The rhetorical mode of

expression may be said to consist in using language in such a way as to bring about certain preferred interpretations. Compare, for example, an apparently bare statement, "The sun sets," with the rhetorical statement, "The Sun drove his chariot beyond the waters of the western seas." To the ancient mind the last statement would suggest a particular kind of order and meaning in the universe—in other words, a cosmos. . . . Rhetoric . . . stands between us and the fear of something which, even if it is not chaos, is disconcerting.[5]

Dorigen's friends would use the courtly garden merely as *vitaille*, as psychic sustenance which may stand temporarily between Dorigen and the black rocks, but which is not intended to replace them. But the rhetoric of the courtly garden becomes total fantasy and escape in the person of Aurelius.

This opposition between colors of rhetoric as *vitaille*, on the one hand, and as magic, fantasy, *appearence*, on the other, provides the basis for the overall narrative shape of the Franklin's Tale and also for the smaller sequences produced by the Franklin's rhythmic modulations from one image or episode to another. The narrative as a whole, apart from these modulations, moves from sea through garden and courtly lament to the climax in the magician's illusory obliteration of the rocks, then back through Dorigen's complaint and the three acts of generosity culminating in the magician's refusal to hold the squire to his contract. If we include the headlink and the Franklin's closing *demande* to the audience, this pattern is quite clearly one of withdrawal and return—into and out of a very literary world which, at its furthest point from actuality, attains to a condition of total rhetoric in the magical illusion. Closely connected to this narrative pattern is the fact that the Franklin's attention seems to shift from his audience to his subject and back to the audience. He begins in the headlink, in terms of a complex social situation involving the Squire, his son, the Host, and the other pilgrims. From this he moves into a tale with obvious attractions for him and, though he always maintains firm control, he is at times visibly affected so that his attention to his audience becomes secondary. After Dorigen's suicide complaint, however, he seems newly aware of the demands of the storytelling situation; the pace of the narrative is quickened, the tale and the moral are modified to provide the audience with *vitaille* which will have made the fabulous entertainment worthwhile. Thus the tale, which is about the functions and dangers of recreation, is itself an exemplary recreative act, a comment and improvement on the Squire's entertainment. The interpretation which follows will trace some of the moments which comprise this act and articulate the contours of the pattern.

After opening with a brief profile of the scene and characters, the Franklin turns to the other pilgrims and delivers his *sentence* on patience. The profile of

Dorigen and Arveragus[6] is thereby generalized; it becomes a contribution to the marriage debate and to the topic of *maistrie*. The Franklin's focus on the actual frame-world and his corresponding emphasis on the tale as an old story serving an exemplary purpose are evident in the lines which introduce the plot:

> Who koude tell, but he hadde wedded be,
> The joye, the ese, and the prosperitee
> That is bitwixe an housbonde and his wyf?
> A yeer and moore lasted this blisful lyf,
> Til that the knyght of which I speke of thus,
> That of Kayrrud was cleped Arveragus,
> Shoop hym to goon and dwelle a yeer or tweyne
> In Engelond, that cleped was eek Briteyne,
> To seke in armes worshipe and honour;
> For al his lust he sette in swich labour;
> And dwelled there two yeer, the book seith thus.
> Now wol I stynten of this Arveragus,
> And speken I wole of Dorigen his wyf,
> That loveth hire housbonde as hire hertes lyf.
> For his absence wepeth she and siketh,
> As doon thise noble wyves whan hem liketh.
> She moorneth, waketh, wayleth, fasteth, pleyneth;
> Desir of his presence hire so destreyneth
> That al this wyde world she sette at noght.
>
> (803–21)

The Franklin makes it clear that the demands of the chivalric life and ethos, which seem to have for him the patina of the golden age, conflict with the demands of the more routine and bourgeois *trouthe* of marriage. Arveragus was not called away by a Crusade: he decided arbitrarily ("shoop hym") to spend a year or two away from home because he set "al his lust" in the pursuit of worship and honor; and, as the book says, he extended "swich labour" to the upper limit, so that there is some reason for the strain on Dorigen's patience. Whatever appeal "thise olde gentil Britouns" may have for the knight of the shire, who seeks worship and honor closer to home, he sees that the ideal will have to be tempered, indeed contaminated, if *trouthe* is to serve a life which may be more mundane but is equally precious. Arveragus's labor is too purely self-directed to harmonize with the complex social obligations which the Franklin sees as centered in home and marriage. All this, of course, draws out an implication which the Franklin only touches on in passing, but

I feel that the implication is reinforced by the actual context in which the Franklin's awareness of his audience sets it: the context of the marriage debate, the values represented by the Squire and his tale, the Franklin's portrait in the General Prologue, and the animation of that portrait in the dialogue following the Squire's Tale.

The Franklin immediately attenuates this impression of Arveragus by his lightly ironic treatment of Dorigen. She has friends, after all, matters are not as bad as she makes them, she should know (as he knows) that everything will turn out for the best. Her friends insist that "causelees she sleeth hirself, allas!" (825), and Arveragus considerately sends "lettres hoom of his welfare, / And that he wol come hastily agayn" (838–39). The tone of his aside to the audience suggests that he does not take Dorigen's plight as seriously as she does:

> By proces, as ye knowen everichoon,
> Men may so longe graven in a stoon
> Til som figure therinne emprented be.
> So longe han they conforted hire, til she
> Receyved hath, by hope and by resoun,
> The emprentyng of hire consolacioun,
> Thurgh which hir grete sorwe gan aswage;
> She may nat alwey duren in swich rage.
>
> (829–36)

From this point on, the Franklin confronts his fiction more directly; his asides and disclaimers, especially in the approach to the magician's triumph, reveal his involvement in the tale rather than his awareness of the audience, and this involvement is of course most clearly discernible, as we shall see, in his protestations against magic. The temporal boundaries of this period of involvement are roughly marked by Dorigen's two complaints, and it is within this period that we find the Franklin's major digressions, descriptions and other devices which interrupt or decelerate the narrative—it is here, in other words, that he lingers over or forcibly disengages himself from those aspects of the tale which claim his interest.

The serious trouble in the tale is shown to be caused by Dorigen's urge to amuse herself. She has just given the squire her "fynal answere" to his plea for mercy, but instead of breaking off she detains him, no doubt simply to pass the time—"after that in pley thus seyde she" (988):

> . . . whan ye han maad the coost so clene
> Of rokkes that ther nys no stoon ysene,

> Thanne wol I love yow best of any man,
> Have heer my trouthe, in al that evere I kan.
>
> (995–98)

The wish, though real, is voiced as idle chatter, and the language of courtly promise is a more or less ironic recognition on Dorigen's part of the impossible proposition to which the squire's rhetoric reduces.[7] Such a reduction is indirectly echoed a few lines later by the Franklin, who reminds us he is a plain-speaking man while reporting that the garden party has served its proper function for all but one of the guests:

> . . . sodeynly bigonne revel newe
> Til that the brighte sonne loste his hewe;
> For th'orisonte hath reft the sonne his lyght,—
> This is as muche to seye as it was nyght!—
> And hoom they goon in joye and in solas,
> Save oonly wrecche Aurelius, allas!
>
> (1015–20)

Having thus aligned himself with the anticourtly forces of common sense, and smiled at the self-pitying squire, the Franklin proceeds to impersonate Aurelius in an elaborately rhetorical complaint which takes us further away from the treacherous sea: the God of black rocks is replaced by pagan deities called on to fulfill the squire's impossible wish; the sun, which cannot hear his pleas, is replaced by Apollo (1029–37); and Christian actuality disappears behind the more archaic world of projected and "preferred interpretations":

> Lord Phebus, dooth this miracle for me.
> Preye hire she go no faster cours than ye;
> I seye, preyeth your suster that she go
> No faster cours than ye thise yeres two.
> Thanne shal she been evene atte fulle alway,
> And spryng flood laste bothe nyght and day.
> And but she vouche sauf in swich manere
> To graunte me my sovereyn lady deere,
> Prey hire to synken every rok adoun
> Into hir owene dirke regioun
> Under the ground, ther Pluto dwelleth inne,
> Or nevere mo shal I my lady wynne.
>
> (1065–76)[8]

This is of course asking too much—"He nyste what he spak"—and Aurelius will have to be satisfied with natural magic, a second-best type of miracle in which, through astrological mumbo-jumbo, actuality is concealed behind the rhetoric of *apparence.*

As the Franklin goes on to narrate the events leading up to the fulfillment of the illusion, he is at pains to dissociate himself from "swich folye," and to distinguish proper from improper uses of magic.[9] At the same time, he reveals what seems a fairly thorough familiarity with the magician's instruments and techniques, so that one finds it hard to believe he did not himself study that book "of magyk natureel" at Orleans (1124–25). Thus after remarking at line 1267 that "I ne kan no termes of astrologye," he lets fly a twenty-four-line salvo of jargon by way of describing the magician at work (1273–96). The tone, however, is not one of fascination but one of impatience—"he went through all this nonsense to produce this disruptive illusion" (cf. 1270–72, 1291–96). The Franklin's attitude here must apply to the whole tale and not merely to magic, since so large-scale an illusion is credible only as make-believe or only to the superstitious. As this section of his tale comes to its unrealistic climax, he seems to be reminding us that this is, after all, the creation of "thise olde gentil Britouns" who "in hir dayes / Of diverse aventures maden layes" (709–10).

The Franklin makes it clear that he is by no means against magic per se, and his descriptions are sufficiently circumstantial to raise questions in our minds concerning the possibility that he may be recalling his own experiences. Aurelius's brother, seeking to cure the squire, remembers:

> That whiles he was at Orliens in Fraunce,
> As yonge clerkes, that been lykerous
> To reden artes that been curious,
> Seken in every halke and every herne
> Particular sciences for to lerne—
> He hym remembered that, upon a day,
> At Orliens in studie a book he say
> Of magyk natureel, which his felawe,
> That was that tyme a bacheler of lawe,
> Al were he ther to lerne another craft,
> Hadde prively upon his desk ylaft;
> Which book spak muchel of the operaciouns
> Touchynge the eighte and twenty mansiouns
> That longen to the moone, and swich folye
> As in oure dayes is nat worth a flye,—

> For hooly chirches feith in oure bileve
> Ne suffreth noon illusioun us to greve.
>
> (1118–34)

Magic is a lust as natural to *young* clerks as courtly love is to young squires: "So priketh hem nature in hir corages." The mixture of motives—holy day and holiday—which characterizes the Canterbury pilgrimage also affects youthful scholars, who go to France not only in search of the normal university curriculum but also to "seken straunge artes, / To ferne halkes, kowthe in sondry londes."[10]

The Franklin, who knows the dangers of *curiositas*, reminds us that the bachelor went to Orleans "to lerne another craft," a phrase whose practical ring suggests a contrast to the *folye* which was *prively* pursued. But such folly has a proper place in life, a recreative function described by the squire's brother:

> I am siker that ther be sciences
> By whiche men make diverse apparences,
> Swiche as thise subtile tregetoures pleye.
> For ofte at feestes have I wel herd seye
> That tregetours, withinne an halle large,
> Have maad come in a water and a barge,
> And in the halle rowen up and doun.
> Somtyme hath semed come a grym leoun;
> And somtyme floures sprynge as in a mede;
> Somtyme a vyne, and grapes white and rede;
> Somtyme a castel, al of lym and stoon;
> And whan hem lyked, voyded it anon.
> Thus semed it to every mannes sighte.
>
> (1139–51)

Like tale telling and dancing in gardens after dinner, magic may contribute to the delight of what is for the Franklin the essential social occasion. Here is not only a harmless but a healthy display of rhetorical powers for the pleasure of others as well as oneself, and here the spectator may humor in play those urges and fantasies (both *derke* and idyllic) which are dangerous if not afforded some controlled, public forms of release. The magical items in the above list provide a representative sampling of aristocratic activities and appeal to a representative range of affections.

In the next part of the narrative the Franklin goes out of his way to create an excuse for dwelling at greater length on this function of magic. One may

speculate that his dismissal of natural magic as nonsense may have some
roots in his own curious and futile labors over a book of formulas, and that
fiction, which replaces magic, is the only medium in which these vestigial fantasies may be sanely reflected. Thus as the improbable content of the tale approaches the saturation point, the Franklin allows himself a peculiarly
realistic and Franklinlike interlude. Aurelius and his brother meet "a yong
clerk romynge by hymself" on the outskirts of Orleans, and after greeting
them "in Latyn thriftily" he pulls his magic on them:

> . . . he seyde a wonder thyng:
> "I knowe," quod he, "the cause of youre comyng."
> And er they ferther any foote wente,
> He tolde hem al that was in hire entente.
>
> (1175–78)

Our attention is diverted from the "wonder thyng" by the brief but telling
hint of the clerk's eagerness to display his accomplishments, and by the lines
which immediately follow, when the Franklin changes tone and reminds us
of a fact that makes vanities of all accomplishments but *pacience*:

> This Briton clerk hym asked of felawes
> The whiche that he had knowe in olde dawes,
> And he answerde hym that they dede were,
> For which he weep ful ofte many a teere.
>
> (1179–82)

This brief insertion adds point to the succeeding interlude in which the
Franklin seems quite clearly to identify himself with the magician. The account of the magically induced, illusory hunting, hawking, jousting, and
dancing is sandwiched between a report on the magician's larder ("Hem
lakked no vitaille that myghte hem plese") and a call for dinner (1183–1218).
The Franklin's concerns are comically projected into the tale, and the charm
of the final section is heightened by the repeated line indicating pride in
clerkly possessions, "Into my studie, ther as my bookes be" (1214, cf. 1207). His
excited response to the "sighte merveillous" he is imagining causes a momen-
tary lapse into the first person: "And farewell al oure revel was ago" (1204).
The fact that Aurelius is seeing a show and not actually touring the clerk's
property does not emerge until the *voyded* at line 1195, so that the reality of the
illusion is initially stressed; after this point the visions are more selectively
aimed at the squire's *plesaunce* and, as in a dream, are made to vanish in a

moment of preclimactic pleasure. For the squire's courtly feast of Barmecide, the clerk substitutes the real if prosaic fulfillment of *vitaille*. The illusions of human rhetoric—magic, courtly love, fiction—are given qualified approval as amusements for the social hour. The lyric and escapist and narcissistic tendencies, to which these illusions appeal, are contained; they are put into play as elements of a narrative, life-sustaining, and social experience.

This interlude has very little to do with the story proper and seems therefore to delay the unavoidable climax. Having thus temporarily withdrawn, the Franklin returns to his unpleasant business:

> At after-soper fille they in tretee
> What somme sholde this maistres gerdon be,
> To remoeven alle the rokkes of Britayne,
> And eek from Gerounde to the mouth of Sayne.
>
> (1219–22)

The clerk, who shares the narrator's interest in the "wel arrayed hous" and life, proceeds to interpose an uncourtly obstacle:

> He made it straunge, and swoor, so God hym save,
> Lasse than a thousand pound he wolde nat have,
> Ne gladly for that somme he wolde nat goon.
>
> (1223–25)

But Aurelius dismisses him with an airy gesture: "Fy on a thousand pound!" (1227).

Aurelius and the magician no sooner set off for Brittany than the Franklin again interrupts the narrative, this time with a literary and periphrastic digression:

> . . . this was, as thise bookes me remembre,
> The colde, frosty seson of Decembre.
> Phebus wax old, and hewed lyk laton,
> That in his hoote declynacion
> Shoon as the burned gold with stremes brighte;
> But now in Capricorn adoun he lighte,
> Where as he shoon ful pale, I dar wel seyn.
> The bittre frostes, with the sleet and reyn,
> Destroyed hath the grene in every yerd.
> Janus sit by the fyr, with double berd,

And drynketh of his bugle horn the wyn;
Biforn hym stant brawen of the tusked swyn,
And "Nowel" crieth every lusty man.

(1243–55)

The passage is like a sequence of emblematic yet realistic miniatures from a Book of Hours. The sequence paradigmatically visualizes both the total thrust of the narrative and the personal atmosphere—the teller's sensibility—by which it is suffused. The Franklin describes the season first in terms of an Aurelian Phoebus declining into winter lust, then in terms of a *burel* Janus waiting out the bitter spell in festive warmth and looking forward to the time of new birth. It was the Phoebus of "burned gold with stremes brighte" to whom Aurelius had prayed for his now-imminent fulfillment in Capricorn; from this standpoint the wintry image may be an objective correlative of Dorigen's plight: as the courtly experience reaches its climax this menacing image suggests its true nature. And the last four lines may then be read as a shift to a more optimistic image of the season. The whole sequence, with its sense of quickly passing time, has a proleptic effect: the Franklin overleaps the moment of jeopardy to console us with a happy forecast.

But this is more than an evasive digression; it is an emblem, an instructive embodiment, of the Franklin's view of life. The Franklinlike Janus does not only replace the Squirelike Phoebus in the sequence of images; he succeeds him in the sequence of life and experience. The Phoebus image interprets life as a decline from the golden age and green gardens of youth; the wish to abolish time and perpetuate May is companion to this view; the pessimistic view and the escapist wish are the complementary sides of the pleasure principle. Against this is set the figure of Janus, a god of seasons and of the hearth who presides *bifrons* over the setting and rising of the sun, over the transition from the old year to the new, over war and generation. The future toward which Janus looks is not a mere recurrence of vernal nature. He looks toward the new birth commemorated and anticipated in *Nowel*, though in a broad rather than a strict Christian sense: the Franklin's *Nowel* is a wintry festival which helps to sustain *pacience* through the bitter season. If the original "payen rite" no longer provides sufficient reason for feasting, good cheer may now be justified as an earnest of the good news—the news, namely, that life does not run down irreversibly from youth's golden age but that future gains may outweigh past losses. Something of this message is apparent in the very treatment of the image: Janus conflated with the Franklin, the Roman god with the worldly but Christian Englishman who revives the ancient figure and festival in the new context of his own vision.

The digressions and interludes just examined present instances in which magic, *vitaille*, and entertainment are temperately indulged and thus play a useful role in the rhythm of man's life. Expressing the Franklin's norms, they imply the extent to which the behavior of the characters in the tale violates those norms. Thus we see him periodically disengaging himself from the plot and projecting contrasts of scene or situation which reaffirm the happy balance achieved by Epicurus's own son. This rhythmic alternation between interlude and plot makes itself felt fairly early in the tale, and I should like to add two more instances to those discussed above. The first is very brief and occurs just after Dorigen has dismissed the wretched squire with her seemingly impossible demand. Within his account of the squire's exaggerated and literary behavior, his growing isolation, the Franklin frames a contrasting vignette of normal social life—the life of Dorigen and her friends—in the garden:

> "Madame," quod he, "this were an inpossible!
> Thanne moot I dye of sodeyn deth horrible."
> And with that word he turned hym anon.
> Tho coome hir othere freendes many oon,
> And in the aleyes romeden up and doun,
> And nothyng wiste of this conclusioun,
> But sodeynly bigonne revel newe.
>
> (1009–15)

The second example occurs after Aurelius's outlandish prayer to Phoebus. The Franklin turns with some distaste from his woebegone lover and embraces a fact which promises to dissipate the threat of a courtly affair. The measure of his involvement and relief is suggested by his sudden apostrophe to Dorigen:

> Dispeyred in this torment and this thoght
> Lete I this woful creature lye;
> Chese he, for me, wheither he wol lyve or dye.
> Arveragus, with heele and greet honour,
> As he that was of chivalrie the flour,
> Is comen hoom, and othere worthy men.
> O blisful artow now, thou Dorigen,
> That hast thy lusty housbonde in thyne armes,
> The fresshe knyght, the worthy man of armes,
> That loveth thee as his owene hertes lyf.
> No thyng list hym to been ymaginatyf,

> If any wight hadde spoke, whil he was oute,
> To hire of love; he hadde of it no doute.
>
> He noght entendeth to no swich mateere,
> But daunceth, justeth, maketh hire good cheere;
> And thus in joye and blisse I lete hem dwelle,
> And of the sike Aurelius wol I telle.
>
> (1084–1100)

These interludes seem as natural to the Franklin as breathing, and as important. Images of needful recreation, they also provide him with *his* recreation. They repeat in smaller compass the dominant rhythm of withdrawal and return, play and work, self-indulgence and social responsibility—in literary terms, the lyric and narrative inflections which shape his act of telling as they express his life.

The Franklin's interruptions during the central portion of the tale do not strike us as primarily intended to produce certain effects on his audience; they seem rather to rise from the effects of the tale on him. I do not mean by any stretch of the imagination to suggest that his story makes him flinch and seek relief in digression; his tale is comic not tragic, and he obviously relishes the whole situation. But his absorption in his subject matter, his reasons for wanting to tell a tale of this sort, are more apparent and unguarded during this part. However fantastic the "apparence or jogelrye" is, he takes it seriously as symbolic of certain dangerous human tendencies, and his ability to suggest this symbolic dimension is a sign of his control. But *control* implies something to be controlled, and I think we must see a more immediate kind of interest reflected in the parts of the tale dealing with magic. Because he shows himself knowledgeable in the very magic which he treats with distaste, his distaste seems directed toward a vestige or memory of his own youthful folly as well as toward the superstitions and fantasies of a relatively archaic "Breton" imagination. And the distaste seems proportional to the present or past attractiveness of these fantasies. Both his attitude toward magic and his familiarity with it are evident in the account he gives of the magician at work:

> So atte laste he hath his tyme yfounde
> To maken his japes and his wrecchednesse
> Of swich a supersticious cursednesse.
> His tables Tolletanes forth he brought,
> Ful wel corrected, ne ther lakked nought,
> Neither his collect ne his expans yeeris,
> Ne his rootes, ne his othere geeris,
> As been his centris and his argumentz

> And his proporcioneles convenientz
> For his equacions in every thyng.
> And by his eighte speere in his wirkyng
> He knew ful wel how fer Alnath was shove
> Fro the heed of thilke fixe Aries above,
> That in the ninthe speere considered is;
> Ful subtilly he kalkuled al this.
> Whan he hadde founde his firste mansioun,
> He knew the remenaunt by proporcioun,
> And knew the arisyng of his moone weel,
> And in whos face, and terme, and everydeel.
>
> (1270–88)

In spite of his impatience, he seems to betray a certain grudging admiration for the magician's craftsmanship. But this is almost the last significant digression in the tale. Shortly after, Aurelius confronts Dorigen with the fait accompli, and this leads to the complaint which is a turning point not only in the tale itself but also in the teller's attitude toward it.

The Franklin allows Dorigen to complain for 102 lines and "a day or tweye, / Purposynge evere that she wolde deye" (1457–58) rather than submit to Aurelius. Actually, her purpose changes—or to be more accurate, suicide is not her real intention at all. This is a Scheherazade situation in parody: Dorigen feels capable of going through "mo than a thousand stories . . . touchynge this mateere" (1411–12), and she reels off exempla of noble women sufficient to keep her talking to herself until Arveragus comes home. Her list of examples falls rhetorically into two sections. The first seven examples—six of them suicides and one a martyr to chastity—lead her resoundingly to the wrong conclusion:

> What sholde I mo ensamples heerof sayn,
> Sith that so manye han hemselven slayn
> Wel rather than they wolde defouled be?
> I wol conclude that it is bet for me
> To sleen myself than been defouled thus.
> I wol be trewe unto Arveragus,
> Or rather sleen myself in som manere.
>
> (1419–25)

This rather vague and indecisive plan opens the way for fifteen more examples in a sequence which curves gradually upward until it ends with a small group of women who outlived their husbands—three or four killing themselves only after their husbands had died, and five or six not at all famous for having surrendered their own lives in this worthy cause. Though the Franklin interrupts her before she has finished, and Arveragus finds her still at it three days later, the included sample completely expresses and rounds off its function as therapy. Dorigen's current way of passing time is better than staring at black rocks, and this time her *pacience* is rewarded.

The pattern of her complaint is curiously similar to the pattern of the Franklin's Tale. For one thing, it is clear that she has read and enjoyed "thise stories" of exemplary women merely for their own sakes. Her delight in old books is amusingly conveyed at the beginning of the complaint by her inclination to dwell on the scenes she envisages, e.g.:

> Whan thritty tirauntz, ful of cursednesse,
> Hadde slayn Phidon in Atthenes atte feste,
> They comanded his doghtres for t'areste,
> And bryngen hem biforn hem in despit,
> Al naked, to fulfille hir foul delit,
> And in hir fadres blood they made hem daunce
> Upon the pavement, God yeve hem meschaunce!
> For which thise woful maydens, ful of drede,
> Rather than they wolde lese hir maydenhede,
> They prively been stirt into a welle,
> And dreynte hemselven, as the bookes telle.
>
> (1368–78)

The first group of seven examples occupies forty-four lines, the last group of fifteen only thirty-one. The more detailed vividness of the first seven tableaux encourages her to see herself cast as lead tragedienne, so she moves more briskly through the second group and picks happier instances whose exemplary function outweighs their fictional immediacy.

After Dorigen's complaint, the Franklin himself increases the narrative pace: there are no extended digressions or descriptions, and the effect of a rapid denouement is produced by a syntax whose dominant mode is parataxis: "and then . . . and then . . . and then . . ." We might see this pattern in complaint and tale as another embodiment of seasonal rhythm—the fantasy is indulged and safely spent, giving way to other, perhaps healthier, impulses. In both cases we see pleasure first and profit after. But of course there is another motive in the fact that the Franklin, unlike his soliloquizing heroine, is responsible to an audience. Dorigen's prolixity perhaps makes him apologetic, for he seems to grow less patient with his tale and more concerned for the patience of his audience:

> "Allas," quod she, "that evere was I born!
> Thus have I seyd," quod she, "thus have I sworn"—
> And toold hym al as ye han herd bifore;
> It nedeth nat reherce it yow namoore.
>
> (1463–66)

> Paraventure an heep of yow, ywis,
> Wol holden hym a lewed man in this
> That he wol putte his wyf in jupartie.
> Herkneth the tale er ye upon hire crie.
> She may have bettre fortune than yow semeth;
> And whan that ye han herd the tale, demeth.
>
> (1493–98; cf. 1546–56, 1592–94, 1621–24)

The Franklin's consciousness of his audience cuts two ways, as the second passage above shows; he is alive to the mutual obligations of teller and listener, to the need for self-control on both sides because of the limits of time and patience. This shift of attention from tale to audience is underlined in a peculiar manner: the Franklin projects it onto his characters. Most noticeable and significant is the compunction about brevity which the squire evinces: he answers and releases Dorigen "in fewe wordes" (1525) and concludes his brief plea to the clerk with "ther is namoore to telle" (1584) and his explanation (shortened by the Franklin's summary at lines 1598–1602) with "This al and som; ther is namoore to seyn" (1606). The same sentiment is evident in the couplet with which clerk and Franklin cooperate in sending off the former: " 'It is ynogh, and farewel, have good day!' / And took his hors, and forth he goth his way" (1619–20). Even Arveragus's sympathetic question at line 1469—"is ther oght elles, Dorigen, but this?"—takes on a certain comic quality in the shadow of his wife's still-echoing encyclopedia of noble wives.[11] One senses an embarrassed haste in the final section, as if all the characters are helping the Franklin apologize to his audience for the heroine's filibuster. This indicates that the decorum of tale telling, the obligation to one's audience, comes now to hold the Franklin's attention and replace the more personal concerns which the tale reflected during the central portion of the narrative. The characters are also affected by the Franklin's effort to convert the old tale into an exemplum. Thus the clerk, in the above passage (1610–12), describes an exemplary clerk, and the squire concludes his act of generosity by making Dorigen and himself exempla of wifehood and squirehood:

> . . . heere I take my leve,
> As of the treweste and the beste wyf
> That evere yet I knew in al my lyf.
> But every wyf be war of hire biheeste!
> On Dorigen remembreth, atte leeste.
> Thus kan a squier doon a gentil dede
> As wel as kan a knyght, withouten drede.
>
> (1538–44)

Paull Baum's feeling that the last four lines should be assigned to the Franklin testifies to the extent to which the teller's extrafictional interest at this point dominates his fictional characters.[12]

The *demande* which concludes the tale is an abrupt gesture, a little forced, and it seems like a superficial bow in the direction of "morality." Its very salience, however, serves its function: it is intended to stir up a debate on generosity—a debate not among Chaucer's readers, but among the Franklin's auditors. Both the gesture and its content have a social thrust: the latter reveals an effort to convert the "olde gentil" lay into a parable touching on problems of contemporary interest—the transfer of the old ideals of knighthood to clerkly and commercial enterprises. If the private and aristocratic idyll is to be justified, it must be capable of translation into some more mundane and practical sphere of public activity. In the gesture itself, the Franklin moves back to the level of generalization, the atmosphere of topical discussion among pilgrims with which he began his tale. And he has modified the topic as well as the tale, for if he took his cue from the marriage debate, he has, through the agency of the tale, shifted to a new topic which is perhaps closer to his heart. The *fre* act performed by each character entails jeopardizing or sacrificing something he prizes—the knight's reputation, the squire's lust, the clerk's profit—in the interest of a socially directed *trouthe*. Each in his own way has had his pleasure and indulged it beyond the limits of that temperance which would have rendered it useful: the knight's urge "to seke in armes worshipe and honour," the squire's pursuit of the courtly life, the clerk's delight in magic. Though the knight initiates the chain of generous acts and provides the model, the Franklin's emphasis is mainly on the clerk, for it is here that the theme of *gentilesse* is transferred from the literary context of the former age to the actual context of the new social ideals:

> Everich of yow dide gentilly til oother.
> Thou art a squier, and he is a knyght;
> But God forbede, for his blisful myght,
> But if a clerk koude doon a gentil dede
> As wel as any of yow, it is no drede!
> Sire, I releesse thee thy thousand pound.

And, as if to confirm his affinity with the clerk, the Franklin has him conclude the penultimate line of his speech with the key word:

> For, sire, I wol nat taken a peny of thee
> For al my craft, ne noght for my travaille.
> Thou hast ypayed wel for my vitaille.
> It is ynogh, and farewel, have good day!
>
> (1608–19)

The Franklin's awareness of the social context of narration stands in sharp contrast to the comic insensitivity of the Squire toward his audience, and it fulfills the rhythm which dominates the Franklin's behavior. It is as if he has had the pleasure of his tale "as in his tyme," and now he considerately hastens to wind things up without further trying his auditors' patience. Having given rein to his fantasy and (hopefully) entertained others as well as himself, he will conclude with something relevant and instructive. So at the end, he actively engages his companions by resorting to a tactic not unlike the Nun's Priest's "taketh the fruyt," though perhaps with less explicit emphasis on "lat the chaf be stille." And, like the Nun's Priest, he enjoys the "pleyn delit" of his tale as long as possible and does not definitely offer the *fruyt, vitaille*, until the closing *demande*.

Notes

1. Donaldson, whose brief commentary on the Franklin's Tale is most suggestive, notes the narrator's "translation of all that is ideal in courtly love . . . into terms of a happy marriage. This splendidly illustrates bourgeois aspiration to aristocratic virtues, with inevitable redefinition—and less inevitable purification—in the context of bourgeois practicality. . . . His idea of marriage is a far finer thing than the immorality of courtly love, as it is also far finer than the commercial drabness of much contemporary bourgeois marriage" (E. T. Donaldson, *Chaucer's Poetry* [New York, 1958], p. 926). My debt to these insights will become more obvious in the following discussion.

2. Quotations from Chaucer are from *The Works of Geoffrey Chaucer*, ed. F. N. Robinson, 2d ed. (Boston, 1957).

3. Cf. also 1021–30, 1080–86, 1101–3. The Franklin's treatment of Aurelius is wittily embodied in this comparison: the plight of Narcissus suits him better, and in more ways, than does that of Echo.

4. On reviewing these remarks, it seems to me that they stand in need of some qualification, and that indeed they may appear either inconsistent or inaccurate in the light of my subsequent discussion. There *are* interruptions and descriptions reflecting the narrator's interests, and one *may* feel that the complaints of Aurelius and Dorigen are disproportionately long. The digressions, however, occur during the central portion of the tale and belong to a controlled pattern or structure which enriches the meaning of the tale. The lyric declamation is dramatically motivated and also, as we shall see, contributes to the Franklin's main theme. I have decided to let the remarks stand because this comparison between Franklin and Squire seems essentially correct, especially as just qualified.

5. *Chaucer's Poetry*, p. 941.

6. Chaucer's spelling of the hero's name seems to depart from the form—Arviragus—used by the previous authors (see F. N. Robinson's note, p. 723). His change allows *vera-, trouthe*, to appear in the name and, as in the case of golden Aurelius, enforces his typicality.

7. Donaldson's comment on this is interesting but it misses the tone of the passage by treating the promise as too solemn a matter: "while she is making it clear to Aurelius that he is not living up to her ideas of how men should behave, she apparently makes an analogy between his bad behavior and nature's in allowing the ugly rocks to remain where they are. She then combines her two irritations by promising to love Aurelius on the rather cruel condition that he remove the rocks. In substance, she promises to be untrue to her own nature if Aurelius manages to rearrange creation" (*Chaucer's Poetry*, p. 925).

8. Aurelius's speech is as a whole an amusing performance, full of directions to the gods reminding them pedantically of their functions, e.g.:

> Youre blisful suster, Lucina the sheene,
> That of the see is chief goddesse and queene
> (Though Neptunus have deitee in the see,
> Yet emperisse aboven hym is she).
>
> (1045–48)

9. E.g., 1132–34, 1264–66, 1270–72, 1291–93.

10. During the fourteenth century, Orleans was a great center for both classical and legal studies; it has less relevance to ancient Bretons than to the Franklin who, in his own modest way, seems to have had some experience and connections in both the law and letters.

11. One wonders whether the question is apprehensive, or perhaps ironic.
12. "Notes on Chaucer," *MLN* 32 (1917): 377.

Further Reading

Like Marshall Leicester's essay on the Wife of Bath's Tale, Harry Berger's essay is a fine example of New Critical close reading, attentive to tone and underwritten by a generous humanism. For a different interpretation with similar presuppositions, see Mary J. Carruthers, "The Gentilesse of Chaucer's Franklin," *Criticism* 23 (1981): 283–300. Other critics have been less positive about the Franklin, although the tale remains a favorite. The Franklin has been seen as an epicurean sensualist who is confused about marriage, as a social climber, and as unfairly harsh to Dorigen while being excessively forgiving of Arveragus. See, for example, Robert P. Miller, "The Epicurean Homily on Marriage by Chaucer's Franklin," *Mediaevalia* 6 (1980): 151–86; Nigel Saul, "The Social Status of Chaucer's Franklin: A Reconsideration," *Medium AEvum* 52 (1983): 10–26; Stephen Knight, "Ideology in the Franklin's Tale," *Parergon* 28 (1980): 3–31; and Felicity Riddy, "Engendering Pity in the Franklin's Tale," in *Feminist Readings in Middle English Literature: The Wife of Bath and All Her Sect*, edited by Ruth Evans and Lesley Johnson (London, 1994), pp. 54–71. In "Why Chaucer Calls the Franklin's Tale a Breton Lai," *Philological Quarterly* 51 (1972): 365–79, Kathryn Hume provides an illuminating answer. Richard Firth Green, *A Crisis of Truth: Literature and Law in Ricardian England* (Philadelphia, 1999), pp. 1–40, provides an expert commentary on the key word "trouthe" (see also his discussion on pp. 329–33). Paul Strohm, *Social Chaucer* (Cambridge, 1989), pp. 84–109, discusses oaths in Chaucer's England.

The Pardoner's Dilemma

LEE PATTERSON

◆　◆　◆

For because [the sinner] believes himself to be assailed by attacks
from every side, despairing of salvation, he always grows in
wickedness. . . . He scorns his return, despairs of grace, glories
in sin; yet nonetheless, as a witness of his wickedness, he has fear
within. And although it seems on the outside as if he commits
evil deeds boldly, yet nonetheless within himself he trembles
because of them.

FEW OF THE PERFORMANCES in *The Canterbury Tales* have generated as
much critical controversy as the Pardoner's Prologue and Tale. The disagreement is fundamental: is his performance motivated by an uncertain
sexuality or by an apparent scorn for religion? Is Chaucer representing a psychology shaped by what his time would have considered sexual deviancy? Or
is he exploring the condition of a man who ostentatiously scorns, yet secretly desires, the salvation offered by medieval Christianity? In this essay I
shall argue that the Pardoner is best understood as a man struggling with a
religious dilemma that was well understood—and deeply feared—in his
own time.

The rationale for reading the Pardoner in sexual terms derives from a line
in the General Prologue, where the narrator speculates—"I trowe"—that
the Pardoner is "a geldyng or a mare" (691). This implies that the Pardoner is a
castrate or a homosexual. For modern readers, for whom sexual identity is a
crucial determinant of selfhood, this line immediately places sex at the center
of the picture. Two other aspects of the tale encourage them to keep it there.
One is the Old Man whom the three rioters of the tale meet in their quest to
kill death, a figure who describes himself in eerily Oedipal terms.

Ne Deeth, allas, ne wol nat han my lyf.
Thus walke I, lyk a restelees kaityf,
And on the ground, which is my moodres gate,
I knokke with my staf, bothe erly and late,
And seye "Leeve mooder, leet me in!"

(727–31)

Equally tempting are the false relics that the Pardoner carries "biforn hym in his lappe" (686). After he has finished his tale he turns to the Host and asks him to make an offering and kiss these relics. The Host responds with an outburst famous for its scatological violence:

I wolde I hadde thy coillons in myn hond
In stide of relikes or of seintuarie.
Lat kutte hem of, I wol thee helpe hem carie;
They shul be shryned in an hogges toord!

(952–55)

Thus the Oedipal dream of a return to the mother (as expressed by the Old Man) is here punished by the paternal threat of castration—a psychoanalytic scheme as neat as any modern reader could want. Not surprisingly, recent criticism has focused almost exclusively on the Pardoner's sexuality.

But if we explore the presence in Chaucer's own time of the themes of castration and homosexuality the results are surprising. A careful search reveals that in late medieval England, castration was virtually unknown and that homosexuality was of far less cultural import than a modern reader might expect.[1] Unlike continental practice, in England *no* civic statutes outlawing sodomy—the term used for all forms of what the Middle Ages thought were "unnatural" sex acts, but designating especially sexual acts between men—were enacted, and the records of the church courts (where sodomy cases would therefore have been tried) show a remarkable record of disregard. Richard Wunderli has examined 21,000 cases brought before the London church courts between 1470 and 1516; of these 21,000 cases, only one concerned sodomy, and the defendant was excommunicated for non-appearance.[2] In his examination of the records of the church courts for Herefordshire and Worcestershire, David Klausner did not find a single case of prosecution for sodomy.[3] It is hard to avoid the conclusion that sodomy, as either social practice or ideological construct, was not a major presence in Chaucer's cultural world.[4] So far as I know, there is no recognizable representation of sodomy or what we might call the "sodomitical personality" in the literature of the time—with the possible exception, of course, of the Pardoner.[5] Whatever sexual acts may have been performed, whatever habits may have been formed, or whatever subcultures may have existed, sodomy seems not to have entered into the cultural discourse of late medieval England so as to leave a mark on the legal record.

The upshot of these facts is that the Pardoner's actual (by which of course we mean fictional) sexuality was, for Chaucer and his audience, likely to have been of far less interest than it is to readers today. If neither castration nor sodomy seem to have mattered much as historical facts or conceptual beliefs in fourteenth-century England, perhaps we should concentrate instead on what they might have meant symbolically. The medieval justification for proscribing sodomy is that it is nonproductive. The central fact about the Pardoner, for Chaucer, is neither that he is physically maimed nor that his sexual habits make him a social outcast but that he is to be understood as sterile not in a physical but in a *spiritual* sense.

This claim is supported by the fact that, in Chaucer's immediate environment, there was a powerful, subtle, and widespread discourse of spiritual or religious sterility that fits the Pardoner with surprising aptness. This discourse, sometimes labeled Wycliffite or Lollard, might better be called, more simply and broadly, "reformist." As historians of late medieval English religion recognize, the reformist impulses of the period expressed themselves in a wide range of ways, many of them entirely orthodox.[6] Some aspects of this reformist impulse were shared by both Langland and Chaucer, although doubtless neither would have described himself as Wycliffite or Lollard. Indeed, Chaucer makes it clear in the Man of Law's Epilogue, where his idealized Parson is accused of being a Lollard, that the term can be used simply as a slur to stigmatize an earnest sincerity in religious matters. The extent to which Chaucer personally shared this sincerity is unclear, but that it interested him as a topic for poetry—as did most things in his world—is undeniable.

In Chaucer's account of the Pardoner, the crucial issue from a reformist perspective is the contemporary debate about the nature of clerical service. This debate focused on two related issues, simony and preaching. For the reformists, simony meant not simply the buying of church offices but the selling of any spiritual good for a material reward. In other words—and this is central both to late medieval English piety in general and to the Pardoner in particular—simony was a materialism that took the literal for the spiritual, the sign for the signified. As one reformist text put it, "to take or give a temporal thing for a spiritual thing . . . is simony."[7] The grossest form of simony was exactly what the Pardoner does: the selling of indulgences.[8] Merchandising indulgences is simoniacal for two reasons. First, it sells the spiritual benefit of pardon for money: "to take money for [pardons] is to sell God's grace and so simony, and then both parties are cursed of God and man";[9] as another text says, with special relevance to the Pardoner, it is simony to sell "a full indulgence 'a poena & a culpa.' "[10] Second, since indulgences are merely outward signs, they are spiritually ineffective: the only form of pardon worth having is God's, which can be received only through grace and, especially, contrition. The reformist contempt for what is called "feigned indulgences or pardons"[11] is scathing and relentless:

> lustful men tell . . . how their greedy confessors absolve them, as they say, of sin by a little lead not weighing a pound, hung with an hempen thread on a little piece of calfskin, painted with a few black marks of ink.[12]

To believe that a piece of paper can bring forgiveness is an empty formalism equivalent to that of the Pharisees who wore phylacteries on their heads: woe to those who "for a bull purchased of a false pardoner, through a false assertion and simony of silver, and they pay him then a penny and lay it on their heads, [think that] they are absolved of all their sins."[13]

Moreover, the fourteenth-century reformists reinvoked, with special intensity, a traditional understanding that simony could be metaphorically expressed as sodomy.[14] The logic of this interpretation is given by one of the reformists' heroes, Richard FitzRalph, archbishop of Armagh, who argued that to substitute the material for the spiritual is a crime against the "law of Nature."[15] Given this interpretation, reformists understood Christ's words in Matthew 10.15 as referring to simoniacs: "Amen I say to you, it shall be more tolerable for the land of Sodom and Gomorrah in the day of judgment, than for [simoniacs]." Over and over again, this passage was applied to simoniacs, as in the following discussion:

> For like Judas they sell truth, for Christ is truth, for money or love of worldly things. And since they sell truth—that is, a spiritual good—for money or worldly things they are cursed simoniacs and heretics. . . . At Judgment Day there shall be less pain for Sodom and Gomorrah, that were destroyed because of sin, than to those men that will not receive Christ's disciples and his gospel, nor live after the teaching of Christ's gospel.[16]

Noting as we go that Judas is here the first simoniac, we can see that sodomy exists in reformist literature far less as a sexual sin than as a sin against the church. In the *Lanterne of Light*, in a long list of those who dwell with the devil, the author first lists sexual sinners—"lechers, fornicators, adulterers, men who commit incest—that is, those who befoul their own kin—and all unclean men and women that are in orders or are professed"—and then those who commit sins against the church: "There are hypocrites, sodomites, sacrilegers, and sellers of sacraments."[17] Here sodomites are included not among the carnally licentious but the spiritually corrupting.

We can now infer that the Pardoner may be thought to be a mare—a sodomite—because he is a simoniac. But why a gelding? While the selling of indulgences was the most prevalent form of simony in Chaucerian England, it was not considered the worst. Reformist literature of the period repeats with relentless insistence that a cleric's most important duty is preaching: "the highest service that men have on earth is to preach God's word."[18] For the reformists, false preaching is the worst form of simony. Moreover, false preaching is defined in terms that are relevant precisely to the Pardoner. Preaching can be corrupt in two related ways. The first is when it is used in order to extract money from the audience. The other is when it strays from the strict exposition of the scriptural, and especially the Gospel, text, into what reformists call "chronicles and poems and gossip," "japes and tattle," "controversies [and] rhymes," or—most relevant to the Pardoner—"fables [that] distract people."[19] Indeed, preachers who lard their sermons with "chronicles, with poems, and [with] dreams and many other useless tales . . . wander into many fleshly lusts": homiletic errancy entails sexual vagrancy.[20] And this use of fables is seen as a way of preparing the audience for donations: false preachers "sow fables, chronicles, and lies in order to rob the poor people afterward," and they "preach fables and flattery & lies . . . to deceive the people of faith and a good life and rob them of their worldly goods."[21]

The same objection to a style of preaching trivialized by the use of exempla and *fabula* is made by Chaucer's Parson, who cautions the Host that "Thou getest fable noon ytoold for me" (X.31). This Parson is described in the General Prologue in terms that invoke many of the central reformist values for the clergy—including the fact that he would "Cristes gospel trewely . . . preche" and that "His parisshens devoutly wolde he teche" (481–82)—and who, in the Man of Law's Epilogue, is accused by the Host of being a Lollard for objecting to blasphemy.[22] Like all reformist sermons, the Parson's sermonlike tale is in fact almost completely devoid of exempla. But the Pardoner's sermon not only itself largely consists of an exemplum but is interspersed with brief exemplary narratives of Lot, Herod, Attila, "Stilboun," and Demetrius. As he says:

> Thanne telle I hem ensamples many oon
> Of olde stories longe tyme agoon.
> For lewed peple loven tales olde;
> Swiche thynges kan they wel reporte and holde.
> (435–38)[23]

And all of his sermon rhetoric is designed to extract money from his audience, as he boasts: "For myn entente is nat but for to wynne" (403). He is evidently one of those who, as the reformists charged, have "committed adultery with the law of God, and *turn it away from its nature*, to please the people. And so with begging, and pride in their speaking, they sell God's word, as one who would sell an ox."[24]

Similar definitions of the "spiritual lechery"[25] of false preaching as an "unkynde" offense against nature, a spiritual sodomy worse than bodily sodomy, appear throughout reformist texts. Preaching *ought* to be a way of begetting God's children with the seed of his word:

> Since God's word, by which men should spiritually engender God's sons, is
> better than the physical seed by which the body of man is engendered, and
> these prelates misuse this better seed, then they commit a greater sin than
> did the sodomites that wasted their physical seed; for always the better that
> a thing is, the worse and the more abominable is its misuse. . . . Such
> prelates that preach Christ's gospel in this way are more abominable and
> more enemies of God and his people than were the cursed men of Sodom
> and Gomorrah.[26]

Preachers should, the reformists say, "make children in God, and that is God's work, who has wedded the Church."[27] Where are these children to be begotten? Jesus Christ is our father and his spouse is "our mother holy Church"— a traditional formulation[28]—who "bears in her womb souls to be born into bliss but never without the help and the grace of our Lord Jesus Christ,"[29] grace that is made possible through the spiritual seed of preaching. The sowing of this seed, in another text, takes place "in the field of this Church," the church that is the mother of all Christians.[30] These metaphors are surely relevant to the central scene of the Pardoner's Tale, where the Old Man knocks on his mother's gate with his staff and asks for entrance. But we have already found enough here to explain the relevance of the narrator's speculation on the gelding/mare possibility. As a simoniac who both sells spiritual goods and fails to sow God's seed in the field of holy mother church, the Pardoner would have been seen by a contemporary audience as impotent twice over.

But fourteenth-century reformist literature is not exclusively committed to sexual images of religious infertility. There are several other relevant topics found in this reformist literature. Both traditional and reformist texts use the parable of the withered fig tree to describe the false preacher. The fig tree cursed by Christ (Matthew 21:18–22, Luke 13:6–9, Mark 11:12–14) is typically understood throughout the Middle Ages as figuring the false preacher who displays abundant words but is empty of works.[31] Preachers who feed their audience with fables are

> trees without fruit, twice dead, and the roots are torn up. . . . and they
> should bear spiritual fruit as do other trees at harvest time, but they are
> without fruit, as was the fig tree that Christ cursed, for neither in preach-
> ing nor in a good life do they profit people's souls. And thus they are twice
> dead, dead in body and in soul, dead in this world and in the next, dead in
> their own person and dead in helping other men.[32]

Note the double death of damnation: dead in the body and dead in the soul. False preachers are also represented as Judases who are, as one text puts it, "dead in themselves" as well as "slayers of men's souls [and] more abominable to God . . . *than the cursed sin of Sodom,* that for hideous sin sank into hell."[33] The connection between the simoniac and Judas, already noted above, is intimate: one reformist text says that priests who commit simony are not just like Judas—"they say with Judas, 'What will you give me if I give him to you?' "—but are actually worse than Judas. He sold Christ bodily, but in exchanging spiritual benefits—prayers, sermons, or pardons—for material goods, they are selling Christ spiritually.[34] This knotting of simony, sodomy, and the figure of Judas is important for the Pardoner for, as we shall see, Judas provided Chaucer with a crucial model for the central symbolic event of his tale, the Old Man's knocking with his staff asking for reentrance to his mother.

The general reformist concern with churchmen defrauding the poor[35] is often associated specifically with the depredations of pardoners—and even more specifically with pardoners who carry false relics:

> There comes a pardoner with stolen bulls and false relics, granting more
> years of pardon than will come before Judgment Day in exchange for
> worldly goods. . . . and this pardoner claims more power than ever Christ
> granted to Peter or Paul or any apostle, in order to draw alms from poor,
> bedridden neighbors that are known to be feeble and poor, and to get it for
> himself and to waste it sinfully in idleness and gluttony and lechery.[36]

Needless to say, relics, whether false or true, were themselves a target of reformist literature—although they were less often attacked in the vernacular texts (as opposed to Wyclif's Latin writings) than other observances that were seen as idolatry pure and simple.[37]

This brings me to the final and most important aspect of late medieval English religion that can help us to understand the Pardoner in terms current in

Chaucer's world: its insistence on the priority of the inner to the outer, of the meaning to the form, of the spirit to the letter, in every aspect of religious life. This concern lies behind and supports the entire reformist enterprise. It is expressed in the most explicit way in the persistent interpretation of various late medieval religious practices—pilgrimage, image worship, indulgences, auricular confession, alms giving—as idolatry. In his treatise on the Ten Commandments Wyclif argued that the Second Commandment—forbidding the making and worship of idols—is the most important because it forbids all sins and prescribes all theological and moral virtues.[38] To worship something other than God as if it were God, whether it be money, food, or an image, is idolatry. As a vernacular text says: "The worship of cursed idols is the beginning, cause and end of all evil; . . . for as many idols as a man has, so has he deadly sins."[39] Idolatry is to take the letter for the spirit, the sign for the signified. In a language almost as old as Christianity itself, idolatry is a kind of fornication; idolaters "take to signs as to common whores."[40] One reformist text, listing the sins caused by idolatry, claims that it causes "especially the foul and horrible sin of Sodom, of both men and women."[41] The logic of this claim is, once again, that to take the sign as a signified rather than a signifier is to turn it from its natural purpose: like sodomy, it is a spiritually fruitless sin against nature.[42] This is, at heart, the source of the objection to indulgences. Remission of sins is accomplished not by "bulls of pardon" but "true contrition": it is only when "a sinner has inward sorrow for his sins [that] he shall be saved."[43]

In sum, then, we can see that Chaucer's Pardoner embodies a whole range of issues that are both central to the reformist piety of Chaucer's time and logically interdependent. He is a simoniac who sells spiritual goods; a false preacher who performs only for money and who relies on exempla rather than biblical exegesis; an exploiter of the poor, including widows; a man who offers pardon *a poena et a culpa* while ignoring the need for contrition. In short, he is a spiritual sodomite sunk in the gross commercialism and materialism that perverts religious truth. Does this mean that sodomy and castration as at least potentially *literal* characteristics of the Pardoner are irrelevant? On the contrary, in granting them an insinuated albeit uncertain existence Chaucer forces the reader to confront the problem upon which the Prologue and Tale turn—the relation of the material to the spiritual. Are we to read the Pardoner as a body or a soul, materially or spiritually, as a person or a symbol? In other words, Chaucer aligns the *process* of interpretation with the *content* of that which is to be interpreted. We do not simply observe the Pardoner but experience in our efforts at understanding him the central dilemma of his existence.

In the Pardoner, then, Chaucer is offering us not merely a more than usually sophisticated instance of religious satire that draws upon the most highly charged terms of religious discussion current at the time—an established symbolic terminology. His real brilliance is in *psychologizing* these religious issues. The Pardoner is not merely a poster child for religious abuses but a deliberate and self-conscious one, whose relation to that which he scorns is highly ambiguous. The Pardoner serves to demonstrate the truth of reformist claims about empty formalism not merely by displaying them but by *internalizing* them, not merely by revealing the death of the soul that is brought about by literalism but by *experiencing* it. Moreover, he is himself aware of his own dilemma, so that he becomes both an instance and a *victim* of institutional decadence: he is a religious personality who recognizes the inefficacy of the religious practices he promotes without being able to believe that those that *are* effective are available to him. He is therefore not merely in danger of damnation but knows of his danger, indeed focuses upon it with obsessive anxiety. The Pardoner exemplifies and internalizes reformist piety: he is at once within and outside the church, demonstrating at once the need for reform and the relentlessness of its demands. As always, Chaucer explores the social realities of his world from within the perspective of the individual consciousness.

The ostensible purpose of the Pardoner's Prologue is to demonstrate that he knows himself to be "a ful vicious man" (459) motivated by an entirely "yvel entencioun" (408). Tyrannizing the priest and his parishioners, and willfully undermining the penitential system of which he is an agent, the Pardoner appropriates and debases even the scriptural image of the dove by which medieval preaching was typically legitimized:

> Thanne peyne I me to strecche forth the nekke,
> And est and west upon the peple I bekke,
> As dooth a dowve sittynge on a berne.
>
> (395–97)

And throughout he insists upon the almost allegorical simplicity of his own motives—"I preche of no thyng but for coveityse" (424)—and glories in his own hypocrisy: "Thus kan I preche agayn that same vice / Which that I use, and that is avarice" (427–28). Delightedly wringing the last penny from a widow with starving children, he consigns the souls of his audience to an infernal black-berrying. Always the rhetorician, he at once offends the censorious *gentils* and titillates the raucous lower elements (represented by Harry Bailly) by playing to the full the role of the deliberate sinner, the man who has chosen with open eyes the path to his own damnation. Simultaneously entertaining and horrifying his audience, he adopts excess as a strategy by which he can at once reveal and conceal himself.

But in reality his hyperbole betrays the more complicated self it seeks to hide. Insisting early and often that his motives are brazenly simple (403–4, 423–24, 432–33, 461), he also claims—and repeats the claim—that he is doing good works:

> But though myself by gilty in that synne,
> Yet kan I maken oother folk to twynne
> From avarice, and soore to repente.
>
> (429–31)

> For though myself be a ful vicious man,
> A moral tale yet I yow telle kan.
>
> (459–60)

What makes these claims persuasive is his own response to them, for in both cases he hastily withdraws from disturbing complications to the comforting simplicity of an unqualified avariciousness. "But that is nat my principal entente," he insists, "I preche nothyng but for coveitise" (432–33), and he continues to claim that his moral tale serves only as a device "for to wynne" (461). And in both these cases, when his own complexity might become visible to himself and to his audience, he cuts off his line of thought with a misdirected and defensive conclusion: "Of this mateere it oghte ynogh suffice" (434), "Now hoold youre pees!"—although only he has been speaking—"my tale I wol bigynne" (462). These fugitive and embarrassed self-defenses show the Pardoner acknowledging in his spirit values he subverts in his working, a complication that occurs again in the famous benediction with which he closes his Tale:

> And lo, sires, thus I preche.
> And Jhesu Crist, that is oure soules leche,
> So graunte yow his pardoun to receyve,
> For that is best, I wol yow nat deceyve.
>
> (915–18)

In sum, he is by no means as unambiguously impenitent as he claims, and his attempt to reduce himself to the simplicity of allegorical evil itself witnesses to the painfully divided consciousness from which he seeks to escape. By turns derisory and hesitant, vaunting and awkwardly candid, the Prologue reveals in its very lack of clarity a spirit in conflict.

If the Prologue presents a theatrical self-representation that reveals as it conceals a man who yearns for a redemption he simultaneously disdains, this same ambivalence controls the Tale. The Pardoner wants his audience to take his Tale literally, as a simple exemplum that means *radix malorum est cupiditas*. But when read spiritually, the Tale is a moral allegory about the Pardoner himself, and it figures not avarice but despair. On the one hand, the rioters enact the Pardoner's life of self-damnation. Brazenly impenitent—"And ech of hem at otheres synne lough" (476)—they enact a perverse imitation of the ultimate pardoner, Christ. "Deeth shal be deed, if that they may hem hente!" (710) is their claim; and as R. A. Shoaf has pointed out, "The cry of the prophet [Hosea], 'o death, I will be thy death,' exegesis consistently understands as the triumphant claim of Christ the Redeemer."[44] They engage in the imitation of God symbolically as well: together a parodic Trinity—"we thre been al ones" (696)—they enact as well a dark Eucharistic ritual as "the yongeste of hem alle" (804) serves bread and poisoned wine. And when, like the Pardoner, they issue from their tavern to misperform their divine mission, they receive their just desserts with terrifying efficiency. In the guise of a story of three rioters, the Tale presents us with the facts of the Pardoner's case and the future that (he fears) awaits him.

The penitential meaning of the Pardoner's history, with its tortuous inner complexities, is most powerfully expressed in the figure of the Old Man. Rather than the saintly wise man of the analogues, a philosopher, or hermit, or even Christ, the Pardoner presents a figure who accurately reflects his own contradictions. Like the Pardoner, the Old Man proffers advice both needful—"Agayns an oold man, hoor upon his heed, / Ye sholde arise" (743–44)—and perilous: "turne up this croked wey" (761). Also like the Pardoner, he knows the truth but is himself unable to use it. In the terms of the story, the Old Man knows where Death is to be found but cannot find it himself, while he has won through to a gentle wisdom that has done little to relieve his own suffering. Hence, like the Pardoner at the end of his Tale, he too offers a closing benediction—"God save yow, that boghte agayn mankynde, / And yow amende!" (766–67)—that is in the event self-excluding. For the Old Man's fate is to remain ever unregenerate, whether this be expressed in the scriptural terms of exchanging age for youth or in the penitential terms of exchanging the "cheste" of his worldly goods for the "heyre clowt" of penance.[45] Like the *quaestor*—the Latin term for a pardoner—whom he faithfully expresses, the Old Man is condemned to a life-in-death of Cain-like wandering, and in his fruitless penitential yearnings he has descended into the hell of despair. Living death, wandering, and sterility: these are the characteristics of despair—the fatal belief that one's sins are so great that they cannot be forgiven—and they are characteristics shared by the Old Man and by his creator and *alter ego*, the Pardoner.

Despair is the condition of yearning for salvation but remaining impenitent because one believes that one's sinfulness cannot be forgiven, of wanting to confess but being unable to confess. The essence of despair as a religious idea is most fully expressed in the Old Man's account of how he knocks on mother earth for an entrance that is denied him. Chaucer's source for this scene derives from a very specific symbolic discourse of medieval religious culture. In the Middle Ages, the classical figure of Oedipus became linked with the theological condition of despair, the agency of this linkage being the biblical figure of Judas. According to medieval exegetes, while Cain was the Old Testament type of despair, it was his New Testament fulfillment Judas who expressed in the most painful and uncompromising form the fatal economy of this spiritual suicide. As religious writers endlessly repeated, Judas sinned more in hanging himself—that is, in choosing an impenitent self-destruction—than he did in selling Christ. In order both to explain such impenitence and yet to reaffirm the power of divine mercy, the Middle Ages provided Judas with a legendary history derived from the narrative of the Theban Oedipus but now rewritten in penitential terms. According to this legend, Judas was exposed as an infant by his parents in an effort to evade a prophecy that he would bring ruin to them and to his race. He became, however, the adoptive son of a foreign king and queen. But in an envious rage he killed their natural son, a Cain-like act of fratricide for which he was driven out. Becoming then the trusted servant of Pontius Pilate (or, in some versions, Herod), he stole some apples from an orchard, and in the course of this Adamic violation he killed the orchard's owner, who was (unbeknownst to him) his father. When he then married the man's widow he completed the fatal Oedipal curse.

When Judas and his mother learned of their relationship, they sought forgiveness from the new teacher, Jesus Christ. This request is meant to demonstrate God's capacity for forgiveness and renewal: Judas displayed, in the words of one text, "the condition, grief and tears of true penitence," and Jesus promised to save him from despair if he would "worthily repent." But the lure of his evil origin was too great, and with his betrayal of Christ and final despairing suicide a story that was designed to argue for the power of penitential conversion came finally to illustrate a darker lesson about the compulsions of wickedness. As Oedipus was called back to his mother, so is Judas called back to his original nature; and the paternal injunction of penance— "you can be saved if you will worthily repent"—is rejected by him both now and forever. Despair is the inability to change: the man in despair cannot get rid of the self of illicit desires in order to assume the reborn self of innocence, no more than the Pardoner's Old Man can find a young man who will exchange his youth for the Old Man's age, no more than the Old Man can exchange his own chest of worldly goods for the hair cloth of penance.

It is as a figure of despair driven by incestuous yearnings that the Old Man of the Pardoner's Tale invokes the figure of Judas. And he also invokes him, and his Old Testament prefiguration, Cain, in his condition of endless wandering. Cain must wander because the earth, having been polluted with his brother's blood, now refuses to receive him. As Augustine says, "He indeed sought for death, but no one would give to him what he had himself given to his brother."[46] As for Judas, in hanging himself he reinvokes Cain's exclusion: according to the exegetes, he died suspended between earth and heaven because neither men nor angels would accept him. Hence, apparently, the Old Man's hopeless knocking on the earth with his staff—

> And on the ground, which is my moodres gate,
> I knokke with my staf, bothe erly and late,
> And seye "Leeve mooder, leet me in!"

—a gesture that is at once violent and pathetic.

Also important here is a strikingly apt biblical text whose relevance to this scene has never been explored.[47]

And there was a man of the Pharisees, named Nicodemus, a ruler of the Jews. This man came to Jesus by night and said to him: Rabbi, we know that thou art come a teacher from God; for no man can do these signs which thou dost, unless God be with him. Jesus answered and said to him: Amen, amen, I say to thee, unless a man be born again, he cannot see the kingdom of God. Nicodemus saith to him: How can a man be born when he is old? Can he enter a second time into his mother's womb and be born again? Jesus answered: Amen, amen, I say to thee, unless a man be born again of water and the Holy Ghost, he cannot enter into the kingdom of God. That which is born of the flesh is flesh: and that which is born of the Spirit is spirit. Wonder not that I said to thee: You must be born again. The Spirit breatheth where he will and thou hearest his voice: but thou knowest not whence he cometh and whither he goeth. So is every one that is born of the Spirit. Nicodemus answered and said to him: How can these things be done? Jesus answered and said to him: Art thou a master in Israel, and knowest not these things? Amen, amen, I say to thee that we speak what we know and we testify what we have seen: and you receive not our testimony. If I have spoken to you earthly things, and you believe not: how will you believe, if I shall speak to you heavenly things? (John 3:1–12)

For exegetes Nicodemus was an instance of the heretic or schismatic who longed to join the Christian community but remained hesitant: hence the secret nighttime visit. Although he was, as Augustine said, divided in his thought, his literal understanding was struggling toward the spiritual, his oldness yearning to put on youth.[48] That Nicodemus is later, in John 19:39, described as bringing myrrh and aloes to anoint Christ's body is taken to indicate that indeed rebirth is possible, that there are no lost souls. Could any text better illustrate the Pardoner's spiritual condition?[49]

Finally, the relics. It is certainly the case that the Pardoner associates his relics with his sexuality: he carries them in a "male," or purse, in his lap, and he offers them to the Host in a way that is clearly (and self-consciously) sexually challenging: come kiss my relics. It is also the case that the Host's riposte invokes a connection between testicles ("coillons" [952]) and relics. This passage derives its inspiration from a discussion in the *Roman de la Rose* where Reason and the Lover are debating whether the relation of sign to signified is natural or merely conventional: Reason says it is conventional (and therefore unstable) and uses as her example the fact that one could call those objects that are venerated in churches *coilles* rather than *reliques*.[50] Clearly an association between relics and the male sexual organs is present here.

To understand this association, we need to consider how relics were regarded in late medieval England. As scholars of medieval religion have pointed out, relics provided a living and immediate relationship between the believer and the holy. In the relic, the holy was *materially* present. The relic was, as Margaret Aston has put it, "a special sort of bridge between the visible and the invisible."[51] It was in part because of this connection that the bread of the sacrament began to take on the quality of a relic.[52] An unshakable faith that the material was imbued with the spiritual inspired Hugh of Lincoln when he bit off one of the fingers of the corpse of Mary Magdalene, explaining to the dismayed onlookers that this was not unusual since he ate the Host whenever he partook of the Eucharist.[53] So too, the efficacy of a relic could be tested by placing upon the reliquary a cloth and then weighing it afterward to measure the physical amount of spiritual power it had absorbed.[54] The point of the relic was not that it was a sign of holiness but that it was *itself* holy: it erased the line between the material and the spiritual. Moreover—and this is the most important point, explained by Caroline Bynum—relics erased the line between material and spiritual in the most definitive way possible: their very existence confirmed the promise of the resurrection of the body.[55] This is one of the meanings of the so-called likeness reliquaries that emerged in the later Middle Ages: the jewel-encrusted golden container that modeled the arm or hand or finger it contained was itself a prefiguration of the resurrected body that all the saved would receive in heaven.[56]

This powerful doctrine is deliberately mocked by the Pardoner with his fake relics. For him, the line between the material and the spiritual can only be crossed parodically. In carrying his fake relics next to his genitals, he associates them with that which most fully represents corporeality—as Leo Steinberg has reminded us with his discussion of the representation of the genitals of the infant Jesus.[57] Finally, when the Host jokes that he will cut off the Pardoner's testicles and enshrine them in a hog's turd (a gross parody of a likeness relic), his statement has at least three possible but incompatible meanings. One is that he is threatening to castrate the already effeminate Pardoner. A second is that he is threatening to turn the Pardoner into a *eunuchus Dei*, a castrate for Christ, and thus to prepare him for the sanctity that would then make his body parts appropriate objects for veneration. And third, the Host conspires with the Pardoner in mocking not merely the capacity of relics to bear spiritual power but the resurrection of the body itself: the Pardoner's body will be partitioned and fragmented, not with the promise of wholeness and transformation but rather with the threat of corruption and decay. This last meaning is most likely, given the Host's acknowledgment of mutual gamesmanship: "I wol no lenger *pleye* / With thee, ne with noon oother angry man" (958–59). What the Host cannot understand, however, is that the Pardoner's mockery of the resurrection of the body is not merely cynical sport. Rather it expresses his frustration and pain at being unable to believe in what would save him. "Unhappy man that I am, who shall deliver me from the body of this death?" (Rom: 7:24)[58] Paul answered his own question with the statement about the resurrection of the body that underwrites the Pardoner's performance, as the Pauline metaphor of sowing and the central theme of the overcoming of death suggest:

> But some man will say: How do the dead rise again? and with what manner of body shall they come? Senseless man, that which thou sowest is not quickened, except it die first. . . . So also is the resurrection of the dead. It is sown in corruption; it shall rise in incorruption. It is sown in dishonor; it shall rise in glory. It is sown in weakness; it shall rise in power. It is sown a natural body; it shall rise a spiritual body. . . . Behold, I tell you a mystery. We shall all indeed rise again. . . . In a moment, in the twinkling of an eye, at the last trumpet; for the trumpet shall sound and the dead shall rise again incorruptible; and we shall be changed. For this corruptible must put on incorruption; and this mortal must put on immortality. . . .

O death, where is thy victory? O death, where is thy sting? (1 Cor: 15:35–55)

The Host's joke mocks this great speech of consolation and confirms the Pardoner's worst fear—not the fear of exposure as a eunuch, nor of punishment as a sodomite, but rather the fear of the double death of the body and the soul. That this fear is expressed in terms of the Pardoner's body, his false relics, and the hog's turd is, we can now understand, all too appropriate. For it is the Pardoner's literalism, his *spiritual* corporeality, that makes it impossible for him to read the spirit in the letter, to recognize his corruptible body as a mere prefiguration of that which is incorruptible and eternal. What motivates the Pardoner most powerfully is the one thing that all human beings have in common—not sexuality, but something equally basic and finally more important: mortality. In him, Chaucer demonstrates the medieval belief that the spirit is inescapable, that salvation is always available.

Notes

The epigraph is from Gregory the Great, *Moralia in Iob*, 12.40 (*PL* 75:1007).

1. Detailed evidence for this claim is presented in the original version of this essay, Lee Patterson, "Chaucer's Pardoner on the Couch: Psyche and Clio in Medieval Literary Studies," *Speculum* 76 (2001): 638–80.
2. Richard M. Wunderli, *London Church Courts and Society on the Eve of the Reformation* (Cambridge, 1981), pp. 83–84.
3. David N. Klausner, ed., *Records of Early English Drama: Herefordshire, Worcestershire* (Toronto, 1990). The absence of cases of sodomy was communicated to me personally by Professor Klausner.
4. Wunderli, *London Church Courts*, also notes that "we can never know for sure from the silence of the records. Perhaps such acts were considered serious enough to be handled in a higher church court or by the bishop personally" (p. 84). Wunderli concludes, however, that "a lack of defamations for sodomy does, I believe, argue for a probable low incidence of sodomy" (p. 84).
5. The other exception is *Cleanness*, which survives in a single manuscript and is often thought to be, as in Allen J. Frantzen's reading, addressed to the clergy: "The Disclosure of Sodomy in *Cleanness*," *PMLA* 111 (1996): 451–64. On the other hand, Elizabeth Keiser argues in *Courtly Desire and Medieval Homophobia: The Legitimation of Sexual Pleasure in* Cleanness *and Its Contexts* (New Haven, Conn., 1997), that the poem was written for an elite gentry audience, for whom the attack on sodomy was understandable

within the context of a culture that valued heterosexual pleasure highly and in which "the realm of sensuality and its erotic refinements—still marked as feminine—are explicitly legitimated as essential components in the male's self-realization through love" (p. 139). Much the same argument can be made, I believe, about Alain de Lille's *De planctu naturae*, where heterosexual generation is also celebrated as a response to the Catharist heresy that Alain attacks in his *De fide Catholica*. See Roger French and Andrew Cunningham, *Before Science: The Invention of the Friars' Natural Philosophy* (Aldershot, England, 1996), pp. 104–8.

6. According to Anne Hudson, *The Premature Reformation: Wycliffite Texts and Lollard History* (Oxford, 1988), " 'Conservative Lollardy' is sometimes very close to 'radical orthodoxy' " (p. 279).

7. James Henthorn Todd, ed., *An Apology for Lollard Doctrines* (London, 1842), p. 52. The *Apology* later says that simoniacs "are sellers of doves, for they sell spiritual things" (p. 57). I have translated the Middle English of the reformist texts into modern English.

8. An indulgence is a grant from the Church that releases the sinner from a certain amount of the purgatorial punishment or *poena* incurred because of sin, but not from the guilt, or *culpa,* of sin. That can only be forgiven by God. Thus when the Pardoner says that he can "assoille," or absolve people from sin (387, 913, 933, 939)—that is, from the guilt of sin—he is promising more than even an honest pardoner could accomplish.

9. F. D. Matthew, ed., *The English Works of Wyclif Hitherto Unprinted*, EETS, o.s. 74 (London, 1880), p. 66. This work will subsequently be referred to as *EWW*.

10. Lilian M. Swinburn, *The Lanterne of Li3t*, EETS, o.s. 151 (London, 1917), p. 76.

11. *EWW*, p. 80.

12. Cited by Hudson, *Premature Reformation*, p. 300; see also *EWW*, p. 82. The "lead" refers to the seal attached to a document.

13. Gloria Cigman, ed., *Lollard Sermons* (Oxford, 1989), p. 113. For more on pardoners as simoniacs, see G. R. Owst, *Literature and Pulpit in Medieval England* (Cambridge, 1933), p. 373, n. 3; and G. R. Owst, *Preaching in Medieval England* (Cambridge, 1926), p. 105.

14. This interpretation is present in William Peraldus, *Summae virtutum ac vitiorum*, 2 vols. (Antwerp, 1571), 2.34 and 2.74 (see John Wyclif, *De Simonia*, edited by Dr. Herzberg-Fränkel and Michael Henry Dziewicki [London, 1898], p. 8, n. 24), and is undoubtedly of long standing. The connection between Wyclif's treatise and the portrait of the Pardoner in the General Prologue was first made by Terrence A. McVeigh, "Chaucer's Portraits of the Pardoner and Summoner and Wyclif's Tractatus de Simonia," *Classical Folia* 29 (1975): 54–58; see also George J. Engelhardt, "The Ecclesiastical Pilgrims of the *Canterbury Tales*: A Study in Ethology," *Mediaeval Studies* 37 (1975): 287–315; Melvin Storm, "The Pardoner's Invitation: Quaestor's Bag or Becket's Shrine?" *PMLA* 77 (1982): 810–18; Eugene Vance, "Chaucer's Pardoner: Relics, Discourse, and Frames of Propriety," *New Literary*

History 20 (1989): 723–45; and Richard K. Emmerson and Ronald B. Herzman, *The Apoca-lyptic Imagination in Medieval Literature* (Philadelphia, 1992), pp. 171–81.

15. Cited by Owst, *Literature and Pulpit*, p. 244.

16. *EWW*, p. 26; see also p. 248 and Wyclif, *De Simonia*, pp. 8–9.

17. Swinburne, *Lanterne*, pp. 131–32.

18. Thomas Arnold, ed., *Select English Works of John Wyclif*, 3 vols. (Oxford, 1869–71; henceforth referred to as *SEWW*), 3.143. The relation of the Pardoner to traditional pre-scriptions for preaching has been explored by Alastair Minnis, "Chaucer's Pardoner and the 'Office of Preacher,' " in *Intellectuals and Writers in Fourteenth-Century Europe*, edited by Piero Boitani and Anna Torti (Tübingen, 1986), pp. 88–119; see also Alan J. Fletcher, "The Preaching of the Pardoner," *Studies in the Age of Chaucer* 11 (1989): 15–35, and Gregory W. Gross, "Trade Secrets: Chaucer, the Pardoner, the Critics," *Modern Language Studies* 25.4 (1995): 1–36. Minnis touches on Wycliffite texts but does not deal with the material de-scribed here, while Fletcher dismisses Wycliffite material as irrelevant to the Pardoner's orthodox audience. The connection among sodomy, simony and preaching is discussed by Monica Brzezinski Potkay, "*Cleanness*'s Fecund and Barren Speech Acts," *Studies in the Age of Chaucer* 17 (1995): 99–109 (106–9), although without mention of the Pardoner.

19. These passages derive from *EWW*, pp. 124, 438, and Anne Hudson, ed., *Two Wycliffite Texts: The Sermon of William Taylor 1406, The Testimony of William Thorpe 1407* (Oxford, 1993), p. 19. Both of these objections—to using preaching as a prelude to begging and to the use of fables or exempla—are part of the traditional language of antifraternal-ism, and go back at least to William of St. Amour in the mid-thirteenth century; see Penn Szittya, *The Antifraternal Tradition in Medieval Literature* (Princeton, 1986), p. 53. But as is typical of the anti-clericalism of the late fourteenth-century described by Wendy Scase, *Piers Plowman and the New Anticlericalism* (Cambridge, 1989), these terms came to be applied to many kinds of clerics, including pardoners.

20. Swinburne, *Lanterne*, p. 55.

21. *EWW*, pp. 105–6.

22. According to Margaret Aston, it is "wholly probable" that the description of the Parson in the General Prologue would have identified him to a contemporary audience as having "Lollard inclinations" (*Lollards and Reformers. Images and Literacy in Late Medieval Religion* [London, 1984], p. 16 and note).

23. On the Pardoner's use of exempla, see Siegfried Wenzel, "Chaucer and the Lan-guage of Contemporary Preaching," *Studies in Philology* 73 (1976): 138–61.

24. *SEWW*, 3.123; emphasis added.

25. *EWW*, p. 10.

26. Ibid., p. 56. The designation of ineffective preaching as sodomitical is applied in one text even to those who refuse to listen to a sermon with the proper attentiveness; see Cigman, ed., *Lollard Sermons*, p. 201.

27. *SEWW*, 3.143–44.

28. Ibid., 3.125, 3.144; Swinburne, *Lanterne*, pp. 95–96, 133.

29. Swinburne, *Lanterne*, p. 31.

30. *SEWW*, 1.95–6.

31. I have discussed the exegesis of this metaphor, and its presence in the tale in the oak tree under which the rioters find their deaths, in Patterson, *Chaucer and the Subject of History* (Madison, Wis., 1991), pp. 404–5.

32. *EWW*, p. 307.

33. *SEWW*, 3.470; italics added.

34. Todd, *Apology*, p. 58; see also *EWW* p. 167, *SEWW*, 3.471, and Swinburne, *Lanterne*, pp. 92–93.

35. *EWW*, pp. 130, 214.

36. Ibid., p. 154. For other examples of pardoners and relics, see Owst, *Preaching in Medieval England*, pp. 108–9, pp. 109–10, and p. 110, n.1; and above, n. 13.

37. See Hudson, *Premature Reformation*, pp. 304–5; J. F. Davis, "Lollards, Reformers and St. Thomas of Canterbury," *University of Birmingham Historical Journal* 9 (1963): 1–15; and Aston, *Lollards and Reformers*, pp. 89–90. There is even evidence that Lollards themselves engaged in their own form of relic collecting: when a Lollard was burned as a heretic in the early fifteenth century, his ashes were gathered by the faithful and preserved (Hudson, *Premature Reformation*, p. 172).

38. John Wyclif, *De Mandatis divinis*, edited by Johann Loserth and F. D. Matthew (London, 1922), p. 162.

39. Todd, *Apology*, pp. 87–8.

40. Swinburne, *Lanterne*, p. 41.

41. Cigman, *Lollard Sermons*, p. 114.

42. A scriptural source for this connection between idolatry and sexual deviance is Romans 1:21–27.

43. *EWW*, p. 160.

44. R. A. Shoaf, *Dante, Chaucer, and the Currency of the Word: Money, Images, and Reference in Late Medieval Poetry* (Norman, Okla., 1983), pp. 220 and 274 n. 18.

45. Drawing on scriptural texts, Robert P. Miller, "Chaucer's Pandoner, the Scriptural Eunuch, and the Pardoner's Tale," *Speculum* 30 (1955): 180–99, identifies the Old Man as the *vetus homo* of sin, the antithesis of the *novus homo* who has been reborn, and he points out the Old Man's thwarted penance: "He desires 'an heyre clowt to wrappe' himself in—i.e. the hair shirt of penance, and he wishes to be buried: for the Old Man must be crucified and buried that the New Man may live" (197).

46. Augustine, *Contra Julianum* (*PL* 45:1555).

47. I am indebted to a Yale undergraduate, Andrew Hongo, and his teacher David Quint, for bringing this allusion to my notice. Lawrence Besserman, *Chaucer and the*

Bible: A Critical Review of Research, Indexes, and Bibliography (New York, 1988), does indicate the possibility of this allusion, but adds a question mark.

48. Augustine, *In Joannis evangelium tractatus CXXIV* (PL 35.1484). See also Bede, who follows Augustine in seeing this passage as referring to heretics and schismatics, and for whom the mother to be reentered is "Ecclesia mater, quae generat novit" (PL 94.198); John Scotus Erigena, who stresses the relation of the visible to the invisible, the letter to the spirit (PL 122.315–18); and Peter Comestor, *Historia scholastica* (PL 198.1560), who emphasizes Nicodemus's status as a learned man.

49. The only other vernacular text that I know in which an allusion to John 3.1–12 occurs is the *Chevalier de la charrete* by Chrétien de Troyes. Two young knights warn Lancelot that to cross the sword bridge is no more possible "than for a man to enter the womb of his mother and be reborn" ("ne que li hom porroit antrer / el vantre sa mere et renestre"): Mario Roques, ed., *Le Chevalier de la charrete* (Paris, 1963), ll. 3056–57, p. 93. Given the religious implications of Lancelot's quest into "the land from which, once they have entered there, neither clerk nor noble ever returns" (1904–6), the notion of spiritual rebirth has an evident appropriateness.

50. This argument was first made, not for the Pardoner's Tale but for Chaucer's source for this passage in the *Roman de la Rose*, by R. Howard Bloch, *Etymologies and Genealogies: A Literary Anthropology of the French Middle Ages* (Chicago, 1983), pp. 128–58.

51. Margaret Aston, *England's Iconoclasts*, vol. 1: *Laws against Images* (Oxford, 1988), p. 402.

52. See G. J. C. Snoek, *Medieval Piety from Relics to the Eucharist: A Process of Mutual Interaction* (Leiden, 1995).

53. Ibid., p. 28.

54. Ibid., p. 13.

55. Caroline Walker Bynum, *The Resurrection of the Body in Western Christianity, 200–1336* (New York, 1995). The importance of the resurrection of the body as a warrant of eternal life is vividly illustrated by the medieval habit of burning heretics, as is explained by R. C. Finucane, "Sacred Corpse, Profane Carrion: Social Ideals and Death Rituals in the Later Middle Ages," in *Mirrors of Mortality: Studies in the Social History of Death*, edited by Joachim Whaley (London, 1981), pp. 40–60 (58).

56. Ellert Dahl, "Heavenly Images: The Statue of St. Foy of Conques and the Signification of the Medieval 'Cult-Image' in the West," *Acta ad archaeologiam et Artium historiam pertinentia* 8 (1979): 175–92.

57. Leo Steinberg, *The Sexuality of Christ in Renaissance Art and in Modern Oblivion* (New York, 1983).

58. Chaucer quotes this line in the Parson's Tale: "Who shal delivere me fro the prisoun of my caytyf body?" (X.344).

Further Reading

This essay was originally written to argue that models of interpretation that rely upon psychoanalytic accounts of behavior mislead the reader into ignoring medieval materials that can provide more reliable interpretations. The most celebrated psychoanalytic reading of the Pardoner's Prologue and Tale—one that should be read in conjunction with this essay—is by Carolyn Dinshaw, *Chaucer's Sexual Poetics* (Madison, Wis., 1987), pp. 156–84. The primary emphasis of much contemporary work on the Pardoner is on his presumed sexuality: see, for instance, Glenn Burger, "Kissing the Pardoner," *PMLA* 107 (1992): 1143–56; Steven F. Kruger, "Claiming the Pardoner: Toward a Gay Reading of Chaucer's Pardoner's Tale," *Exemplaria* 6 (1994): 115–39; and Robert S. Sturges, *Chaucer's Pardoner and Gender Theory: Bodies of Discourse* (New York, 2001). An essay that combines a concern with sexuality and medieval attitudes toward language is Rita Copeland, "The Pardoner's Body and the Disciplining of Rhetoric," in *Framing Medieval Bodies*, edited by Sarah Kay and Miri Rubin (Manchester, England, 1994), pp. 138–59. Essays that use medieval evidence to argue that the Pardoner would be understood by a medieval audience not as homosexual or impotent but as an excessive womanizer are Richard Firth Green, "The Pardoner's Pants (and Why They Matter)," *Studies in the Age of Chaucer* 15 (1993): 131–45; and C. David Benson, "Chaucer's Pardoner: His Sexuality and Modern Critics," *Medievalia* 8 (1982): 337–46. For other discussions of the prologue and tale as essentially religious, see Linda Georgianna, "Love So Dearly Bought: The Terms of Redemption in *The Canterbury Tales*," *Studies in the Age of Chaucer* 12 (1990): 85–116; and Alan J. Fletcher, *Preaching, Politics, and Poetry in Late-Medieval England* (Dublin, 1998). A fine psychological (rather than psychoanalytic) reading of the Pardoner is provided by H. Marshall Leicester, " 'Synne Horrible': The Pardoner's Exegesis of His Tale, and Chaucer's," in *Acts of Interpretation*, edited by Mary J. Carruthers and Elizabeth D. Kirk (Norman, Okla., 1982), pp. 25–50.

Empathy and Enmity in the Prioress's Tale

STEPHEN SPECTOR

◆ ◆ ◆

Midway through the impassioned prayer that precedes her tale, Chaucer's Prioress alludes to the Incarnation in terms of joined contraries conveying sublime paradox:

> O mooder Mayde, O mayde Mooder free!
> O bussh unbrent, brennynge in Moyses sighte,
> That ravyshedest doun fro the Deitee,
> Thurgh thyn humblesse, the Goost that in th'alighte,
> Of whos vertu, whan he thyn herte lighte,
> Conceyved was the Fadres sapience.[1]

The force and economy with which these contradictions are joined are rhetorically heightened by the chiastic structure of the first of these lines, "O mother Virgin, O virgin Mother noble." The following line too is structurally compressed, juxtaposing contraries in the "unburnt, burning" bush, a familiar type of Mary, who "was fyred brente not, for she was moder without losse of maydenhod."[2] In the next two lines, the Prioress astonishingly transforms the Gospel account of the Incarnation, in which Gabriel tells Mary that the Holy Spirit will come upon her, and the power of the Most High will overshadow her (Luke 1:35). In the nun's fervent reworking, it is instead the Virgin who ravishes the Holy Ghost down from the Deity! Yet the heat and energy suggested in the word *ravyshedest* are paradoxically contained, like the flames of the burning bush, within the chastity of the Conception.[3] And the fact that Mary ravishes the Holy Ghost through her humility, compelling or possessing through acquiescence, further extends the paradox in this prayer. The joining of contraries in paradox is thus as crucial to the Prioress's prayer as the joining of contradictions in irony is to her General Prologue portrait. But there is still another contradiction here: that the Prioress, whose faith and emotion seem so shallow and misplaced in the General Prologue, should utter so ardent a prayer at all.

Much of the mystery and delight of Chaucer's poetry issues from the marriage of such contraries, the reconciliation of the apparently irreconcilable, often in wonder and surprise, if not in peace. As much as any of Chaucer's pilgrims, the Prioress embodies a juxtaposition of such polarized qualities. A bride of Christ, she is nonetheless described as if she had stepped out of an Old French romance. Her ecclesiastical authority seems subverted in the General Prologue by her spiritual superficiality. Yet this shallowness is later shown, in her prayer, to conceal a burning religious fervor. And her genteel spotlessness in the General Prologue is shockingly contrasted in her tale by the bloody child cast in a dung pit. She is undeniably a creature of love, however compromised, and yet she embeds in her tale an animosity, directed toward Jews, that is as passionate as her prayer. Wordsworth observed that her tenderhearted sympathies are set off against her fierce bigotry, and D. S. Brewer says that the Prioress is the gentlest of the pilgrims who tells the only cruel and fanatical tale.[4] Talbot Donaldson notes in her tale a "strange mixture of delicacy and horror."[5] "Jewels and jakes," says Alan Gaylord; "charm and depravity," says Ian Robinson.[6] And, we must add, love and hate.

This essay is an exploration of the intersection of love and hate, and of the unresolved play between these and other contradictions in Chaucer's presentation of the Prioress. I attempt here to discover the connectedness in her contraries and to deconstruct the moral dichotomy in her depiction of Christian and Jew. In the process, I review historical scholarship on Christian-Jewish relations in the late medieval period in order to challenge the assertion that Chaucer himself necessarily participated in a universal intolerance toward Jews.

LONG BEFORE THE advent of poststructuralism, critics detected the subversions that pervade the Prioress's description and problematize her tale. The Prioress's intention is not complex: she attempts to illustrate the simple beauty of her faith by offering a beautiful and simple miracle of the Virgin. In so doing, she valorizes innocent faith while rejecting the cursed Jews, whom she presents as the enemies of naive devotion. Her tale is thus intended to represent and vindicate her own qualities. For most of the twentieth century, however, critics have observed the ways in which the Prioress's qualities differ from themselves. And in recent decades, they have debated the degree to which these differences complicate and undermine her simple intention. In consequence, the profound conflicts in so shallow a pilgrim have been reproduced as conflicts in readings of the text.

Chaucer's description of the Prioress is itself a matter of spirited debate. Despite nearly general critical agreement that he wrote this portrait with restraint and even affection, virtually every line has provoked conflict among readers. The Prioress's age and appearance are an extreme case: some critics regard her as young and beautiful, others as old and overgrown. True, beautiful medieval foreheads were large, but D. W. Robertson, Jr., says that the Prioress's signified stupidity or lack of discretion.[7] Gordon Harper says that a forehead a span broad would scarcely conform to any notion of beauty.[8] And F. N. Robinson's note on this line questions whether a nun's forehead shouldn't have been covered in any case. Harper, in an essay titled "Chaucer's Big Prioress," takes the fact that the Prioress "was nat undergrowe" to mean that she was unusually large, even fat, and he makes a dastardly reference to her as bulbous. But Muriel Bowden says that being "nat undergrowe" means that she is well proportioned, and Talbot Donaldson and John Block Friedman assume that the Prioress's figure is good.[9] The gentle Prioress threatens to become a different creature for each reader, so that for Sister M. Madeleva, a sensible, mature nun, the Prioress is one too.[10] And for G. K. Chesterton, the Prioress is a spinster, but particularly English, with a special kindness to animals so much valued by the English gentry today.[11] The Prioress's tale has, as we shall see, undergone similar shape shifting.

John Livingston Lowes gave classic expression to the contradictions and subversions in the Prioress's portrait by observing that she is a religious who is described by language appropriate to a romance heroine. The manner of her smile, the choice of her name, and indeed her entire description are, said Lowes, "steeped in reminiscences of the poetry of courtly love," creating a "delightfully imperfect submergence of the woman in the nun."[12] The General Prologue portrait, in fact, is constituted of qualities that seem mislocated and misdirected. The Prioress's concern for physical spotlessness, for example, parodies the true interest of a religious, the safeguarding of spiritual spotlessness. Worse, this passage is modeled on the advice of the sinful figure La Vieille in the *Roman de la Rose*, who recommends such table manners among women's wiles to attract men. Sister Madeleva, one of the staunchest defenders of the Prioress, denies irony in the portrait, arguing that her table manners, for instance, reflect the nun's natural desire to keep her habit clean.[13] Arguments of this kind are valid in themselves, but they fail to consider the context of the passage, both in the portrait and its source. And they account neither for the manner of presentation, the language employed, nor what is left unsaid.

There is further misdirection and mislocation in the Prioress's *conscience and tendre herte*. The irony is conveyed, as Bowden points out, by the fact that it is a mouse that calls forth the Prioress's sympathy, not the suffering of her fellow man.[14] God and neighbor are the true objects of charity, adds John Steadman, who observes that the falseness of the Prioress's choice of objects is made obvious by contrast with the Plowman.[15] Robertson notes that this passage, like much of the portrait, proceeds by anticlimax, raising expectations by referring to conscience, charity, and pity, and then descending to the trapped mouse that benefits from those qualities.[16] And Chauncey Wood, developing Stanley Fish's idea that readers make anticipatory judgments, or partial closures, says that the reference to conscience is one of many instances in this portrait in which the reader is teased into a false expectation, only to be surprised by what follows.[17]

The reader's expectations are similarly misled by the portrait as a whole. It does not, for instance, prepare us for the passion of Eglentyne's prayer, which is presumably concealed beneath the "chere of court." We are similarly surprised by her tale. Critics have often found the Prioress of the General Prologue to be charming, possibly beautiful, but spiritually superficial, oversentimental, conflicted, and, to some scholars, stupid. Yet there is no hint within the portrait of the outburst of intolerance that will follow. Quite the contrary, the focus is on love. This love is misdirected and made pathetic, as in the Prioress's tears for suffering mice. And sacred and profane love are conflated, as emblematized in the Prioress's motto. But the central theme remains love, not hate, and the newcomer to Chaucer, having read the General Prologue description, may well expect the Prioress's Tale to speak of love, however confused, and perhaps of the rescue of nuns in distress.

In fact, the Prioress does tell a tale of love, and of rescue, a miracle of the Virgin. The story begins with a *litel clergeon*. This *litel child* attends a *litel scole* where, while studying his primer one day, he hears the older children singing the antiphon *Alma redemptoris mater*. He does not understand the Latin, and fails in his attempts to have it explained to him, but it is sufficient for him to know that the song is in praise of Mary. This innocent learns the song by rote, and sings it twice a day as he passes among the city's Jewry, a place

> Sustened by a lord of that contree
> For foule usure and lucre of vileynye,
> Hateful to Crist and to his compaignye.
> (490–92)

The Jews are provoked, and the Prioress evokes both their traditional association with the devil and their assumed willingness to kill in defense of their law:

> Oure firste foo, the serpent Sathanas,
> That hath in Jues herte his waspes nest,
> Up swal, and seide, "O Hebrayk peple, allas!
> Is this to yow a thyng that is honest,
> That swich a boy shal walken as hym lest
> In youre despit, and synge of swich sentence,
> Which is agayn youre lawes reverence?"
> (558–64)

With allusions recalling the conspiracy against Christ and the slaughter of
the innocents, the Prioress tells that the Jews hire a murderer, another
cursed Jew, who seizes the child, cuts his throat, and casts him into a privy.
Referring to Herod (another allusion to the slaughter of the innocents),
then to Cain's killing of Abel, the nun reaches an emotional pitch reminiscent of her prayer:

> I seye that in a wardrobe they hym threwe
> Where as thise Jewes purgen hire entraille.
> O cursed folk of Herodes al newe,
> What may youre yvel entente yow availle?
> Mordre wol out, certeyn, it wol nat faille,
> And namely ther th'onour of God shal sprede;
> The blood out crieth on youre cursed dede.
> (572–78)

The Jews wickedly lie to the child's mother, denying that the boy ever passed
through the Jewry. But through the intercession of the Virgin, the dead child,
his throat cut, sings the *Alma redemptoris mater*. The Christian folk hear the song
and send for the provost. With torment and shameful death, the provost kills
the Jews who knew of the murder, dragging them by horses, then hanging
them, acts of which the gentle Prioress implicitly approves. The child then explains that Mary herself, the "welle of mercy," has brought about the miracle,

placing a grain under his tongue, bidding him to sing the anthem, and then expressing a distinctly maternal consolation and assurance:

> My litel child, now wol I fecche thee,
> Whan that the greyn is fro thy tonge ytake.
> Be nat agast; I wol thee nat forsake.
>
> (667–69)

The martyr's "litel body sweete" is finally buried in a tomb of clear marble. The Prioress concludes by beseeching young Hugh of Lincoln, slain by "cursed Jewes" in a ritual blood slaughter, to intercede, so that merciful God, because of his mercy, will multiply his mercy on us "synful folk unstable." This juxtaposition of condemnation and mercy, the damned and the saved, the objects of hate and of sentimentality, crystallizes the contraries that inform her tale.

Many early critics took no notice of any such contraries. Instead, they spoke of the tale as a perfect illustration of the miracle-of-the-Virgin genre. George Lyman Kittredge, praising the Prioress's dignity and daintiness, speaks of the tale as "infinitely pathetic," never mentioning the Jews.[18] Chesterton says that the Prioress's Tale is beautiful, and Nevill Coghill calls it one of the sweetest expressions of Chaucer's special feeling for the Blessed Virgin, conveying the beauty of holiness and of Christian triumph.[19] Wordsworth did speak of the bigotry set off against tenderness in the tale; but, as Florence Ridley notes, this did not stop him from rendering the tale in modern English.[20] Even Lowes, who so elegantly expressed the incongruities in the Prioress's portrait, speaks of her in ways that suggest affection and delight, betraying no sign of disturbance: he characterizes her description as "delicately ironical," "exquisitely sympathetic," "delightfully imperfect."[21]

The fact is that before the Holocaust much informed opinion about the Prioress's Tale was undisturbed by her treatment of the Jews, which was often not noticed at all.[22] Instead, her tale was praised for its beauty and perfection. This is significant and must be given full weight, for if it was so in our own century, one cannot expect Chaucer to have necessarily felt differently. For Kittredge and the others, and perhaps for Chaucer too, the Prioress's stereotyping of vicious Jews was no more serious a matter than the Man of Law's treatment of the heathen Surryens, who also commit murder to defend their law, instigated by Satan's instrument, the Sowdanesse.

Since the Holocaust, by contrast, the question of anti-Semitism has been a central point of discussion about the Prioress. R. J. Schoeck argues that Chaucer presented the tale in order to denounce the ritual-murder libel, and George K. Anderson calls the Prioress a vapid anti-Semite.[23] Several scholars, including

Talbot Donaldson, Ian Robinson, Alfred David, and Donald R. Howard, have distinguished Chaucer's own views from the Prioress's, citing his greater awareness of Christianity and the posture of the Church, or his other personal qualities.[24] Others, notably Ridley and Albert B. Friedman, have refuted these assertions about the reputed tolerance of the Church, noting the ubiquity of anti-Jewishness at the time and its pervasiveness in Christian piety.[25] Under such cultural circumstances, this line of argument suggests, the Prioress's bigotry loses significance. Her cruelty is manifest only from a point of view impossible to the Middle Ages, says Brewer, and David questions whether any medieval reader would have perceived the ironies in miracles of the Virgin that are apparent to the modern mind.[26] Ridley (p. 5) argues that the Prioress "and the rest of her credulous countrymen" regarded Jews "as strange, mysterious, and therefore sinister." Hardy Long Frank asserts that Jews were universally considered to be devils in late medieval Christendom.[27] And Friedman (p. 120) considers it foolish to expect Chaucer to have been above the narrow beliefs of his age when broad-mindedness was impossible for Pascal, 250 years later.

This critical impasse over the horizons of Chaucer's possible attitude toward Jews illustrates with particular clarity the influence of history and ideology on critical perspectives. Readers' responses, already divided by the contraries in the Prioress's portrait, have been further distanced by recent experience. Several post-Holocaust scholars, sensitized by the barbarism of the twentieth century, have looked for greater civility in the fourteenth, at least in the transcendent person of Chaucer. They implicitly view earlier assessments of the tale as naive and insensitive (like the Prioress herself) precisely because those views were conceived in innocence of the horrific consequences of intolerance that we have seen in our time. Other scholars have challenged the validity of applying such a modern sensibility to a medieval text. Their position is reinforced by more radical contemporary critical claims that broadly dismiss the notion of Chaucer as a man who transcended the influences of his period—who was in his time but not of it. The possibility that Chaucer escaped conventional prejudices will be rejected by some advocates of this view as a relic of a discredited Whig historiography.[28]

BOTH SIDES OF THIS DEBATE deserve reexamination. The assumption of an inescapable and constant medieval hatred of Jews in which Chaucer necessarily shared is drastically oversimplified. The actual historical picture across Europe over a period of centuries was far more complex. Many prominent medieval Jewish historians have concluded that enmity toward Jews, though widespread and often calamitous, was not universal. As the appendix below demonstrates, along with official oppression and popular hatred, there were many recorded gestures and declarations of respect and amity between individual Gentile and Jew. These interactions often occurred in spite of formal proscriptions, which themselves help document the behavior they were designed to suppress.

On the other hand, Chaucer's own attitude toward Jews is probably irretrievable. Beliefs and prejudices of this sort are often prelogical and are not always discernible from an author's writing. This is particularly true of the portrayal of the Jews, which since the patristic period had typically been axiomatic rather than observed or deduced.[29] In *The Canterbury Tales*, the issue is further complicated, of course, by the fact that narratives are assigned to tale tellers and often colored by irony. Moreover, to address the question of how Chaucer felt about Jews, one must interrogate the actions neither of Chaucer the pilgrim, nor even of Chaucer the poet, whose masked and fragmented qualities, to the extent that they can be inferred, are part of a posture offered to public view. Rather, one must investigate the inner life of Chaucer the private individual.[30] And there are reasons for skepticism that in issues of this kind a man's personal qualities are necessarily identical with the public ones suggested in his work. Barring new documentary discoveries, we cannot even establish that the issue was in any sense significant to Chaucer. What we can address, however, is the artistic function of the intolerance within the text.

THE ISSUE I WISH to consider here, therefore, is not whether Chaucer was anti-Jewish, but rather how he transformed the conventional intolerance in a traditional miracle of the Virgin in his presentation of the Prioress: why, in short, such an unexpected outburst of hatred is attributed to so gentle a nun.[31] The Parson's references to Jews are merely incidental. But the Jews of the Prioress's Tale play, as I shall try to show, a particularized role that is specifically relevant to Eglentyne. Merely to assert that the Prioress participates in a general hostility toward Jews ignores the context in which they appear in her tale and the function that they serve. Such an approach recalls the important but self-limiting work of the early critics of the General Prologue portrait, who documented historical practices and infractions resembling the Prioress's, but failed to account for the context and the manner of presentation of these elements in the Prioress's description. Moreover, this approach allows a divorce between the tale and the Prioress's character as it emerges in the General Prologue description. This, in fact, is precisely what John Lawlor recommends: he warns that attempting to fit the tale to the General Prologue description must call into play our modern suspicions, so that we will "view dourly any essay into that commonest of medieval modes, the pathetic."[32] But as Edward H. Kelly observes, in order to "more fully appreciate the poet's art of creation, it is necessary to see the description in the General Prologue as artistically functional in understanding the tale."[33]

Critics who have explored the unity of the General Prologue and the tale have in several instances emphasized the Prioress's unscrutinized sensibility or sentimentality, or the inherent association between these qualities and cruelty. Bowden (pp. 99–100) says that the implication of the Prioress's sympathy for mice rather than men is reinforced in her tale, in which she tells with perfect blandness of the tortures visited upon the Jews. Donaldson says, "Emotionalism that excludes the intellect—as it does in the Prioress' Tale—can be a dangerous thing, for the psychological transition from exquisite sensibility to bloodshed is an easy one."[34] Bertrand Bronson also puts the blame on the nun's "shallow sensibility," which, he says, is the obverse of cruelty.[35] Gaylord links sentimentality and brutality in describing the Prioress's actions, and Ian Robinson says that the Prioress's sentimentality is so thoughtless as to become wicked.[36] Ridley, taking a different approach, considers the tale a humorless display of naïveté, ignorance, blind vehement devotion, and (following Kittredge) suppressed maternal longing (p. 29).

Questions remain, however. Bowden's point about the Prioress's misplaced sympathy in the General Prologue does not explain the nun's explosion of enmity or her abundant sympathy with the *clergeon*. And though sentimentality and shallow (or heightened) sensibility can accompany and conceal cruelty, they need not cause it and are not invariably associated with it. The same is true of the naïveté, ignorance, and blind devotion that Ridley mentions. Current psychoanalytical thinking about intolerance proceeds, as we shall see, along very different lines. As for Kittredge's notion of thwarted motherhood, I think that it is mistaken, a "partial closure" inspired by the Prioress's sympathy for small animals and the little boy. For in her prayer, the Prioress emphatically adopts the perspective not of a mother, but of a child, with motherhood relegated to the nurturant Virgin Mother, whose guidance and strength Eglentyne beseeches.

THE PRAYER, which serves as prologue to her tale, is the key to reconciling the Prioress's contraries. Beautiful and moving when considered in itself, this rarely examined prayer provides the missing elements that connect the portrait and the tale. And it reveals how the empathy and enmity in her tale are precisely suited to her character—or, rather, how her character is suited to the tale. The prayer begins with a versifying of Psalm 8:

> O Lord, oure Lord, thy name how merveillous
> Is in this large world ysprad—quod she—
> For noght oonly thy laude precious
> Parfourned is by men of dignitee,

> But by the mouth of children thy bountee
> Parfourned is, for on the brest soukynge
> Somtyme shewyn they thyn heriynge.
>
> (453–59)

This psalm, Sister Madeleva informs us (p. 30), is the first of several allusions in the prayer to the Little Office of the Blessed Virgin. The psalm also appears in the Mass for the Feast of the Holy Innocents, and so links the prayer to the liturgical and scriptural reminiscences of the slaughter of the innocents in the tale.[37] Beyond that, the psalm serves as the text, as it were, for her tale, which illustrates praise from the mouth of a child. But, just as in our reading of the General Prologue portrait, we are surprised by what follows: the significance of these lines is transformed in light of the final stanza of this prayer, for the image of the nursing child refers not to the *clergeon* but to the Prioress herself:

> My konnyng is so wayk, O blisful Queene,
> For to declare thy grete worthynesse
> That I ne may the weighte nat susteene;
> But as a child of twelf month oold, or lesse,
> That kan unnethes any word expresse,
> Ryght so fare I, and therfore I yow preye,
> Gydeth my song that I shal of yow seye.
>
> (481–87)

The *clergeon* is seven years old, beyond infancy, but the Prioress images herself as still an infant. These lines display, in fact, the specificity with which the Prioress's qualities are reproduced in her tale. As a child of twelve months old or less, she places herself at the age of the innocents to whose slaughter her tale refers. Moreover, she mirrors herself in that other innocent, the *clergeon*. The simple, faithful child becomes the repository of her own simple, childlike faith. Like her, he is *sowded to virginitee*, "made fast in virginity," because he dies a virgin. His devotion, like hers in the General Prologue, is expressed only in song. And just as the *clergeon* is unaware of the meaning of his song, knowing only that it praises Mary, so we are told only of the *sound* of hers and her manner of singing.[38] Both the nun and the child are filled with devotion for Mary, and for both, fervor substitutes for substantial understanding. Both are untutored in the suffering and compassion that inform Christianity. The child, after all, is only beginning to learn his primer. And, significantly, the primer is a source of the Prioress's prayer. For the primer contains the Little Office of the Blessed Virgin, which the Prioress paraphrases in the prayer.[39]

The nun's frailty and vulnerability also reemerge in the child. In her prayer, Eglentyne stresses her childlike weakness, her frail inability to sustain her song.[40] And in her tale, the helpless child has his throat cut so that he can no longer sing. The treatment of his body also recalls the Prioress's portrait: she is obsessed with cleanliness, and the *clergeon* is killed by the forces of foulness and defilement, who cast his body in the uncleanest of places. Mary's intervention in the tale further identifies the Prioress with the *clergeon*, for he is saved by a miracle that answers the nun's own request of Mary: declaring that she is like a child, scarcely able to speak, Eglentyne prays that Mary will guide her song. In the tale, this actually happens to the child: he is rendered literally unable to speak, and Mary does guide his song. And the Prioress realizes her own desire for spotlessness through him by placing him among the 144,000 virgins of Apocalypse 14, who are *sine macula*, "without spot," and who, as she says, follow the "white lamb celestial."

The function of the Jews in the tale lends specific meaning to the Prioress's outburst of enmity. By assigning this tale to the Prioress or, more correctly, by creating the Prioress and matching her so precisely with the tale, Chaucer introduced a detailed self-referentiality between teller and tale. In consequence, the Jews in the tale are not generalized bogeymen, as they may appear to be in the analogues or in the tale considered in isolation. Rather, in signifying threats to childlike innocence, to virginal spotlessness, and to simple faith, the Jews are made to endanger the very qualities that Chaucer embodied in the nun. They are the foul representatives not only of spiritual stain, but also of physical defilement, which issues from their entrails. As such, they symbolize the most offensive possible contrary to the immaculate Eglentyne. The nonspecific anti-Jewishness of the tale and its analogues is thus translated into the Prioress's revulsion at the qualities that constitute her own negation.[41]

This treatment of the Jews offers a striking parallel to the dominant psychoanalytical model of intolerance, in which the bigot localizes in the Jew the unwanted or threatening elements of his internal or external world.[42] A similar paradigm informs the cycle drama, in which the Jews represent precisely those qualities that the good figures must expel from themselves.[43] In terms of literary rather than psychological projection, the Jew in the Prioress's Tale, as in the cycles, is a highly specific figure signifying a precise danger to the Christian. Deconstructed in this way, the conflict *between* faith and disbelief in these texts is seen as a conflict *within*, and the radically marginalized figure of the Jew emerges as central.[44]

Madame Eglentyne's enmity is aimed, then, at figures whose role is profoundly relevant to her. The same is true of her empathy. And this reveals the self-referentiality of the sentiment in which the Prioress bathes the *clergeon*: her loving approbation of the child with whom she shares so many qualities is, finally, love of self. Her love is thus misdirected, just as her pity and tenderness are in the General Prologue. But this does not negate her love of Mary, as is only fitting in a pilgrim so thoroughly composed of contraries, who reconciles in her nature such various expressions of love. In fact, this joining of personal and spiritual love recreates the ambiguity of the Prioress's love in the General Prologue, reenacting the imperfect submergence of the woman in the nun. In the end, though, it is Mary's perfect love that prevails in the tale, drawn down from heaven by the child's simple, unthinking, but ardent devotion. The nun thus vindicates her own qualities by having Mary reward them with the maternal love that the Prioress, in her spiritual infancy, requires.

Ultimately, much of the unresolved tension in the presentation of the Prioress centers on the question of love. The nun's love is confused, compromised. In the prayer and tale, by contrast, Mary's abundant love is unambiguous. And so in the tale Eglentyne, the humble, thorny brier rose, has Mary, the noble "white lylye flour" of her prayer, bestow her love to redeem virginal innocence from the forces that endanger it.[45] In so doing, Mary redeems the Prioress too and vanquishes ambiguity from the motto *Amor vincit omnia*. This is the triumph of love in the Prioress's Tale. But it occurs only within the tale. In this regard, Eglentyne recalls the Wife of Bath, whose magical tale of marital peace and accord is incongruous with her own experience of marriage.[46] Similarly, the Prioress is assigned a tale that appears to miraculously transcend the misdirections and ambiguities in her portrait. The tale does not negate the contradictions in her makeup, however, but rather completes the restless Chaucerian marriage of contraries.

Appendix: The Horizons of Tolerance

Anti-Jewishness was inherent in Christian doctrine, and hostility toward Jews was widespread even a century after they had been expelled, as was the case in England when Chaucer wrote. Viewed telescopically, the official and popular intolerance toward Jews was generally progressive, and the principal events concerning them during the fourteenth century were marked by persecution, violence, and expulsion.[47] Having been expelled from England in 1290, they were evicted from all royal possessions in France in 1306. After returning to France in 1315, they were attacked in 1320 by the so-called Pastoureaux, or Shepherd Crusaders, and were expelled again in 1322 after being accused of conspiring with lepers to poison wells. They were reinvited to France in 1359, but expelled definitively from most districts in 1394. In Germany at the time of the Black Death (1348–1349), Jews were charged with well poisoning and burned en masse. Some cities, like Ratisbon and Vienna, successfully defended their Jews. But most German cities were emptied of Jews, many of whom went to Poland. Those who returned to their towns in Germany often did so under less favorable economic and political agreements than had previously obtained. And in 1391 in Spain, a progrom movement accompanied by forced conversions anticipated events of a century later, when the Jews were expelled from that nation in 1492.

By Chaucer's lifetime (ca. 1343–1400), the European Jews had been widely abused and oppressed. Nationalist and economic pressures in concert with religious fervor, popular prejudice, and pogromist violence had spurred many communities to degrade and ultimately expel the Jews.[48] Theologically, their guilt and spiritual infirmity had by then long been a commonplace. Chaucer would have been well aware that in both religious literature and popular belief, the Jews were traditional symbols of evil, perfidious and threatening allies of the devil.[49] Did he and all other Gentiles inevitably share this view? As recent criticism asserts, people are ineluctably affected by the ideology and social determinants of their time. But the specific responses to such influences are always individual and incalculable. The issue of intolerance provides a test case. Modern experience teaches that the reaction to highly propagandized prejudice can be contradictory, labile, even uncanny.[50] Medieval anti-Judaism differed in important ways from the racially based anti-Semitism practiced in the twentieth century.[51] But along with that earlier hostility too, and despite the proscriptions and condemnations that it engendered, there are many signs of a crosscurrent of mutual tolerance between Christian and Jew. Moreover, the evidence suggests the existence of more than mere formal tolerance, which could, after all, be negotiated on the basis of self-interest, or purchased, or grudgingly conceded on theological grounds: there are in addition gestures and expressions of mutual respect and personal regard.[52] As Salo Baron (11:120–21) observes, Jews were often despised and haunted, especially at critical moments in history. But despite it all, Jews and Christians

> often maintained far closer social relations (even in the obscure realm of sex) than one might expect in the light of the stringent segregationist laws and preaching on both sides. (11:119–20)

Baron (11:187) adds that friendly daily exchanges often went unreported. But the closeness of relations between the groups can be inferred as, for example, from the lavish efforts that had to be expended in order to cut off such contacts.

An explicit doctrine tolerating Jewish residence in Christian communities had been evolved in the patristic period and developed by Bernard of Clairvaux and Thomas Aquinas. From the thirteenth century, the Jews were technically *servi camerae*, or the king's serfs.[53] Jacob Katz notes that many Jews achieved high political standing, as evidenced by the fact that they were permitted to bear arms in France and Germany well into the thirteenth century.[54] Baron (11:114) adds that Jews were never prohibited from carrying arms in Italy or Spain. Katz asserts that despite oppressive rules and ideologies of separateness on both sides, neighborly and even friendly relations between Jews and Christians always occurred. The religious symbolism that permeated each community was a further barrier to social penetration, but, says Katz, Jews and Christians nevertheless often met in a friendly spirit.

Although the two communities remained socially unintegrated, common features marked their social lives. Jews and Gentiles shared practices and beliefs and sometimes enjoyed common literary interests.[55] And in large measure, depending on the time and place, they dressed alike and spoke alike.[56] From the thirteenth century, Jews were required to wear a badge, undoubtedly an important step in their social degradation. The badge was not uniformly enforced during the medieval period, however.[57] And Baron (11:187) notes that it was imposed on Jews precisely because it was needed to distinguish them from Christians, with whom they had close relations.

Social interaction occurred in direct defiance of segregative laws. During the famous disputation in Paris in 1240, the Jewish spokesman is reported to have said that, contrary to talmudic prescription:

> [W]e do sell cattle to Gentiles, we enter into companionship with them, we stay with them alone, we entrust our infants to them to be suckled in their own homes, and we do teach *Torah* to a Gentile, for there are many clerics able to read Jewish books. (Quoted in Katz, p. 108)

Despite formal prohibitions, Gentile and Jew gave gifts to one another until the end of the period.[58] Close personal ties appear to have developed. Israel Abrahams reports, for example, that Immanuel of Rome, Dante's Jewish imitator, required special consolation on Dante's death in 1321. Abrahams observes that no theological prejudice stood in the way of the mutual regard between the Christian poet and the Jew and notes that Immanuel wrote in an Italian sonnet:

> Love has never read the *Ave Maria*, Love knows no law or creed. Love cannot be barred by a *Paternoster*, but to all who question his supreme power Love answers, "It is my will."[59]

Friendships between the groups, according to Abrahams (pp. 420, 426) were especially notable in Italy, where Jews and Christians played cards together and ate, drank, and danced together. Sentimental attachment is attested elsewhere in Europe as well during Chaucer's lifetime. Guido Kisch notes, for example, that German law books reveal outspokenly friendly attitudes between individual Jews and Gentiles in the late fourteenth and the fifteenth centuries. Such utterances, Kisch concludes, gain weight because they were evidently free expressions, made openly in court, of popular sentiment in favor of Jews (*Germany*, p. 326). Abrahams (p. 426) cites the isolated but piquant instance of a Christian in Frankfurt who in 1377 applied the friendly epithet *selig* to a deceased Jew. Relationships between the sexes in this century often went well beyond friendship. Though formal marriage was not recognized unless one of the parties converted, affairs, common-law marriages, and concubinage between Christian and Jew were frequent. So many Mediterranean Jews kept Christian concubines that this practice was often attacked by Jewish moralists.[60] Illicit relationships between Jews and Gentiles are also documented in France, Zurich, and Constance.[61] Each side tended to be more permissive if its own males had relations with females of the other religion, and Baron (11:82–84) observes that Christian popular literature in some cases sympathetically depicted the seduction of Jewish girls.

Expressions of personal respect and evidently of friendship—or at least of personal diplomacy—are documented from the fifteenth century as well. Despite long-standing warnings from both sides about defilement through exposure to the other's religious ceremonies, for example, social contact did occur at such events. A Sicilian Christian, to cite one instance, served as godfather at a Jewish circumcision in 1484. Baron observes that friendly acts of this sort were normally taken for granted, and so passed unnoticed by official documents.[62] In Germany, friendly exchanges of gifts in connection with religious rituals were frequent. In Wiener Neustadt, for example, the eating of cakes that a Christian had brought to a Jewish wedding was officially permitted by R. Israel Isserlein. Isserlein also approved of Jews giving gifts to Christians, including clerics, for New Year's, as well as on a Jewish holiday, the *Lag be-'omer*.[63] German Gentiles and Jews were sufficiently friendly, in fact, to provoke a Church council to forbid them to bathe, eat, or drink together.[64] Numerous similar prohibitions in German secular law books further witness the amicable relationships that then existed (Kisch, *Germany*, p. 326). Sexual relations between Gentile and Jew are also documented from the fifteenth century: in the Orthodox German community of Ratisbon, for example, three Jews were prosecuted within the space of seven years (1460–1467) on that charge, and several were reported awaiting trial.[65] In Italy in 1418, Jewish leaders complained about the sexual laxity of Italian Jews, many of whom considered Gentile women "permitted to them." And in Spain, personal associations with Gentiles were so close, and sexual relations so common, that some Jews attributed their downfall in that country to their excessive rapprochement with their Christian neighbors. A final illustration of trusting relationships between Christian and Jew in defiance of official regulation is the fact that fifteenth-century popes employed Jewish doctors in spite of papal decrees opposing such services.[66]

Most of the acts and gestures cited above were inspired by actual social contact between the groups. Whether Chaucer ever met Jews is purely speculative.[67] But even where personal interaction was unlikely, thoughtful people were capable of assessing Jews on their merits, rather than as a stereotypically damned and demonic people. In fourteenth-century England, for example, several religious and literary figures acknowledged the piety and ethicality in Jewish behavior.[68] Langland conceded, albeit grudgingly, that Jews were kinder to their needy fellows than were Christians.[69] The homilies of John Bromyard praise the Jews' piety, care for the poor, and heroic suffering for their faith, as well as their avoidance of searing.[70] Thomas Brunton's printed sermons consider Jews superior to Christians in moral and religious practice.[71] Richard Rex notes that Wyclif and others argued that Jews, Saracens, and pagans could be saved on the basis of their virtuous acts.[72]

At least some fourteenth-century continental poets viewed the Jews more sympathetically than did religious polemic, treating them as human beings who were victimized by their historical circumstances. The German poet Heinrich der Teichner, who was active from about 1340 to 1375, wrote, for example, "Many a man, who is himself much worse, bears an unjust grudge against the poor Jew." Jan van Boendale (de Clerk), a Flemish poet of the first half of the fourteenth century, wrote of the Jews:

> Want mi dunct emmer dat si
> also wel menschen syn als wi
> ende oec comen van Adame.

[It always seems to me that they are human beings like us and have also come from Adam].[73]

Respect toward Jews and the potential for friendship with them is prominently portrayed in the *Decameron*, the most suggestive analogue to *The Canterbury Tales*.[74] In the second tale of the first day, Neifile describes an intimate friendship between a Christian and a Jewish merchant named Abraham. The tale repeatedly emphasizes Abraham's integrity, goodness, learning, and modesty. It is his wisdom, in fact, that ultimately leads him to convert, for he realizes that a religion that can survive the spiritual decadence of its princes in Rome must be favored by God! The subsequent tale also portrays a wise Jew, Melchisedech, whose actions illustrate the declared lesson of the tale: that good sense can save a man from danger. In the process, Melchisedech compares Judaism, Christianity, and Islam to three rings. Originally, there was only one ring, which signified that the son who was given it would inherit the wealth of his family. But in one generation a man had three virtuous and obedient sons whom he loved equally. So he had two more rings made, each virtually indistinguishable from the first. According to this parable, God gave the three religions to equally beloved peoples; each carries out God's commandments, and, says Melchisedech, the question of which is the true heir remains unsettled. These tales demonstrate the possibility of displaying Jews in a distinctly positive light. Melchisedech's contentions about the status of Judaism, though placed in a distant setting, are nonetheless remarkable. And the affection between the Christian and the Jew in Neifile's tale is represented emphatically and without apology, firmly suggesting that Boccaccio's audience would have regarded such a relationship as unexceptionable.

A caveat: though some of the instances cited here evidence long-standing patterns, others are isolated and possibly exceptional. At least some of them may belie private conviction. Their cumulative testimony demonstrates, however, that the historical position and experience of the Jews were far more complex than the simple assumptions that the Prioress's Tale and its literary and theological matrix suggest. The degradation of the Jews of medieval Europe was widespread and often agonizing. But there were other views and other voices than the Prioress's, and several of them indicate that the horizons of potential tolerance were less drastically constricted than has sometimes been supposed.

Notes

1. *The Riverside Chaucer*, gen. ed. Larry Benson, 3d ed. (Boston: 1987), VII:467–72. All subsequent quotations from Chaucer's works are taken from this edition.

2. *The Myroure of oure Ladye*, EETS ES 19 (1873), ed. John Henry Blunt, p. 296.

3. The word *ravyshedest* in its primary sense suggests "took by force" and, most extremely, "raped." James Winny, for example, glosses the word as "seized, took possession of" (*The Prioress' Prologue and Tale* [Cambridge, 1975]). Even rendered in its mildest sense as "drew, attracted," this word attributes a far more active role to Mary than she has in the Gospel story (compare Latin *raptus* and Paul's use of the word in 2 Cor.

12:1–4). The verb *lighten* means not only "make light, render cheerful" or "illumine," the possible renderings in Robinson, or "cheer, gladden," the gloss in the *Chaucer Glossary*, but also "set on fire." These senses, following the image of the burning bush, sustain the paradox of sexualized asexuality that characterizes the passion of the prayer.

4. D. S. Brewer, *Chaucer* (London, 1953; rpt., 1961), p. 151.

5. E. T. Donaldson, *Chaucer's Poetry* (New York, 1958; rpt., 1975), p. 1096.

6. Alan T. Gaylord, "The Unconquered Tale of the Prioress," *Papers of the Michigan Academy of Science, Arts, and Letters* 47 (1962): 632; Ian Robinson, *Chaucer and the English Tradition* (Cambridge, 1972), p. 153.

7. D. W. Robertson, Jr., *A Preface to Chaucer* (Princeton, N.J., 1962), p. 246.

8. Gordon H. Harper, "Chaucer's Big Prioress," *Philological Quarterly* 12 (1933): 310.

9. Muriel Bowden, *A Commentary on the General Prologue to the Canterbury Tales*, 2d ed. (London, 1969), p. 95; Donaldson, *Chaucer's Poetry*, p. 1044; John Block Friedman, "The Prioress's Beads 'of Smal Coral,'" *Medium Aevum* 39 (1970): 301; cf. Thomas Blake Clark, "Forehead of Chaucer's Prioress," *Philological Quarterly* 9 (1930): 312–14.

10. Sister M. Madeleva, "Chaucer's Nuns," in *Chaucer's Nuns and Other Essays* (New York, 1925), p. 21ff.

11. G. K. Chesterton, *Chaucer* (London, 1932; rpt., 1965), pp. 202–3.

12. John Livingston Lowes, "Simple and Coy," *Anglia* 33 (1910): 440–51.

13. Madeleva, "Chaucer's Nuns," pp. 13–15.

14. Bowden, *Commentary*, p. 99; Jill Mann adds that medieval satirists traditionally contrasted excessive tenderness for animals with indifference to human suffering (*Chaucer and Medieval Estates Satire* [Cambridge, 1973], p. 132).

15. John M. Steadman, "The Prioress' Dogs and Benedictine Discipline," *Modern Philology* 54 (1956): 3.

16. Robertson, *Preface*, p. 246.

17. Chauncey Wood, "Chaucer's Use of Signs in His Portrait of the Prioress," in *Signs and Symbols in Chaucer's Poetry*, ed. John P. Hermann and John J. Burke, Jr. (University, Ala., 1981), pp. 89–91.

18. George Lyman Kittredge, *Chaucer and His Poetry* (Cambridge, Mass., 1925), pp. 175–78.

19. Chesterton, *Chaucer*, p. 171; Nevill Coghill, *The Poet Chaucer* (London, 1949), pp. 22, 138.

20. Florence H. Ridley, *The Prioress and the Critics* (Berkeley, Calif., 1965), p. 2.

21. John Livingston Lowes, "The Prioress's Oath," *Romanic Review* 5 (1914): 368; Lowes, "Simple and Coy," 442.

22. Sister Madeleva, "Chaucer's Nuns," says that the tale tells just the sort of story "that Sisters are telling to the smaller and even the grown children in Catholic boarding schools the world over to-day . . . that the children clamor for again and again and never tire of hearing" (pp. 37–38). Robert Kilburn Root, in discussing the Prioress's

Tale in 1906, attributed the "senseless persecution" of the Jews in European history to the "fact" that the Jews were rich while the Christians were poor. He added that the Christians' belief in the Jews' murderous practices "could hardly have sprung up without some sort of foundation" in fact (*The Poetry of Chaucer* [Boston, 1906], p. 191)! Thomas R. Lounsbury, by contrast, as early as 1891 denounced the "folly and fanaticism" that underlie the tale (*Studies in Chaucer* [New York, 1891; rpt., 1962], 2:490–91).

23. R. J. Schoeck, "Chaucer's Prioress: Mercy and Tender Heart," in *Chaucer Criticism*, ed. Richard Schoeck and Jerome Taylor (Notre Dame, Ind., 1960; rpt., 1965), I:245–58; George K. Anderson, "*Beowulf*, Chaucer, and Their Backgrounds," in *Contemporary Literary Scholarship*, ed. Lewis Leary (New York, 1958), p. 41. The term "anti-Semitism" is appropriate to a modern rather than a medieval context; see n. 51 below.

24. Donaldson notes that unlike the narrowly limited Prioress, Chaucer, an intelligent man and a great poet, was in no way limited (*Chaucer's Poetry*, p. 1097). Ian Robinson, *Chaucer and the English Tradition* (London, 1972), p. 152, says that it would be surprising if a responsible public servant like Chaucer were as simple-minded and savage as the Prioress. Alfred David, drawing the valid analogy between the tale and a fairy story, says that Chaucer, unlike the Prioress, is "very much aware that fairy-tale justice and Christian mercy are incompatible" (*The Strumpet Muse* [Bloomington, Ind., 1976], p. 209); Donald R. Howard in *The Idea of the Canterbury Tales* (Berkeley, Calif., 1976), p. 277, says that it is out of the question that the tolerant, open-minded, and empathetic Chaucer could have failed to note the Prioress's moral blindness.

25. Ridley, *The Prioress*, p. 5ff.; Albert B. Friedman, "The Prioress's Tale and Chaucer's Anti-Semitism," *Chaucer Review* 9 (1974–1975): 118–29.

26. Brewer, *Chaucer*, p. 151; David, *Strumpet Muse*, p. 207. Robert Worth Frank, Jr., observes that anti-Semitism is a standard constituent element in the genre of the Miracle of the Virgin ("Miracles of the Virgin, Medieval Anti-Semitism, and the Prioress's Tale," in *The Wisdom of Poetry: Essays in Early English Literature in Honor of Morton W. Bloomfield*, ed. Larry D. Benson and Siegfried Wenzel [Kalamazoo, Mich., 1982], p. 179).

27. Frank also cites examples of tolerance and benevolence toward Jews, however. See his "Chaucer's Prioress and the Blessed Virgin," *Chaucer Review* 13 (1978–1979): 355, 358. Compare Schoeck, "Chaucer's Prioress," pp. 255–56; and Howard, *Idea of the Canterbury Tales*, p. 279.

28. See Lee Patterson, *Negotiating the Past* (Madison, Wis., 1987), ch. 1. Patterson asserts (p. 74) that *The Canterbury Tales* stood in ideological opposition to the dominant formations of its period. I take this to support the contention I develop below that Chaucer need not have shared in the prevailing intolerance of his time.

29. James Parkes observes that Christian texts had, since the early days of the Church, portrayed Jews not in terms of their contemporary relationships or circumstances, but rather in accordance with their scriptural roles (*The Conflict of the Church and the Synagogue* [New York, 1969; rpt., 1977], pp. 220, 374f.). In Augustine's formulation, the

Jew remained doctrinally "stationary in useless antiquity." This characterization of
the Jew as frozen in time applied, of course, to the characterization itself. By the thirteenth century, however, Church scholars had to respond to the realization that Judaism had in fact evolved since the first century; see Jeremy Cohen's "Scholarship and
Intolerance in the Medieval Academy: The Study and Evaluation of Judaism in European Christendom," *American Historical Review* 91 (1986): 592–613.

30. This argument differs in emphasis from Donaldson's in his famous essay
"Chaucer the Pilgrim," which reaches somewhat different conclusions about the distinctions among Chaucer the pilgrim, the poet, and the man. Though these three
figures bore a close resemblance to one another and "frequently got together in the
same body," Donaldson says, Chaucer the poet subsumed the other two. Interestingly, much of this discussion treats the portrayal of the Prioress. Donaldson asserts
that Chaucer the man, like his pilgrim persona, would have found the Prioress
charming; Chaucer the poet, by contrast, noted her many imperfections and incor-
porated her inharmonious parts into an inseparable whole (*Publications of the Modern
Language Society* 69 [1954]: 928–36; reprinted in *Speaking of Chaucer* [New York, 1970], pp.
1–12). Responses to Donaldson have included the observation that writers project
some element of themselves into any character and the question as to whether anyone knows his "real" self well enough to present or conceal it (see Donald R.
Howard, "Chaucer the Man," *PMLA* 80 [1965]: 337–43; reprinted in *Chaucer's Mind and
Art*, ed. A. C. Cawley [New York, 1970], pp. 31–45). But the disjunction between the
suggestion of the poet's personality in the text and the historical indications about
Chaucer the man has also been noted. See, for example, George Kane, *Chaucer* (Oxford, 1984), pp. 9–10.

31. Gaylord, "Unconquered Tale" (p. 631), cites the brutality of attitude, action,
and imagery in the tale, and observes that the brutality of the Prioress's language in
the tale "tends to belie the total softness and sweetness of the lady who swears by Saint
Loy." Albert B. Friedman, "The Prioress's Tale," denies this and argues that the line "I
seye that in a wardrobe they hym threwe" (572) reveals the Prioress's "fastidious hesitation in mentioning this unpleasant but necessary detail" (p. 126). I disagree: the line
can equally well be read as charged with indignation.

32. John Lawlor, *Chaucer* (London, 1968), p. 131.

33. Edward H. Kelly, "By Mouth of Innocentz: The Prioress Vindicated," *Papers on
Language and Literature* 5 (1969): 363. In this essay I attempt to occupy a middle ground
between Kittredge's claim (*Chaucer and His Poetry*, p. 155) that the tales exist for the
sake of developing the pilgrims as characters, and more recent arguments that the
pilgrims are not recognizably motivated characters. I contend that in portraying
the Prioress, Chaucer developed a stock literary figure in surprising ways, in part
by matching her with a tale that both inspired and complicated his characterization
of her.

34. Donaldson, *Chaucer's Poetry*, p. 1097. Cf. Howard, *Idea of the Canterbury Tales*, who says that the Prioress's simplicity and air of elegance lead her into a deplorable frame of mind (p. 276).

35. Bertrand H. Bronson, *In Search of Chaucer* (Toronto, 1960), p. 78.

36. Gaylord, "Unconquered Tale," p. 632; Robinson, p. 150.

37. See Marie Padgett Hamilton, "Echoes of Childermas in the Tale of the Prioress," in *Chaucer: Modern Essays in Criticism*, ed. Edward Wagenknecht (New York, 1959), pp. 88–97.

38. Audrey Davidson notes the unusual beauty of the *Alma redemptoris mater* and its emphasis on the motherliness of Mary, factors that make the anthem appropriate in a tale told by Madame Eglentyne ("*Alma Redemptoris Mater*: The Little Clergeon's Song," *Studies in Medieval Culture* 4 [1974]: 459–66).

39. See Beverly Boyd, "Young Hugh of Lincoln and Chaucer's The Prioress's Tale," *Radford Review* 14 (1960): 1–5.

40. Donald W. Fritz interprets this assertion in terms of the topos of the "inexpressible" in "The Prioress's Avowal of Ineptitude," *Chaucer Review* 9 (1974–1975): 166–81.

41. Other scholars have also noted the Prioress's affinity with the child, but have reached different conclusions from mine. Gaylord, in his perceptive and good-humored "The Unconquered Tale of the Prioress" (p. 634), says that the Prioress keeps the tale at the emotional and intellectual level of a child, evidencing her "arrested development." Maurice Cohen says that Eglentyne's sadomasochism toward the Jews is anal-erotic ("Chaucer's Prioress and Her Tale: A Study of Anal Character and Anti-Semitism," *Psychoanalytic Quarterly* 31 [1962]: 232–49). Sherman Hawkins takes her spiritual childishness as the starting point for the *clergeon* too, and develops a learned patristic argument about the child's spiritual growth: the pit and the murder represent, he says, the literal understanding of Scripture and death to the law ("Chaucer's Prioress and the Sacrifice of Praise," *JEGP* 63 [1964]: 599–624). Albert B. Friedman ("The Prioress's Tale," pp. 124–25) concludes that the Prioress's sentimental sympathy with the *clergeon* leads her to enter too completely into the child's world and to identify with him. He attributes this only to a lack of mature judgment, however, and rejects Gaylord's interpretation of arrested development; he adds that Bronson's assertion that sentimentality is the obverse of cruelty is not relevant here. George J. Engelhardt conjectures that the Prioress, assuming the persona of the child, imagines herself singing unto death the plaint of litigation over the redemption of her convent's liberties ("The Ecclesiastical Pilgrims of *The Canterbury Tales*: A Study in Ethology," *Mediaeval Studies* 37 [1975]: 292–93). And Robert W. Hanning adopts a very interesting feminist perspective, in which the Jews and the child's teachers represent male domination and authority, and the tale expresses the Prioress's vulnerability to men ("From *Eva* and *Ave* to Eglentyne and Alisoun: Chaucer's Insight into the Roles Women Play," *Signs* 2 [1977]: 580–99). I attribute to the Jews their more traditional religious significance.

42. As Gavin I. Langmuir says, psychological (as opposed to cognitive) explanations of intolerance rely heavily on the Freudian concepts of displacement and projection ("Prolegomena to Any Present Analysis of Hostility against Jews," *Social Science Information* 15 [1976]: 701). For a review of Sarte's use of this theory and its application to medieval biblical drama, see Stephen Spector, "Anti-Semitism and the English Mystery Plays," in *The Drama of the Middle Ages*, ed. Clifford Davidson, C. J. Gianakaris, and John H. Stroupe (New York, 1982), pp. 329–30. Freud himself proposed that anti-Semitism is projected resentment against the Church by the "badly christened": those who had Christianity forced on them and deal with their own hostility by identifying similar sentiments in the Jews and vilifying them for it. See Sigmund Freud, *Moses and Monotheism*, trans. Katherine Jones (New York, 1939; rpt., 1967), pp. 116–17.

43. Spector, "Anti-Semitism and the English Mystery Plays," pp. 328–41.

44. One could argue in Derridean terms that the invagination of the text creates a marginal graft, thereby dislocating the text and undermining the narrative intention.

45. Hardy Long Frank, in his fine discussion of the ambiguity in Madame Eglentyne's name, cites two figurative references to the Virgin as the eglantine in the poetry of Gautier de Coinci. In the present context, however, the contrast between the floral symbols is appropriate to the dichotomy between the Prioress and Mary.

46. The Wife's impulse to join in marriages that inevitably result in struggle recalls the joining of restless elements in Chaucer's art itself.

47. Salo Wittmayor Baron comments that when considered as "a single list of pogroms and expulsions, the attacks on Jews appear indeed as an uninterrupted succession of catastrophes. But one must realize that during the thirteenth century (until 1290 in England and 1298 in Germany) there were but relatively few local anti-Jewish attacks with little bearing on Jewish conditions elsewhere. . . . Only the Black Death generated a mass hysteria . . . which had ominous implications for the very survival of European Jewry. . . . However, the then most populous Jewish settlements in Spain, Sicily, southern France, and the Papal States, as well as in Bohemia, Hungary, and Poland, suffered relatively little" (*A Social and Religious History of the Jews*, 2d ed. [New York, 1967], 11:281–82).

48. Guido Kisch argues, however, that nationalism in the modern sense of the word did not influence the treatment of the medieval Jew (*The Jews in Medieval Germany* [Chicago, 1949], pp. 335–37).

49. The Jews and the devil were represented as having a common interest in maintaining the old law. For popular beliefs about the Jews' supposed association with the devil and the Antichrist, see especially Joshua Trachtenberg, *The Devil and the Jews* (New Haven, Conn., 1943).

50. Not all angels wear halos: Gentiles who risked their lives to save Jews during the 1940s sometimes seemed to be unlikely choices for their roles. Many Jews survived the Holocaust because of the protection of the German industrialist Oskar Schindler,

for example. They had good reason to be grateful that the brave and resourceful—but not conventionally moral or religious—Schindler was more faithful to his Jews than to his wife; see Thomas Keneally, *Schindler's List* (New York, 1982). The influence of the Protestant pastor André Trocmé constitutes a partial explanation of why the people of Le Chambon courageously protected Jewish children while other French villagers took no such risk; see Philip P. Hallie, *Lest Innocent Blood Be Shed* (New York, 1979).

51. The etiology of modern anti-Semitism is complex and disputed, but I use the term here as a means of distinction from medieval anti-Jewishness. Langmuir ("Prolegomena," p. 691) asserts that the hostility against Jews about 1900 was very similar to the hostility about 1400; and to the recipient, hostility no doubt does feel the same regardless of its rationalization. But medieval hostility to Jewishness was in large measure theologically inspired: the putative defects it attributed to the Jew could, at least in theory, be washed away by baptism. The most virulent modern "anti-Semitism," by contrast, postulates Jewish racial inferiority that cannot be effaced. Hitler, for example, denounced religiously based political anti-Jewishness as sham anti-Semitism (Lucy S. Dawidowicz, *The War against the Jews 1933–1945* [New York, 1975; rpt., 1978], ch. 1). The term "anti-Semitism," in the sense that Hitler used it, would be anachronistic in discussing medieval attitudes. Another term, "ritual-blood libel," is also inappropriate to the Prioress's Tale, which does not refer to the ritualized slaughter of a Christian child at Passover. The genre of the tale is miracle of the Virgin.

52. One cannot discover the essence of Jewish-Christian relations in a brief survey of the present kind, and that is not my purpose here in any case. I intend only to refute the globally negative assertions about the possibility of amity and respect toward Jews during the period under consideration. I therefore present chiefly positive evidence.

53. Neither legislators nor jurists attempted to define Jewish serfdom clearly. Jews were also referred to as *servitus Judaeorum* and as chests (*cofres*), or treasures, of the king (Baron, *Social and Religious History*, 11:4–5).

54. Jacob Katz, *Exclusiveness and Tolerance* (New York, 1961), p. 6. In this argument Katz depends on Kisch, *Germany*, pp. 119–28.

55. Israel Abrahams says that twelfth-century Jews read Christian love songs and ballads (*Jewish Life in the Middle Ages* [Philadelphia, 1896; rpt., New York, 1978], p. 361). H. H. Ben-Sasson adds that the influence of Christian romances led the author of the *Sefer Hasidim* to draw a comparison between service to God and a knight's loyalty to his lord (*A History of the Jewish People* [Cambridge, Mass., 1969; English translation, 1976], p. 555). It is worth noting in a study of the Prioress's Tale that despite its negative stereotypes about Christian morality, the *Sefer Hasidim* holds the life of Gentiles sacred. It adds that if a Jew is conspiring against a Gentile, every other Jew must foil the plot (see Katz, *Exclusiveness and Tolerance*, p. 101, who follows F. Y. Baer in his discussion of this book). Katz (p. 93) and Ben-Sasson (p. 546) note shared, or at least parallel, religious movements between Jews and Christians.

56. Kisch observes that Jews in northern France dressed indistinguishably from Christians from the twelfth to the fourteenth century, and typically walked bareheaded. In Germany and the rest of Central Europe, by contrast, Jews were distinguished by their horned hats, which they wore of their own free will according to old tradition, as well as by their beards. The famous thirteenth-century miniature of the Jewish minnesinger Süsskind von Trimberg, for example, shows him in fashionable dress except for his pointed hat and beard. In Spain and Italy, Jews had assimilated in dress, though Johannes Purgoldt's early sixteenth-century German law book asserts that Italian Jews were required to wear different clothes from those of Christians. See Kisch, *Germany*, pp. 296–98, and *Forschungen zur Rechts-, Wirtschafts- und Sozialgeschichte der Juden* (Sigmaringen, 1979), pp. 119–20; also Baron, *Social and Religious History*, 11:101, 137. For their own safety, Jews wore the same clothes as Gentiles when traveling, and sometimes even dressed as priests and nuns! (See Ben-Sasson, *History*, p. 623; also Kisch, *Forschungen*, p. 118.) Jews achieved a high degree of linguistic assimilation in their host countries, though dialect differences eventually emerged under the influence of Hebrew and talmudic thinking (Baron, *Social and Religious History*, 11:188, 377n.). Bernhard Blumenkranz observes that Rashi used some 2,000 French words in his biblical and talmudic commentaries and demonstrated a perfect mastery of French (*Histoire des Juifs en France*, ed. Edouard Privat [Toulouse, 1972], p. 26). Kisch says that Jews employed the German language of their native province to annotate and translate Scripture (*Germany*, p. 309). Abrahams (*Jewish Life*, p. 425) notes that Jews in the late Middle Ages also bore the same names as Christians. But compare Blumenkranz, pp. 27–28.

57. The Jew badge was required in 1215 because in many provinces Jews were indistinguishable from Christians and so might "by error" have intercourse with them (see Baron, *Social and Religious History*, 9:28). The badge was not generally worn in France until 1269 and in Castile until the mid-fourteenth century. In Italy, distinguishing marks were common only in the fifteenth century (though earlier in Sicily). In Germany, the distinctive Jewish hat was made obligatory in the thirteenth century; the hat obviated the need for a badge, and no mention is made of the red or yellow wheel as Jewish badge until the fifteenth century. See Kisch, *Forschungen*, pp. 126–27, and *Germany*, pp. 296–97; also Cecil Roth, *A History of the Jews* (New York, 1954; rev. ed., 1970), p. 277.

58. See Baron, *Social and Religious History*, 11:186. In Provence, ca. 1300, R. Menahem Ha-Me'iri said that gift giving to Christians was not only permissible but meritorious (Katz, *Exclusiveness and Tolerance*, p. 117). See R. Israel Isserlein's similar position, discussed below.

59. Quoted from Abrahams, *Jewish Life*, p. 420. It is worth noting that Dante expressed an antagonistic position toward Jews as a people when he urged Pope Boniface VIII to make war on the Jews and Saracens rather than on the Colonnas (Baron, *Social and Religious History*, 11:131).

60. Baron, *Social and Religious History*, 11:81. In Spain, the Church too tried to prevent such illicit relations (see Baron, 9:26).

61. In one noteworthy case, the provost of Paris, Hughes Aubriot, was denounced in 1381 for alleged sexual relations with Jewish women, as well as for allowing baptized Jewish children to be returned to the Jews (see Baron, *Social and Religious History*, 11:85, who concedes that such allegations could have been political; also 11:80). Noting that sexual contacts between Jews and Christians were often cited to demonstrate "la tendance habituelle des Juifs à la débauche," Blumenkranz cites the act of contrition presented in 1300 by Bonfils, "Juif de la Grasse, pour s'excuser des 'crimes quil avoit commis iusqua ce iour la en iouant ou en baisant, embrassant ou connoissant les femmes chrestiennes' " (*Histoire des Juifs*, p. 49).

62. Baron, *Social and Religious History*, 11:186. Abrahams (*Jewish Life*, p. 425) cites the instance of a German knight who reportedly removed the crucifix from his mantel on the frequent occasions that he received Jewish visitors. This, of course, may represent nothing more than an isolated case of politic behavior.

63. Isserlein's ruling on the cakes gave Jews general permission to eat bread prepared by Gentile bakers, except during the ten days of repentance between the New Year and the Day of Atonement (Baron, *Social and Religious History*, 11:186–87).

64. See Abrahams, *Jewish Life*, p. 409; and Baron, *Social and Religious History*, 9:26.

65. Baron, *Social and Religious History*, 11:85. Such illicit relationships continued in Germany: one German law book of ca. 1500 provided that children born to a Jewish father and a Christian mother be removed from the father, baptized, and educated at the father's expense (Kisch, *Germany*, p. 207).

66. Baron, *Social and Religious History*, 11:81, 241; Abrahams, *Jewish Life*, p. 428.

67. Chaucer's response, if he did meet Jews, would also be wholly conjectural. He might have had contact with Jews in 1366, when he was granted a three-month safe conduct in Navarre. This trip may have been connected with the Black Prince's alliance with King Pedro in the civil war in Castile, and perhaps concerned the recall of English mercenaries serving Pedro's opponent, Henry of Trastamara. If Chaucer had dealings with either party, he may well have had contact with Jews. Pedro's court physician and royal treasurer were Jewish, and Henry called Pedro the "Judaized king," who confided only in Jews. Henry for his part was later noted for having many Jewish officials and intimates, and during his reign Jews were accorded great liberty and power in the royal household. Chaucer could also have encountered Jews in France, where one Jewish family was received with esteem at the court of Charles V at the time of Chaucer's diplomatic missions to Paris, Montreuil, and "parts of France" (if, in fact, Chaucer did conduct these missions in 1377, as Froissart reports). Chaucer could have met Jews in Italy, where, Abrahams tells us, friendships between Christians and Jews extended into literary circles. And he may even have come into contact with Jews in England, where they occasionally came to the attention of the court. In

1390, a Sicilian Jew was baptized in the presence of Richard II. In 1392, according to Montagu Frank Modder, a Jewish physician was called to the court to attend Richard. And during most of Chaucer's lifetime, a *domus conversorum* was occupied by converted Jews on the street now known as Chancery Lane in London. Essentially a royal institution, the *domus*, at least earlier in the century, had attracted the warm interest of the king. See Baron, *Social and Religious History*, 11:122, 231; Heinrich Graetz, *History of the Jews* (Philadelphia, 1894; rpt., 1941), 4:129, 150; *Chaucer Life-Records*, ed. Martin M. Crow and Clair C. Olson (Oxford, 1966), pp. 44–53; Haldeen Braddy, "Froissart's Account of Chaucer's Embassy in 1377," *Review of English Studies* 14 (1938): 63–67; Martin M. Crow and Virginia E. Leland, "Chaucer's Life," in *Riverside Chaucer*, pp. xvii–xviii; Leon Poliakov, *The History of Anti-Semitism* (New York, 1961; rpt., 1973), 2:150–51; John A. Crow, *Spain* (New York, 1963), p. 110; Michael Adler, *Jews of Medieval England* (London, 1939), pp. 307–39; Albert M. Hyamson, *A History of the Jews in England* (London, 1908), pp. 127, 130–31; and Montagu Frank Modder, *The Jew in the Literature of England* (Philadelphia, 1944), p. 12 (cited by Ridley, *The Prioress*, p. 13).

68. For a more developed argument that the Jews "were not viewed as ministers of Satan by those Englishmen capable of moral reflection," see Richard Rex, "Chaucer and the Jews," *Modern Language Quarterly* 45 (1984): 107–22.

69. See Schoeck, "Chaucer's Prioress," p. 256; *Piers the Plowman*, ed. Walter W. Skeat (London, 1886; rpt., 1965), B.IX.81–88. Ridley (*The Prioress*, p. 10) correctly points out that in this passage, Langland cites the Jews' virtue in order to shame Christians for failing to behave as well as "Iudas felawes" did (IX.84).

70. See G. R. Owst, *Literature and Pulpit in Medieval England* (Oxford, 1933; rpt., 1966), pp. 177, 418; and his letter to the *Jewish Guardian* (London), 6 August 1926, p. 5 (cited by Rex, "Chaucer and the Jews," pp. 115–16).

71. Cf. Rex, "Chaucer and the Jews," who says (p. 115) that Chaucer must have heard Brunton sermonize on numerous occasions. Rex observes that Gower praised Jews for observing the sabbath. In response to claims that the *Confessio Amantis* is anti-Jewish, Rex cites Ruth M. Ames, "The Source and Significance of 'The Jew and the Pagan,'" *Mediaeval Studies* 19 (1957): 37–47; and notes Gower's praise for "the good Jew Mordecai" in *Mirour de l'Omme*.

72. Rex's admirable and well-intentioned survey attributes this view of salvation to *Mandeville's Travels* and the Parson's Tale, but the passages he cites from these texts do not explicitly demonstrate this point. Compare Ridley's discussion (*The Prioress*, pp. 10–11) of Langland's position on the salvation of the Jews. R. W. Southern considers the growing concern to include unbelievers in the scheme of salvation to be "one of the most attractive features of the period" (*Western Views of Islam in the Middle Ages*, 2d. ed. [Cambridge, Mass., 1978], p. 76; cited by Rex, "Chaucer and the Jews," p. 118).

73. See Kisch, *Germany*, pp. 325, 539–40.

74. Although there is no proof that Chaucer ever read the *Decameron*, it was, as Larry Benson observes, the most famous prose work of his favorite Italian poet. He must have heard of it, and it may well have offered suggestions that inspired the frame of *The Canterbury Tales* (*Riverside Chaucer*, p. 3).

Further Reading

The question of anti-Semitism (or anti-Judaism) has dominated most recent criticism of the Prioress's Tale. In "Postcolonial Chaucer and the Virtual Jew," in *The Postcolonial Middle Ages*, edited by Jeffrey Jerome Cohen (New York, 2000), pp. 243–60, Sylvia Tomasch argues that the tale's anti-Semitism is a function of Chaucer's own views. On the other hand, Lee Patterson, " 'The Living Witnesses of Our Redemption': Martyrdom and Imitation in Chaucer's Prioress's Tale," in his *Temporal Circumstances: Form and History in* The Canterbury Tales (New York, 2006), argues that Chaucer distances himself from the Prioress and provides a historically informed account of the blood libel that figured so prominently in medieval anti-Semitism. Other perspectives on this issue are provided by Sheila Delany, ed., *Chaucer and the Jews: Sources, Contexts, Meanings* (London, 2002); Steven F. Kruger, "The Bodies of Jews in the Late Middle Ages," in *The Idea of Medieval Literature: New Essays on Chaucer and Medieval Culture in Honor of Donald R. Howard*, edited by James M. Dean and Christian Zacher (Newark, N.J., 1992), pp. 301–23; and Richard Rex, *The Sins of Madame Eglentyne and Other Essays on Chaucer* (Newark, N.J., 1995). Bruce W. Holsinger, "Pedagogy, Violence, and the Subject of Music: Chaucer's Prioress's Tale and the Ideologies of 'Song,' " *New Medieval Literatures* 1 (1997): 157–92, argues that the violence of medieval pedagogy is a central aspect of the violence of the tale as a whole.

A Reading of the Nun's Priest's Tale

DEREK PEARSALL

◆ ◆ ◆

THERE HAS HARDLY BEEN A time when the Nun's Priest's Tale has not been appreciated as one of the wittiest and most accomplished poems in the English language. Readers have been delighted by its inexhaustible ingenuity and inventiveness and by its irreverent mockery of the solemn apparatus of human learning and rhetoric; they have warmed to its generous portrayal of the all-too-human foibles and weaknesses of its barnyard hero. If one were looking for Chaucer's most perfect poem—not the one with the loftiest ambitions but the one that most fully achieves the ideas implied in its form—it would certainly be a serious rival to Coleridge's choice, the Miller's Tale. It is a tale also of hidden depths, shoals for the unwary, unplumbable abysses of multiple signification. The development in recent years of more sophisticated techniques of literary analysis has been notable for the light it has thrown on this most sophisticated of Chaucer's poems, but it is likely to remain elusive. Elusiveness is indeed its character, and the life and wisdom it contains are of a kind that must necessarily defy formulation. It is not always easy to resist the temptation to substitute an interpretive paraphrase for one's lived experience of reading a work of literature. The Nun's Priest's Tale, in fact, offers us an explicit invitation to do just that ("Taketh the moralite . . ."). But the effect of accepting the invitation is not merely to miss the joke but to become the butt of it. As in all the best comedy, there is a sharp edge for all pretense and affectation in the midst of the warmth and gaiety. The purpose of this essay, therefore, is not to present an "interpretation" of the poem but to offer some broad lines of approach and some broader contexts in which it may be more fully understood.

Chaucer's knowledge of the fable of the cock and the fox is derived from two sources: a version of the fable as it is told briefly by Marie de France and a version of the episode as it appears in the *Roman de Renart*.[1] At times, the story line that he chooses to follow bears a striking resemblance to that in Marie, and he may have had direct knowledge of her work, though it is possible that his direct knowledge was derived from a version of the fable in a preacher's handbook of exempla. Chaucer's direct knowledge of *Renart* is a more vexed question, given the very small amount of evidence that the work was circulated or well known in England. On the other hand, there are direct verbal parallels with *Renart* which are almost impossible to explain except in terms of Chaucer's familiarity with a written copy of the work or part of the work. It is difficult to believe, for example, that the French forms of expression which provide the basis for these parallels would have survived any intermediary form of oral circulation in England, though it is known that this particular story was popular in England. Chaucer may have known the episode from *Renart* in the form of a copy detached from the main beast epic, but there is some evidence of familiarity with the poem in its full or in a fuller form. The conclusion must be that Chaucer's knowledge of continental literature was, in this case, as in the case of his knowledge of Machaut, Petrarch, and Boccaccio, quite exceptional for his age and that he cannot ever be judged by the norms of expectation for the fourteenth century.

For the accessory paraphernalia of the story and the scatter of allusions to a wide range of learned material, it is clear that Chaucer drew on the riches of a well-stocked mind and a wide reading. The most striking conclusion, however, to emerge from an examination of the sources for the nonnarrative material of the poem is the frequency with which Chaucer returns to some favorite encyclopedic ragbags. The evidence for his extensive knowledge and use of Holkot's commentary on the Book of Wisdom and of the encyclopedic works of Vincent of Beauvais is conclusive, and there are no doubt other, similar works, still to be examined, that he plundered.[2] In this respect, Chaucer's reading is unexpectedly old-fashioned, and the tastes which stimulated that reading (for we can hardly imagine that he read such works solely to provide raw material for his poetry) unexpectedly "medieval." Nevertheless, the literary use to which he put his reading in the Nun's Priest's Tale is one of the supreme examples in our literature of the transmutation of base metal into purest gold.

The existence of the two forms of the Monk–Nun's Priest link can serve to introduce a discussion of the interpretation of the poem. There is no doubt that the existence of the two forms of the link has provided excellent opportunities for the elucidation of Chaucer's developing intentions in fragment VII. The role of the tale as the climax to the longest integrated sequence of tales in the whole of *The Canterbury Tales* can be shown to be thereby reinforced, and a further interest added to the tale in terms of its place in the framework of the tales. In particular, the expansion of the link gives added point, in the Knight's remarks (the original short form was designed for the Host alone), to the emphatic contrast between the Nun's Priest's Tale and the Monk's Tale. This contrast is, in any analysis, an important part of the full meaning of the Nun's Priest's Tale, and the Knight's observations hint, without any laboring of the point, at the laughable inadequacy of "tragedy," at least as it is conceived in the Monk's Tale, and prepare us for the wise and humane accommodation of comedy, as it is evidenced in the Nun's Priest's Tale.

It is necessary to stress, however—and this is the first of a series of objections to a mode of reading now unfortunately all too current—that the primary effectiveness of the contrast between the two tales is in the juxtaposition of the tales as tales, and not in any dramatically conceived confrontation between the Monk and the Nun's Priest as characters. It is possible to see that Chaucer intends us to derive some amusement from the contrast between the Monk and the Nun's Priest, especially the contrast between their horses (the only thing he specifically tells us about the Nun's Priest is that he rides "a jade . . . bothe foul and lene"), but to see the Nun's Priest's Tale as a satire on the Monk's Tale, directed personally by the Nun's Priest against the Monk and prompted by outrage at the latter's ostentation, jealousy of his high position in the ecclesiastical establishment, or contempt for his stupidity, is to deny the essential quality of the tale's humor. To see the Nun's Priest's Tale, further, as the outcome of the Nun's Priest's desire to please the Host or to annoy the Prioress is to make it merely trivial. The humor of the tale, its raison d'être, resides in the "incompetent" mode of narration, in the superb display of irrelevant skills. It can hardly delight us in this way and at the same time be working toward a satirical objective planned and directed by the Nun's Priest as narrator. Even if the two ways of reading the tale are considered to be not completely incompatible, there is no doubt that the latter pales into insignificance compared with the former; it is, indeed, banal. The satirical objectives in the tale are Chaucer's, and the Nun's Priest is his stalking-horse. It could have been anyone, or it could have been, if this were not *The Canterbury Tales*, no

one—in other words, that familiar figure, Chaucer-the-narrator. Any interpretation of the tale that puts the Nun's Priest in the foreground, instead of
leaving him in the background where Chaucer put him, has lost touch with
the important matter of the poem.

As far as the "dramatic" reading of *The Canterbury Tales* is concerned, the
Nun's Priest's Tale is not an extreme or exceptional case, but rather an excep-
tionally clear demonstration of the norm. Chaucer contrived the scheme of
The Canterbury Tales because he wanted it, and he seizes joyfully on the opportunities of dramatic interchange offered by the framework and the links. But
he rarely pursues such matters much beyond the opening lines of a tale, and
no sensible reader would want to pursue them for him, without prompting.
For Chaucer, it is sufficient to have created successfully the illusion that the
narration of a tale is someone else's responsibility. That is the source of his
freedom in the tales and the secret of the artistic energy released there. The
return to the pilgrimage framework at the end of a tale is most often like the
awakening from a dream or, to be more exact, like the return to an illusion of
reality after the experience of a superior reality. It is true that there are occasions in some of the tales when a shadowy projection of the narrator and his
character and circumstances becomes momentarily visible. There is such a
moment in the Nun's Priest's Tale, when the narrator hurriedly disclaims any
intention of dispraising women (4450–4456): it seems highly unlikely that we
are not here invited to recall the Nun's Priest and his relation to the Prioress.
But that is as far as it goes, a sauce to the meal; to pursue interpretation beyond that would be to mistake the sauce for the meal.

The proliferation of "dramatic" interpretations of the tale and the prodi-
gious ingenuity of speculation which has gone into the making of them are
not the products of mere perversity. They have to do with a modern preoccu-
pation with character in literature, and especially with that kind of interest in
character which uses literary texts as a point of departure for groundless speculation about what fictional persons would have been doing if the author had
remembered to tell us. Such readings are very easy to manufacture, since all
they need is an elementary knowledge of human nature and some interest in
mild personality disorders. They need none of the hard work on text, tradition, and genre that might enable us to glimpse, however briefly, the authentic meaning of a poem.

The dramatic interpretation of the Nun's Priest's Tale, however, receives so
strikingly little sustenance from the tale itself that a further explanation of its
popularity seems to be called for. It might be regarded as a simple refuge from
the bewilderment created by the dazzling and many-faceted brilliance of the
tale, but it has much to do, I think, with a misconceived interpretation of the

role of the incompetent narrator. The tale evidently has an incompetent narrator, but to associate this incompetence with the intentions, achieved or unachieved, of a dramatically conceived character is to wreck the whole design of the poem.

To speak of the "incompetence" of the narrator in the tale may seem a dangerous game to play, since there could be nothing more tedious than a genuinely incompetently told tale. What we have in the Nun's Priest's Tale is rather a superbly competent narrator who is telling the wrong tale, or at least telling the right tale the wrong way. It is like a fireworks display that has gotten into the hands of a pyromaniac. It is very important to stress this quality of misdirected competence in the tale, since a number of mistakes have been made in the interpretation of it by readers who are unfamiliar with the techniques of burlesque or the mock-heroic. A case in point is the brief discourse on predestination and free will with which the narrator embellishes his story of Chauntecler's fall (4424–40). This discourse, often described as confused and tortuous by critics, is in fact extremely clear and succinct, a model précis of current views on the theology of predestination. It could hardly have been better done. What has us helpless with laughter is that it should be done at all, in relation to a cock and a fox. The narrator does not, and must not, realize how funny he appears if the comedy is to remain buoyed up; he must have no intention but to tell the tale to the best of his ability. Frequently, his sententious itch is his undoing. As he continues after the last passage referred to, for instance, he has an irresistible urge to moralize on the misfortunes that await a man if he takes a woman's advice (4442–49). The shadow of the Fall descends on the sunlit farmyard, and the prognosis for Chauntecler, it seems, is gloomy. But, of course, the narrator has misinterpreted his own story (and has been followed up the same blind alley by a number of equally sententious modern interpreters), for Chauntecler's problems are caused not by taking women's advice but by not taking his own (4341–43), and what sways him from his own good judgment of the matter is Pertelote's beauty, not her advice. His tale is a truer analogy for, and a more truly comic distortion of, the story of the Fall than he thought, just as his jokes (as about the book of Launcelot [4402]) are funnier than he realizes.

In much of this there are striking parallels between the narrator and his chief character, Chauntecler. Chauntecler is a superbly competent cock, though no songster, and he is an excellent scholar. His analysis of the oracular and significative power of dreams is a model of scholarly discourse, complete with full illustration, citation of authority, and judicious balancing of the evidence (4321). It is not only persuasive but true—true in terms of the weight of medieval authority on the subject and true in the event. Within his discourse, two exempla are told that demonstrate the art of laconic narrative at its most starkly portentous, especially the tale of the murdered man in the dung cart. We are close here to the excellences of the Pardoner's exemplum.[3] It is all very much to the point, and those critics have missed the point completely who complain that Chauntecler is rambling on aimlessly or that he has forgotten his argument in stressing the theme of "Mordre wol out" (4242) or, worse, that the Nun's Priest is satirizing the presence of this theme in the tale of his Prioress. It is essential to the story, on the contrary, that Chauntecler should be doing what he does to the top of his bent; only if this is recognized is the full comedy of the situation released, which is that Chauntecler, for all his eloquence, takes no notice at all of what he says and that furthermore, of course, he could not possibly be saying it (being a cock). Chauntecler's jokes, too, like the narrator's, misfire. He is very pleased with himself for getting the better of Pertelote with a polite mistranslation of an antifeminist tag (4356), and he shares with us a patronizing snigger, but what he does not realize is that his mistranslation is really a true translation: woman is man's confusion because she is his joy and bliss.[4]

What I have outlined so far are some of the basic requirements of burlesque or mock-heroic, which I take to be the genre of the tale. The mention of the allusion to the Fall, however, is a reminder that many modern interpreters would regard laughter as a very poor reward for the effort expended in reading the tale. Starting from the narrator's own injunction to "take the moralitee" (4630), they have subjected the tale to moralistic interpretation or even to systematic allegorical interpretation in the endeavor to extract a lesson that will confirm a certain set of moral and religious values. That the tale is shot through with allusion to serious matters is something no one could deny, and I shall argue presently that the tale has a serious (though very funny) meaning. But the determination of modern interpreters to bend the tale to the exemplification of a single moral or allegorical intent is destructive of its very fabric and has led to some excesses of overinterpretation which are as preposterous as the tale itself.[5] With this said, it must be recognized that moral and allegorical interpretation of the Nun's Priest's Tale has contributed significantly to the fuller understanding of the tale. Those critics, for instance, who have analyzed the aptness of the portrayal of Chauntecler as an image of male vanity, or of the triumph of the lower nature of man over his higher, have certainly recognized an important element in our enjoyment of the tale. The consistent, witty, and generous humanity of the tale is one of its characteristically Chaucerian marvels, but there is no lesson to be learned from this, no little nugget of "moralitee" which we can hoard away for our better edification. For one thing, Chauntecler escapes from the plight his folly has brought him to by the exercise not of his higher reason but of his low cunning, of a technique of flattery that he has learned from his deceiver. There is no lesson to be learned from this, except by animals. Likewise, the presentation of Chauntecler's folly is not true satire, since it is not done from the point of view of a standard of moral values that could be called normative. Moralistic interpreters often comment on Chauntecler's uxoriousness and his fondness for nonprocreative love play (4333) as the cause of his downfall. It will be seen, however, that there are no standards by which we can judge of this matter in relation to cocks and hens—a reasonably continent cock would be no cock at all. Here, as often in the tale, Chaucer employs the juxtapositions of beast fable, the constant switching from awareness of the animals as human to ludicrous awareness of the animals as animal, to deflate pompous interpretations and to snag morality. The embarrassing surfeit of "morals" we are offered at the end of the tale hints at the inadequacy of easy moralizing.

Moralistic interpreters of the poem may be said to have missed its point, but with nothing like the resounding finality with which it has been missed by the exegetical interpreters. At the same time, exegetical interpretation has been valuable in alerting us to allusions and levels of meaning that do indeed need recovery. The ideas of the cock as preacher, or of the fox as diabolical seducer, are certainly present in the tale by implication, as is the explicit series of allusions to the Fall. The effect of this, however, is not to set out for us a diagram of salvation but to take us deeper into the comedy of the tale, and particularly to allow us to enjoy the rich humor of the comedy of survival converted to the comedy of salvation. The inspiration for Chaucer's laughter here has long been neglected but has recently been exposed in a number of essays on Chaucer's debt to the preachers' use of beast fables.[6] It is only in the knowledge of this characteristically medieval exemplary material that we can appreciate how exactly Chaucer caricatures the absurdities of allegorized fable, the joyful irrelevance of stories that have no point matched with allegories that do not work.

To recognize that the tale has no point is the start of understanding. I do not mean by this that it lacks the power to satisfy certain basic appetites that we expect to have satisfied in traditional narratives. In this tale, that appetite is satisfied by the theme of reversal, or "the biter bit."[7] But this is a fact of life, not a point. At the same time, we cannot feel entirely content with a recognition that the tale has no point, and we can perhaps express something more of our response to it by saying that the fact that the tale has no point is the point of the tale. The edifice of human understanding is a noble thing, and the arts of language and rhetoric and learning that bring it into being are noble arts. But man has a tendency to skulk inside this edifice, to mistake it for the reality of his observed world instead of a manmade model of that reality. In the tale, Chaucer takes a few bricks out of the building and allows it to drop around our ears, laughing uncontrollably meanwhile. In so doing, he restores a pristine and uncolored quality to our perception of the nature of language and rhetoric and learning and enables us to see the tricks that we play with them to preserve our high opinion of ourselves.[8] He does so by means of a trick. This surely is a point worth taking, and one specially to be taken by a generation of critics and interpreters who are as fond of telling us what is good for us as were any of Chaucer's preachers.

Notes

1. [The *Lais* of Marie de France were composed in Anglo-Norman in the late twelfth century; the *Roman de Renart*, compiled between 1170 and 1150, was the product of a number of French poets.]

2. [Robert A. Pratt, "Some Latin Sources of the Nonnes Preest on Dreams," *Speculum* 52 (1977): 538–70, argues that a commentary on the biblical Book of Wisdom by Robert Holcot (d. 1349) is one of Chaucer's primary sources; for Vincent of Beauvais, a thirteenth-century compiler of a widely known encyclopedia, see Pauline Aiken, "Vincent of Beauvais and Dame Pertelot's Knowledge of Medicine," *Speculum* 10 (1935): 281–87.]

3. Pratt, "Some Latin Sources," 531–33, has shown clearly how Chaucer has adapted his sources here to reinforce Chauntecler's theme of oracular premonition in dreams and his polite repudiation of Pertelote's view of the "vanite" of dreams.

4. Charles Owen, *Pilgrimage and Storytelling in* The Canterbury Tales: *The Dialectic of Earnest and Game* (Norman, Okla., 1977), p. 137.

5. [Pearsall's target here is the "exegetical tradition" of interpretation which argues that medieval literature should be read according to the same mode of allegorization applied by medieval exegetes to the Bible. Hence, D. W. Robertson, *A Preface to Chaucer* (Princeton, N.J., 1957), argues that when the Nun's Priest's Tale is read allegorically, it is "a story of a priest who falls into the clutches of a friar but escapes just in time when he discovers the essential weakness of the friar's evil nature" (p. 252).]

6. Walter Scheps, "Chaucer's Anti-Fable: *Reductio ad Absurdum* in the Nun's Priest's Tale," *Leeds Studies in English* 4 (1970): 1–10; A. Paul Shallers, "The Nun's Priest's Tale: An Ironic Exemplum," *ELH* 42 (1975): 319–37.

7. Derek Brewer, "What Is the Nun's Priest's Tale Really About?" in *Travaux et Mémoires de l'U.E.R des Lettres et Sciences Humaines de l'Université de Limoges* (Limoges, 1979), p. 22.

8. E. T. Donaldson, *Chaucer's Poetry: An Anthology for the Modern Reader* (New York, 1958), p. 942:

[The rhetorical mode of expression may be said to consist in using language in such a way as to bring about certain preferred interpretations. Compare, for example, an apparently bare statement, "The sun sets," with the rhetorical statement, "The Sun drove his chariot beyond the waters of the western seas." To the ancient mind the last statement would suggest a particular kind of order and meaning in the universe—in other words, a cosmos. This piece of rhetoric was the ancient man's way of reassuring himself that chaos would not come again with the setting of the sun. Today we probably prefer the simplicity of the first statement. Yet "The sun sets" has its residue of rhetoric: we know that the sun does not set but only seems to. We accept this inaccurate and quite rhetorical statement because we are reluctant, even when we know better, to displace ourselves from our inherited position at the center of creation. Rhetoric still stands between us and the fear of something which, even if it is not chaos, is disconcerting. It follows that rhetoric in this sense is something more than language of adornment. It is, in fact, a powerful weapon of survival in a vast and alien universe. In our own time, as in the Middle Ages and in the Age of Homer, rhetoric has served to satisfy man's need for security and to provide a sense of the importance of his own existence and of the whole human enterprise.]

The Nun's Priest's Metamorphosis of Scholastic Discourse

JIM RHODES

❖   ❖   ❖

IN HIS TALE, the Nun's Priest suspends his narrative in order to address a specific theological problem that arises within it. In the familiar and oft-cited passage on free will and predestination (3215–50), theological and literary interests converge on the meaning of philosophical truth. The passage opens with the Nun's Priest wondering if Chauntecleer is destined to perish in the jaws of the fox because whatever God foresees "moot nedes bee," a view he immediately qualifies by adding the comment, "After the opinioun of certein clerkis." The earlier debate between Chauntecleer and Pertelote over the meaning of dreams nicely anticipates and parodies these clerkly debates in their inflexibility and their self-canceling appeals to authority and precedent. Through the parody, the Nun's Priest puts the reader on the alert to his own artful manipulation of language and intellectual distance from the emotions of this debate. When he turns to the aforementioned clerks for an authoritative resolution to the question of Chauntecleer's freedom, he encounters a bewildering welter of opinion:

> Witnesse on hym that any parfit clerk is,
> That in scole is greet altercacioun

> In this mateere, and greet disputisoun,
> And hath been of an hundred thousand men.
>
> (3236–39)

The multiplicity of opinion, only slightly exaggerated, not only attests to the instability of authoritative discourse, it also points to the level of disagreement over the technical vocabulary shared by the clerks. The "mateere" alluded to by the Nun's Priest is justification, which has been described as the single most important issue in the fourteenth century, particularly as it pertains to a theology of reconciliation between God and this world.[1] It had both political and pastoral consequences and it appealed to all levels of fourteenth-century society, from the learned to the "lewed," so much so that we find it debated even among chickens! This is not to make light of the subject or the disputants; rather, in having Chauntecleer and Pertelote discuss fortune, the prophetic power of dreams, and God's justice, the Nun's Priest acknowledges how meaningful these issues are to ordinary individuals. The topic of free will attracted so many lay disputants that Ockham is said to have remarked that "laymen and old women" were poised to challenge theologians in open debate.[2]

To avoid further confusion and for the sake of convenience, I have divided the dominant fourteenth-century views on justification, future contingents, and God's foreknowledge into two main camps, with the understanding that there were innumerable divisions within them. On one side were the traditionalists, like Bradwardine, who followed Augustinian teaching to the effect that God's foreknowledge was his predestination and that human beings could not earn their own salvation or acquire moral virtue prior to grace. In the other camp were the "moderns," sometimes called semi-Pelagians, who argued against philosophical necessitarianism and emphasized instead the moral autonomy of human beings and their capacity to be virtuous *ex puris naturalibus*.[3] The moderns stressed a human being's capacity " 'to do what is in him' (*facere quod in se est*) in order to live well and earn salvation."[4] To offset Augustine's view of predestination and his emphasis on human weakness, the moderns held that individuals were responsible for their salvation, making the event human-centered as well as God-centered. In Ockham's words, human freedom of the will, or liberty, is the basis of human dignity and is the font of moral goodness. Being held responsible for his acts is what makes him deserving of salvation.[5]

The Nun's Priest, who talks himself into as well as out of all kinds of philosophical and theological difficulties, declares his frustration with the utterly intractable nature of this problem: "But I ne kan nat bulte it to the bren, / As kan the holy doctour Augustyn, / Or Boece, or the Bisshop Bradwardyn" (3240–42). The passage may mean that the Nun's Priest defers to the authority of the learned doctors and the bishop, or it may mean that he is unable to rise to the level of their discourse in his effort to arrive at some conclusion. The collective authority of Boethius, Augustine, and Bradwardine, while still substantial and dominant, was undergoing revision in the fourteenth century, particularly in the area of justification, and what the Nun's Priest may be saying has more to do with his impatience with formal theological discourse than with personal incompetence or an inability to penetrate the scholastic language that frames the debate.[6] He seems poised in fact to offer his own critique of scholastic discourse.

For one thing, the Nun's Priest proves he is well versed in the terms of the debate—his summation of Boethius's idea of conditional necessity is as lucid as it is succinct—so when he tells us that he "kan nat bulte it to the bren," he is saying that the problem with language and theological discourse in the fourteenth century makes the whole project of separating fruit from chaff problematical. What theology formerly was able to do, to get at a final or absolute truth, it no longer may be able to do with certainty. He is not denying the existence of truth; rather, like his creator, Chaucer, he is reluctant to make any authoritative claims about the nature of truth.[7] In the absence of metaphysical certainty there may be no essential "bran" to unhusk. The passage underscores the indeterminate nature of all discourse and the authority of none, including the theological, as it is reflected in the proliferation of schools and the increasing heterogeneity of religious theory.

Exasperated, the Nun's Priest breaks off his philosophical meditation, protesting that he will have nothing further to do with "swich mateere"; his tale is of a cock and nothing more. His cock, of course, has everything to do with "swich mateere" and helps us to understand it better. Bradwardine and Augustine, while on the same side in the debate over justification, do not view human nature in identical ways. Augustine considers human dependence on God's grace to be a consequence of the Fall.[8] Bradwardine attributes it to creatureliness; that is, he finds a fundamental flaw in human nature that has always been there.[9] Returning to his beast fable, to creatureliness, the Nun's Priest manages to keep the debate on nature and freedom open, only now he takes up the issue in the context of a fiction. A literary solution should not be imagined as something that only has consequences or significance within the frame of its fiction. As McAlpine points out, the Nun's Priest's Tale "demonstrates the capacity of fiction to project a vision of human reality however remote a fictional world may be in its particulars from human activity."[10] As a moral tale, the beast fable enables the Nun's Priest to move the debate out of the schools and into the arena of everyday life. In a simple barnyard, which doubles as the Garden of Eden, a royal court, the site of Christ's betrayal, the fall of Troy, and the locus of the Peasants' Revolt, among a host of other human catastrophes reminiscent of the Monk's Tale, the Nun's Priest reimagines the broad sweep of history from a bird's-eye view.

Ironically, the Nun's Priest is not "free" to select the topic for his own tale; he is bound by a conditional necessity arising from the Host's disappointment with the Monk's performance:

> . . . this Monk he clappeth lowde.
> He spak how Fortune covered with a clowde
> I noot nevere what; and als of a tragedie
> Right now ye herde, and, pardee, no remedie
> It is for to biwaille ne compleyne
> That that is doon, and als it is a peyne,
> As ye han seyd, to heere of hevyness.
>
> (2781–87)

For all of his lack of finesse and sophistication, the Host displays an intuitive grasp of the suppressed subject of the Monk's Tale: God's hiddenness and the absence of a "remedie" for human fallenness. He expects the Nun's Priest to provide that remedy, if only in the form of comic relief ("Telle us swich thyng as may oure hertes glade") from the Monk's lugubrious narrative. The discussion of free will and destiny in the middle of the Nun's Priest's Tale is no digression or personal indulgence, then; it is an integral part of his answer to the Monk, who has created the impression of a remote and retributive will at work in the universe whose lessons in justice are uneven and imperfect. . . .

The argument against the Monk's Tale, aside from its being too repetitive, has been that his vision is too dark and unrelenting. His stories, Donald Howard says, "present a hopeless world in which man is powerless and the way he tells them reveals his own moral chaos."[11] The Monk's celebrated pessimism may be less a flawed personal vision and more an instance of the theological crisis that coincided with a decline in monastic idealism. As one who "heeld after the newe world the space," the Monk may be experimenting with the theological approach of the "moderns" and entertaining the consequences that ensue from a *deus absconditus*, a God whose acts or motives are hidden from or obscure to human understanding. The more one posits an omnipotent God whose being is unknown, as the moderns did, the more one runs the risk of envisioning a world made exclusively for God in which human beings are in exile and cannot feel at home. Chaucer's Monk is, in several respects, himself homeless. Technically, he remains inside the narrow world of the cloister while habitually journeying outside, unwilling—or no longer able—to abandon the world or the curiosity the world arouses in him. Gerhart B. Ladner informs us that the word *monk,* derived though it is from the Greek word for "sole," does not refer to a monk's solitary life as much as it does to his rejection of all divisiveness and to the perfect single-mindedness of his devotion to God. Chaucer's Monk lacks this unity, making him a kind of *alienus,* a term Ladner associates with "confusion," or the sterile mind of someone not disposed to the order of the right life.[12] Chaucer's Monk appears not to have abandoned altogether his pursuit of holiness ("He yaf nat of that text a pulled hen / That seith that hunters ben nat hooly men") or of truth. He simply no longer expects to find it exclusively in withdrawal from this world. . . . To his credit, the Monk displays none of the hauteur of the Friar and none of the Friar's intellectual disdain toward the likes of the Wife of Bath or the Summoner. However unsuccessful his tale, the Monk's willingness to discuss a philosophical problem in the vernacular does indicate a desire both to break out of the circularity of his argument and to enter the play space of the pilgrimage more wholeheartedly.

   In the person of the Monk, Chaucer has given us a large and expansive figure who has an insatiable appetite for this life and for earthly and physical activity, reflected in the pride he takes in the care of his horses, in sumptuously feeding and clothing himself, and in hunting for game. With the exception of the Wife of Bath, no pilgrim evinces as much enthusiasm as he, at least initially, for telling stories: "I will doon al my diligence, / As fer as sowneth into honestee, / To telle yow a tale, or two, or three" (1966–68). One of the puzzles and disappointments of the Monk's Tale, which stands in the way of his rehabilitation as a narrator, is the absence in his tale of the enthusiasm for literature that he evinces in the General Prologue and in the prologue to his tale. To tell or to teach appears to be his dilemma. His fondness for the exemplum or the moral lesson that can be extracted from it undercuts the impulse of his fictionalizing—evident in the Sampson, Zenobia, and Ugolino episodes—to break out into extended narrative. The Monk's lack of "commitment" to the fictional openness of his tale is emblematic of his unwillingness to declare himself in or out of the monastery or his vocation. He will assert no "remedie" to the human condition until he finds an answer to the question "How shal the world be served?" His tale might best be approached, then, as a kind of intellectual experiment in which he chooses to look at human beings in the light of eschatological disappointment, in their distance from God, and in relationship to whatever consequences obtain from the fact of God's hiddenness or unknowability. Erich Auerbach has pointed out that there was a disposition in the fourteenth century "to free the human emotions from the religious frame, to consider the human tragedy as an absolute, independent of Christ's passion," and this may be what the Monk is doing in his tale.[13] The story of Adam ably illustrates the limits of the Monk's style and vision.

Adam is the paradigmatic "hero" of the Monk's Tale, the figure who brings out all the ambivalence in the Monk and in his tale. First, he affirms the uniqueness of Adam's creation in the image of God: "in the feeld of Damyssene, / With Goddes owene fynger wroght was he" (2007–8). Adam enjoyed the highest degree of dignity of any worldly man in part because he was not "bigetin of mannes sperme unclene," a direct reference to Augustine's idea of how Original Sin is transmitted from generation to generation, which accounts for the weakened nature of Adam's descendants. Adam's Fall, or sin, appears intellectual rather than sexual (Eve is conspicuously absent from the account), because he attributes Adam's Fall to his "mysgovernaunce," which could suggest an inability to control one's sexual appetites but has a stronger sense of Adam's failure to manage his estate properly. The Monk, who takes pride in his management of the monastic property, takes the idea of human responsibility for the created world seriously, a view consistent with the covenantal theology of the moderns. This is intimately connected to the idea of a "remedy" for the Fall, a theme central to . . . the widow's management of her farm in the Nun's Priest's Tale. Adam's Fall "out of [his] hye prosperitee / To labour, and to helle, and to meschaunce" shows the loss of status and dignity suffered by humankind. For the Monk, what now obtains in place of order is mischance, or misfortune, and his gallery of portraits in its disorder brings attention to our plight as contingent beings in a contingent world. Fallenness makes it difficult for the Monk to affirm that human beings have been redeemed or brought back to their original state of dignity. But the Monk does not choose silence or despair as his final response, at least not yet.

The Monk's Adam is like Dante's Adam; his *humanitas* has been separated from his *Christianitas*, and the Monk endeavors to absolve him of his sin in a nonsacramental way, that is, to search for a way for human beings to take possession of their own (historical) nature. The Monk doggedly calls up the past to work it through further, mixing together as he goes along biblical, classical, and mythological figures whose past example may cast new light on present experience. In the course of his narrative the Monk comes across as a kind of pragmatic humanist trapped within a theological vocabulary that has tried to reduce all of human experience to a single central meaning that began with Adam and repeats itself endlessly. To escape, the Monk tries to narrate himself out of a closed system. He shifts from history to story, a medium more open to alternative readings. He does not push his point to a nihilistic end, as Howard fears; he eludes that abyss by adopting a rigidly monological form that forestalls closure by making repetition its hidden subject.

Although the Monk's narrative does not openly show the continuity between the Creation and the Incarnation or the recovery of a christological
dignity inherent in human nature, Richard Neuse has shown that this Monk
has read, and internalized, Dante, which means that he knows the redemption is always implicit because each of the examples he provides represents another Adam—or another Christ—who undergoes his or her agonal struggle
to be. Without denying the horrors of this life or the absence of God from human affairs, the Monk affirms, specifically in the Ugolino and Croesus
episodes, that the human capacity for suffering does bring out in human nature the image of Christ or that which is regenerative.[14]

Neuse's efforts to rehabilitate the Monk and his theological outlook are persuasive and long overdue. It is time we viewed the Monk as a more sympathetic
figure who is saying in his own way that he too cannot "bulte it to the bren." It is
with that in mind that we should receive his last words, "I have no lust to pleye."
The Monk has not lost interest in theology nor in tale telling; he simply has
not found through his recitation a way to combine the two discourses or to rec-
oncile their differences, any more than he can decide where he belongs, in the
monastery or in this world, so his chapel bells accompany him wherever he goes.

If the Monk does not complete the movement from Adam to Christ in his
narrative, the Nun's Priest finishes the story by showing exactly what the Incarnation has meant to human nature and human history. In contrast to the
vast world of the Monk's Tale, the Nun's Priest places us in the enclosed,
present-day world of an English dairy farm, as if to say that the drama of life
occurs in the most humble of circumstances as well as in the exalted. Adam's
"feeld of Damyssene" has been turned into an ordinary barnyard and his labor
into the domestic economy of a humble widow who has learned how to make
herself at home in this world:

> This wydwe, of which I telle yow my tale,
> Syn thilke day that she was last a wyf,
> In pacience ladde a ful symple lyf,
> For litel was hir catel and hir rente.
> By housbondrie of swich as God hire sente
> She foond hirself and eek hir doghtren two.
>
> (2824–28)

If the widow is the subject of his tale, then the dominant theme is one of self-
sufficiency, of her ability to provide for herself and her daughters from what is
available to her in her own yard. The catchword in this passage is "housbon-
drie," which signifies both the widow's judicious use of her resources—her

"governance"—and her marriage to God, with the sly suggestion, in the wake of the Wife of Bath, that Christ is the model for all husbands (see the Wife's appeal to Christ at tale's end, "and Jhesu Crist us sende / Housbondes meeke, yonge, and fressh abedde, / And grace t'overbyde hem that we wedde"). Husbandry functions in the tale as a practical application of the nominalist idea of "doing what is in one." If the widow functions as a metaphor for the church in the fourteenth century, as critics have claimed, then the Nun's Priest gives priority to its pastoral role and apostolic simplicity over its episcopal hierarchy and scholastic learning. Both she and the church serve God by serving this world. As the church in the world, the widow need not get entangled in debates over human freedom and God's powers. Those squabbles are consigned to the rhetors in her hen house!

Although the widow herself may lead something of a monastic existence, once we leave her black-and-white world and enter the technicolor world of the chickens, we are treated to the vibrancy and eroticism of this little world of hers. Chickens prove to be an excellent choice for the Nun's Priest's fable because they cannot fly very high—although Chauntecleer manages to fly just high enough—thus keeping the theological discourse well grounded. If traditional Christian theology is Platonist insofar as it seeks to transpose the essence of human beings out of daily life, Chauntecleer and Pertelote call us back to our origins in nature. Gregory of Nyssa believed Adam, not God, was the inventor of language.[15] Before the Fall from grace, Adam was the name giver, and by giving names to things he elevated their status, gave dignity to them, and redeemed them from mute anonymity.[16] By giving his chickens names, a voice, and subjectivity ("For thilke tyme, as I have understonde, / Beestes and briddes koude speke and synge")—the sheep named Malle sets off the anonymity of the widow—the Nun's Priest "humanizes" or anthropomorphizes them to remind us of what we are capable of *ex puris naturalibus*.

Chauntecleer's understanding of time, for example, "Wel siker was his crowyng in his logge / Than is a clokke or any abbey orlogge," places him squarely in the natural rhythm of life on earth. The analogy between his inner faculty and the abbey clock is one of a series of gestures (another is "His voys was murier than the murie orgon / On masse-dayes that in the chirche gon") that conflate the natural with the spiritual; that is, it collapses the presumed hierarchy that separates the two and infuses the natural order with spirit. Through such analogies, the Nun's Priest restores dignity to natural faculties that orient us to this world; he makes the instincts, or animal nature, a fundamental component of that which is in us.

The most distinguishing of these faculties is the power of language, which originally bound the whole of nature together and which, in this story, is the cause of Chauntecleer's fall. When he succumbs to the flattery of the fox, we see the triumph of language over instinct. Language is also the means to his rise or redemption. Because human beings are not deprived of the power of language—or tale telling—the Fall is not the disaster that leaves us victims to "meschaunce." Human beings once were knowers in the same language that God was the Creator.[17] After the Fall this immediate link was lost and diffused into a multitude of tongues, although the connection can be dimly perceived: "The pure language of names is the 'origin' that has become the 'goal,' inasmuch as its affinity to the divine language of creation lends it the greatest proximity to a state of redemption."[18]

In making Chauntecleer and Pertelote stand-ins for Adam and Eve, the Nun's Priest brings us back to the Garden of Eden not to reenact the Fall, but to resee it or to reinterpret it through the lens of the Incarnation, that is, to present us with an image of *animalitas* striving for union with *rationalitas*. He begins his work of redemption with what appears to be Chauntecleer's outrageous translation of "*In principio* / *Mulier est hominis confusio*," as "Womman is mannes joye and al his blis." If this is intended as a joke, it is not at all clear on whom or for whom the joke is made, women or clerks.[19] Most likely it is a comment on the way clerks interpret texts as they apply to women. The "truth" lies in the interpretation, in the fundamental difference that exists between the authoritative, "clerkly" language of Latin and the English or vernacular version which is always an interpretation as well as a translation and which asserts its own truth or version of reality. Theologically, the translation possesses its own logic, in part because the phrase *in principio*, a medieval commonplace, links the story of Adam's creation in Genesis with the story of Christ's birth in the Gospel of John. The transition is also from Eve to Mary: humankind must experience the Fall and pass through "confusion" in order to know what was true *in principio*, that Adam's creation and Fall contain the seeds of Christ's birth, a point conspicuously absent from the Monk's narrative, but one the Nun's Priest says cannot be omitted from human history or human dignity.

The Nun's Priest's manipulation of the language of this passage provides us with an object lesson that goes to the heart of the language crisis. Shortly after Chauntecleer's mistranslation, the Nun's Priest stages another of his narrative asides. In what may be his most effective defense of the "chaff," or story in itself, the narrator halts his narrative to isolate the "fruit," or truth, of Chauntecleer's ordeal. He shows us Chauntecleer in the full flower of spring, feeling at one with nature and with Madame Pertelote, his "worldes blis." Suddenly, he is struck by the realization that "For evere the latter ende of joye is wo" (3205). The narrator repeats the point, "God woot that wordly joye is soone ago," then drains it of its meaning by exposing it for the cliché that it has become:

> And if a rethor koude faire endite,
> He in a cronycle saufly myghte it write
> As for a sovereyn notabilitee.
>
> (3207–9)

A "rethor," while friendly to poetry, is someone who is adept at separating the fruit from the chaff, although it is possible the Nun's Priest has in mind here the Monk, who sometimes appears to be unsure of the difference between the fruit and the chaff. Technically, a rhetor was someone who wrote in accordance with the school treatises on rhetoric and, as Robert O. Payne reports, the textbooks that were written by the leading teachers of rhetoric "were usually analyses of the art of writing poetry, and in their titles *rhetorica* and *poetica* were more or less interchangeable words."[20] To the Nun's Priest's "rethor," Chauntecleer's adventure—his flight from the beam and his encounters with Pertelote and with the fox—is all so much chaff to be discarded in favor of a preestablished truth. In this context *saufly* probably means "without risk of error" or "with certainty." Not all human experience is the same, however, or reducible to a theorem that can be copied into one's journal. Chauntecleer does not suffer the same fate as his father; he is able to thwart fate and deliver himself from the jaws of the fox, thus turning his woe to high bliss.

For the rhetor's maxim to stand up, it necessarily has to suppress any number of details, the importance of which can never be determined in a single reading. This would seem to be the Nun's Priest's point when he goes on to say, his tongue firmly lodged in his cheek, that "this storie," his fable, is as "true" as is the book of "Launcelot de Lake, / That wommen hold in ful greet reverence" (3212–13). The allusion to Dante's story of Paolo and Francesca is another example of a joy that is short-lived.[21] The comparison with Dante's story problematizes rather than clarifies the tension between Chauntecleer and Pertelote and makes the rhetor's task of extracting a single truth all the more difficult. As a kind of literary joke in a tale of literary jokes, the Nun's Priest treats Dante the way Dante was received, as someone who was writing theology and not poetry. The real point here is that any number of examples can be adduced to illustrate a maxim or truth, but in applying any category one necessarily substitutes it for the individual or existential experience delineated in the narrative, including materials that might subvert the very lesson deduced by the rhetor. The fable or fiction, conversely, aims to generate an unlimited number of possible meanings, especially those that may have been suppressed by tradition or authority.

One of those truths has to do with Eve or women. The Nun's Priest seems determined to show that woman *is* man's worldly bliss even if she was his confusion. First, he shows us that Chauntecleer's wound is self-inflicted. The mermaid's song, a sign of self-destruction, is sung by Chauntecleer and not by Pertelote. Nor is she reducible to the source of his temptation or to mere animal pride. Pertelote makes it clear she is no polysemous text for Chauntecleer or any clerk to read or misread as he sees fit. She evinces her own autonomy, and she too can do that which is in her. She is at once Eve, Mary, Venus, and the widow. She also has the practical intelligence of the Wife of Bath and uses it to provoke Chauntecleer to question authority, especially theological truth. Like the Wife of Bath's hag, she tries to awaken her husband from his solipsism and to teach him to see her as more than a source of physical or sexual bliss.

If, at first glance, Chauntecleer's generous translation of the Latin passage appears to be a case of willed blindness or the inversion of the proper goods that leads to the Fall, in this tale the Fall is shown to be but a fall into this world. In the theological tradition, Chauntecleer has the choice of heeding his higher nature and resisting the "scarlet reed" about Pertelote's eye, or he can fly from the beams and succumb to his animal appetites, as if these dual aspects are separate natures independent of one another. The Nun's Priest takes into account the inescapability of nature, giving us a Chauntecleer who is free within the limits of that nature. Consequently, Chauntecleer's, if not Adam's, fall is inevitable. He cannot remain on his perch where he can only dream of adventures in this world and where he is beset by desire for Madame Pertelote but is prevented from acting because their "perche is maad so narwe, allas!" No, Chauntecleer must descend into the phenomenal world in order to act out his nature.

Once he flies from the beams, Chauntecleer struggles with the burdens of the past under the guise of fate and destiny and in his struggle discovers his freedom. He awakens from his "dream" in the realization that he is an autonomous being who determines his own fate. When he spies the fox lying in the "wortes," his first impulse is to flee, "For natureelly a beest desireth fle / Fro his contrarie, if he may it see, / Though he never erst hadde seyn it with his ye" (3279–81). Once in the jaws of the fox, Chauntecleer does that which is in him: he transforms himself from Adam to Christ (see the way Chauntecleer is identified with Christ in the closing lines of the poem); he brings from potency to actuality what has been present from the beginning, uniting *animalitas* to *rationalitas*, flesh to word. Chauntecleer's dream, while a necessary aspect of his nature and his link with the divine, was unnecessary for his protection. He did not require any forewarning from God, either to identify his enemy or to flee from him and, to balance this off, he did not need any divine intervention to escape from the fox, however subtle this beast of the field. As he remarks once safely in the tree, "For he that wynketh, whan he sholde see, / Al wilfully, God lat him nevere thee!" (3431–32). Now we can see the debate with Pertelote for what it is—an intellectual exercise, like a scholastic disputation, that without lived experience has only limited value or transferability for us.

Against those theologians in the fourteenth century who placed severe limits on the individual's moral autonomy and his capacity to be virtuous out of his own nature, the Nun's Priest shows that the redeemed body can work in harmony with the will and reason, not just against it. The authentic historical subject, as Martin Heidegger would have it, is the one who is capable of resolutely choosing his past. In anticipation of death, this subject is afforded a glimpse of the connected life which reveals to him that the past is a part of one's life and not simply exterior to it.[22] Through his self-recovery, Chauntecleer restores natural man, *homo animalis*, to his original goodness and dignity. Again, the body, along with the soul and reason, manifests the image and likeness of God.

To redeem time, to deliver his promise to the Host for a "remedy" to the Monk's narrative, the Nun's Priest's Tale shows that there is an experience available to human beings on which a new concept of time can be founded, an experience which Agamben describes as "so essential to human beings that an ancient myth makes it humankind's original home: it is pleasure":

> Adam's seven hours in Paradise are the primary core of all authentic historical experience. For history is not, as the dominant ideology would have it, man's servitude to continuous linear time, but man's liberation from it: the time of history and the *cairos* in which man, by his initiative, grasps favorable opportunity and chooses his own freedom in the moment. . . . True historical materialism does not pursue an empty mirage of continuous progress along infinite linear time, but is ready at any moment to stop time, because it holds the memory that man's original home is pleasure.[23]

Agamben goes on to say that the person who has remembered history as he would remember his original home is the true revolutionary and the true seer. Seated on his perch of his "jade," the Nun's Priest sounds like Agamben's theological revolutionary and visionary. In his tale he has looked back to human origins and fashioned, through language, an image of humanity as redeemed.[24] At the close of his tale, he instructs his listeners to take the fruit and let the chaff be still. As we've seen, for the Nun's Priest, the chaff of history does not disappear with the fruit of interpretation. In his economy of play, *fruit* may derive from a late medieval application of *fruitio*, which was part of a widescale and much-discussed "psychology of enjoyment," as developed by Ockham and others.[25] According to A. S. McGrade, Ockham identifies that enjoyment or pleasure not with *delectatio*, but with a sort of volition he calls *dilectio*, which serves as a first cause in his account of human behavior. *Dilectio* can also be translated as "love." The Latin word for enjoyment is *fruitio*, derived from *fructus*, which, McGrade says, connotes a flourishing of the human spirit or the ultimate fruition of a thing's nature. In the operations of the will and reason, which Ockham holds as our highest and noblest powers, we flourish or fulfill our nature and recover our true home, our dignity.[26]

Acting out our nature brings us to "his heighe blisse," Christ's or Chauntecleer's, whichever one prefers.[27] The Nun's Priest has made Chauntecleer in the tree synonymous with Christ on the cross,[28] and he has made the sexual joy experienced by Chauntecleer, "Hym deigned nat to sette his foote to grounde" (3181), interchangeable with the perfect happiness and joy of heaven. Forging a link of identity between Chauntecleer and Christ through his fiction, the Nun's Priest makes bliss predicable of a this-worldly joy and shows that the erotic can be constitutive of the redemptive.

Finally, many readers regard the Nun's Priest's Tale as Chaucer's *ars poetica*, a tale about the act and art of storytelling itself. As such it stands up to the Parson's critique at the end of *The Canterbury Tales* on the limits of fiction as a medium of truth. In his prologue, the Parson invokes the authority of St. Paul to support his rejection not only of fable but also of "all personal speaking that does not confront, in the sacramental language of penance, the sinfulness of the human condition":[29]

> Thou getest fable noon ytoold for me;
> For Paul, that writeth unto Thymothee,
> Repreveth hem that weyven soothfastnesse,
> And tellen fables and swich wrecchednesse.
> Why sholde I sowen draf out of my fest,
> When I may sowen whete, if that me lest?
> (31–36)

As if to avoid the moral ambiguity of the Nun's Priest's Tale, the Parson refuses to tell any fable at all. He issues his admonition to the pilgrims at the outset of his tale as his way of warning them not to mistake the pleasure and amusement of the tale-telling game for the spiritual values of the pilgrimage itself. For the Parson, the distinction between poetry and theology is fixed;

truth, or "soothefastnesse," does not abide in fables—it resides in Scripture as the only sure path to salvation. The Nun's Priest counters the Parson's invocation of St. Paul with his own citation from Paul: "al that writen is, / To oure doctrine it is ywrite, ywis" (3441–42).[30]

As usual, the Host keeps us grounded in the world of the poem, and he sorts through the fruit and chaff of this debate. After giving the Parson the consent of the company to "enden in som vertuous sentence," he cautions the Parson "Beth fructuous, and that in litel space," which is an echo of the Nun's Priest's "fruit," or *fruitio*. Chaucer's poem accommodates the pleasure or enjoyment each pilgrim-teller may derive from his or her text, regardless of its form or content. For the Parson, the Christian or pilgrim flourishes or gains the celestial Jerusalem by the terms of his tale: confession, penance, and satisfaction. The Parson can say unself-consciously that he will tell a "merry" tale, one that promises "pleasaunce leefful." But what is appropriate and desirable to the pilgrim near the goal may not meet the needs of the *viator* in the middle of his journey, who may have a need for narratives that orient him toward this world, such as the Nun's Priest's fable.

The Canterbury Tales survives the solemnizing judgment by the Parson of its fiction, just as the Nun's Priest's Tale overcomes any attempt by a "rethor" to reduce its meaning to a moral function. The integration of the purely fictional world of the animals with the presumed "real" world of the widow and her daughters serves as an emblem of Chaucer's poetic vision. With the flight of the fox and its daring analogy to the Peasants' Revolt, we are abruptly transported back into the black-and-white world of the widow, a peasant herself, who enlists the aid of all the animals as well as the workers on her farm to rout the fox and rescue Chauntecleer. It's as if the whole of nature rises up to offset the depredations of the fox. The "hideous noise" (3393) of the peasants as "they skriked and they howped" threatens to bring the very heavens down. Here we have a perfect example of the chaff of history refusing to be "still"; they demand to be heard, however dissonant or jarring their voices. And the heavens will not fall if Chaucer opens the vast middle of *The Canterbury Tales* to the peasant consciousness of churls like the Miller and the Reeve, or to a wide variety of social discourses which might be suppressed by the authoritative discourse which opens and closes the poem in the epic consciousness of the Knight and the absolutism of the Parson's theological discourse.

If the Nun's Priest's Tale is Chaucer's *ars poetica* and if the language he uses is redemptive, it indicates that in his poetry he is prepared to transform theological discourse, and along with it epic consciousness and tragic consciousness, into the language and experience of everyday life. Because he no longer can "bulte it to the bren," the Nun's Priest's story of Chauntecleer and Pertelote does not arrive at any final resolution to the ambiguities and paradoxes of our experience of time. Nevertheless, in choosing a fiction as his medium, the Nun's Priest's narrative helps us to see that while we were created for this world and this world was created for us, we must live in it in untruth as well as in truth.

Notes

1. Alistair McGrath, *"Iustitia Dei": A History of the Christian Doctrine of Justification* (Cambridge, 1989), p. xi.

2. Margaret Aston, *Lollards and Reformers: Images and Literacy in Late Medieval Religion* (London, 1984), p. 130.

3. For the term *ex puris naturalibus* [Editor's Note: which refers to man "in his natural state," i.e., without the aid of grace], see Heiko Oberman, *The Harvest of Medieval Theology: Gabriel Biel and Late Medieval Nominalism* (Grand Rapids, Mich., 1967), pp. 47–49.

4. Janet Coleman, *Ancient and Medieval Memories: Studies in the Reconstruction of the Past* (Cambridge, 1992), p. 549.

5. Ibid., p. 531.

6. On this point, see Francis Oakley, *The Western Church in the Later Middle Ages* (Ithaca, N.Y., 1979), pp. 132–57.

7. For added discussion on Chaucer's relationship to truth, see Lisa Kiser, *Truth and Textuality in Chaucer's Poetry* (Hanover, N.H., 1991), pp. 1–4.

8. For further discussion of this topic, see Bernard L. Jefferson, *Chaucer and the Consolation of Philosophy of Boethius* (New York, 1916), pp. 72–80. Jefferson states that, unlike Boethius, Bradwardine, Augustine, Jean de Meun, and Dante, Chaucer leaves the question of necessity an open one.

9. See McGrath, *"Iustitia Dei,"* p. 141.

10. Monica McAlpine, "The Triumph of Fiction in the Nun's Priest's Tale," in Robert R. Edwards, ed., *Art and Context in Late Medieval English Narrative* (Woodbridge, England, 1994), p. 94.

11. Donald Howard, *The Idea of The Canterbury Tales* (Berkeley, Calif., 1976), p. 281.

12. Gerhart B. Ladner, *"Homo Viator*: Medieval Ideas on Alienation and Order," *Speculum* 42 (1967): 236–39.

13. Erich Auerbach, *Literary Language and Its Public*, trans. Ralph Manheim (Princeton, N.J., 1995), p. 313.

14. Richard Neuse, *Chaucer's Dante: Allegory and Epic Theater in* The Canterbury Tales (Berkeley, Calif., 1991), pp. 157–59.

15. See John Millbank, *The Word Made Strange: Theology, Language, Culture* (Oxford, 1997), pp. 85–86.

16. For a discussion of this point, see Walter Benjamin, "On Language as Such and on the Language of Man," in *Reflections: Essays, Aphorisms, Autobiographical Writings*, trans. Edmund Jephcott, ed. Peter Demetz (New York, 1978), pp. 322–27; see also Richard Wolin, *Walter Benjamin: An Aesthetic of Redemption* (New York, 1982), pp. 39–42; Michael Jennings, *Dialectical Images: Walter Benjamin's Theory of Literary Criticism* (Ithaca, N.Y., 1987), pp. 94–97.

17. See Benjamin, "On Language as Such," p. 323.

18. See Wolin, *Walter Benjamin*, p. 43; see also Benjamin, "On Language as Such," pp. 328–29. Wolin points out that in Benjamin's analysis, literary works of art as well as Scripture "are legitimate objects of the exegetical quest for the key to redemption" (p. 43).

19. Tom Hahn, "Chaucer and Academic Theology," paper presented at the Seventh International Congress of the New Chaucer Society, 6–11 August 1990, University of Kent, Canterbury.

20. Robert O. Payne, "Chaucer and the Art of Rhetoric," in *Companion to Chaucer Studies*, rev. ed., ed. Beryl Rowland (New York, 1979), p. 42.

21. [Editor's Note: Paolo and Francesca are reading about the love affair between Lancelot and Guenevere when they begin their own adulterous affair, as reported in canto 5 of the *Inferno*.] For a pointed discussion of the Lancelot reference, see McAlpine, "Triumph of Fiction," pp. 81–83.

22. See Howard Caygill, "Benjamin, Heidegger, and the Destruction of Tradition," in *Walter Benjamin's Philosophy: Destruction and Experience*, ed. Andrew Benjamin and Peter Osborne (London, 1994), pp. 1–31, esp. 17.

23. Giorgio Agamben, *Infancy and History: Essays on the Destruction of Experience*, trans. Liz Heron (New York, 1993), pp. 104–5.

24. For further discussion of this point, see David Williams, The Canterbury Tales: *A Literary Pilgrimage* (Boston, 1987), pp. 88–100.

25. See A. S. McGrade, "Ockham on Enjoyment: Towards an Understanding of Fourteenth-Century Philosophy and Psychology," *Review of Metaphysics* 33 (1981): 706–28. See also his "Enjoyment at Oxford after Ockham: Philosophy, Psychology and the Love of God," in Anne Hudson and M. J. Wilkes, eds., *From Ockham to Wyclif* (Oxford, 1987), pp. 63–88.

26. McGrade, "Ockham on Enjoyment," p. 713. See McGrade's comment in "Enjoyment at Oxford" that Ockham believed that human beings were capable of loving God by nature, *ex puris naturalibus*, whereas Bradwardine insisted that without grace we can love only ourselves. McGrade goes on to say that the kind of debates being held at Oxford could have provided a framework for human understanding which poets and others could have utilized in concrete ways, both in understanding how poetry itself

affects us and in understanding or depicting the behavior of actual fictional characters (p. 86).

27. For *bliss*, see Norman Davis, Douglas Gray, Patricia Ingham, and Anne Wallace-Hadrill, eds., *A Chaucer Glossary* (Oxford, 1979), p. 16.

28. For a discussion of this point, see Bernard Levy and George R. Adams, "Chauntecleer's Paradise Lost and Regained," *Mediaeval Studies* 29 (1967): 178–92.

29. Lee Patterson, "The Parson's Tale and the Quitting of *The Canterbury Tales*," *Traditio* 34 (1978): 379.

30. For a penetrating analysis of the Nun's Priest's use of the citation from St. Paul and for the retraction, see Peter W. Travis, "Deconstructing Chaucer's Retraction," *Exemplaria* 3 (1991): 135–58.

Further Reading

These two essays present very different views of the Nun's Priest's Tale. For Pearsall, the Nun's Priest doesn't understand the ironies of his own tale (by no means an unprecedented ignorance in *The Canterbury Tales*), while for Rhodes the narrator is a shrewd if playful analyst of complex contemporary theological and philosophical issues. For a reading that agrees with Pearsall's approach, see Marc Pelen, "The Escape of Chaucer's Chauntecleer: A Brief Revaluation," *Chaucer Review* 36 (2002): 329–35. On the other hand, in "Chaucer's Trivial Fox Chase and the Peasants' Revolt of 1381," *Journal of Medieval and Renaissance Studies* 18 (1988): 195–220, Peter Travis argues that the tale derives from—and comments on—the way in which language and literature were studied in the Middle Ages. Another essay that emphasizes the "schoolroom" quality of the tale is Edward Wheatley, "Commentary Displacing Text: The Nun's Priest's Tale and the Scholastic Fable Tradition," *Studies in the Age of Chaucer* 18 (1996): 119–41. The brief allusion to the Rising of 1381 in the tale has occasioned considerable commentary; see discussions by Richard W. Fehrenbacher, "'A Yeerd Enclosed Al About': Literature and History in the Nun's Priest's Tale," *Chaucer Review* 29 (1994): 134–48; Steven Justice, *Writing and Rebellion: England in 1381* (Berkeley, Calif., 1994), pp. 207–31; and Helen Barr, *Socioliterary Practice in Late Medieval England* (Oxford, 2001).

Suggested Reading

The Middle Ages

Barber, Malcolm. *The Two Cities: Medieval Europe, 1050–1320.* 2d ed. London and New York: Routledge, 2004.

Chazan, Robert. *Fashioning Jewish Identity in Medieval Western Christendom.* Cambridge: Cambridge University Press, 2004.

Cook, William R., and Ronald B. Herzman. *The Medieval World View: An Introduction.* New York: Oxford University Press, 1983.

Fossier, Robert, ed. *The Cambridge Illustrated History of the Middle Ages.* Trans. Sarah Hanbury Tenison. 3 vols. Cambridge: Cambridge University Press, 1986–1997.

Huizinga, Johan. *Autumn of the Middle Ages.* Trans. Rodney J. Payton and Ulrich Mammitzsch. Chicago: University of Chicago Press, 1996 [1924].

Jones, Michael, ed. *The New Cambridge Medieval History: Volume 6, c. 1300–c. 1415.* Cambridge: Cambridge University Press, 2000.

Leff, Gordon. *Dissolution of the Medieval Outlook: An Essay on Intellectual and Spiritual Change in the Fourteenth Century.* New York: New York University Press, 1976.

Moore, R. I. *Formation of a Persecuting Society: Power and Deviance in Western Europe, 950–1250.* Oxford: Blackwell, 1987.

Southern, R. W. *The Making of the Middle Ages.* New Haven, Conn.: Yale University Press, 1953.

——. *Western Society and the Church in the Middle Ages.* Harmondsworth, England: Penguin, 1970.

England in the Time of Chaucer

Alexander, Jonathan, and Paul Binski, eds. *Age of Chivalry: Art in Plantagenet England, 1200–1400.* London: Weidenfeld and Nicolson, 1987.

Coss, Peter. *Knight in Medieval England, 1000–1400.* Dover, N.H.: Sutton, 1993.

——. *Lady in Medieval England, 1000–1500.* Gloucestershire, UK: Sutton, 1998.

Gillespie, James L., ed. *The Age of Richard II.* New York: St. Martin's, 1997.

Gillingham, John, and Ralph A. Griffiths. *Medieval Britain: A Very Short Introduction.* Oxford: Oxford University Press, 2000.

Harriss, Gerald L. *Shaping the Nation: England 1360–1461.* Oxford: Clarendon, 2005.

Hilton, Rodney. *Bond Men Made Free: Medieval Peasant Movements and the English Rising of 1381.* London: Temple Smith, 1973.

Keen, Maurice. *English Society in the Later Middle Ages, 1348–1500.* New York: Viking Penguin, 1990.

Macfarlane, Alan. *Marriage and Love in England: Modes of Reproduction, 1300–1840.* New York: Blackwell, 1986.

——. *Origins of English Individualism.* New York: Cambridge University Press, 1979.

Myers, A. R. *England in the Late Middle Ages.* Harmondsworth, England: Penguin, 1966.

Postan, M. M. *Medieval Economy and Society: An Economic History of Britain, 1100–1500.* Berkeley: University of California Press, 1972.

Saul, Nigel, ed. *Oxford Illustrated History of Medieval England.* New York: Oxford University Press, 1997.

Chaucer and *The Canterbury Tales*

Benson, Larry, Jr., gen. ed. *The Riverside Chaucer.* 3d ed. Boston: Houghton-Mifflin, 1987.

Brewer, Derek, ed. *Geoffrey Chaucer: Writers and Their Background.* London: Bell, 1974.

Brown, Peter. *Chaucer at Work: The Making of* The Canterbury Tales. New York: Longman, 1994.

Cooper, Helen. *Oxford Guides to Chaucer:* The Canterbury Tales. 2d ed. Oxford: Oxford University Press, 1996.

David, Alfred. *The Strumpet Muse: Art and Morals in Chaucer's Poetry.* Bloomington: Indiana University Press, 1976.

Dinshaw, Carolyn. *Chaucer's Sexual Poetics*. Madison: University of Wisconsin Press, 1987.

Hirsch, John C. *Chaucer and* The Canterbury Tales*: A Short Introduction*. Malden, Mass.: Blackwell, 2003.

Knight, Stephen. *Geoffrey Chaucer*. Oxford: Blackwell, 1986.

Mann, Jill. *Feminizing Chaucer*. Cambridge: Brewer, 2002.

Muscatine, Charles. *Chaucer and the French Tradition*. Berkeley: University of California Press, 1957.

Patterson, Lee. *Chaucer and the Subject of History*. Madison, Wisc.: University of Wisconsin Press, 1991.

Pearsall, Derek. *The Canterbury Tales*. London: Unwin, 1985.

Phillips, Helen. *Introduction to* The Canterbury Tales*: Reading, Fiction, Context*. New York: St. Martin's, 2000.

Wetherbee, Winthrop. *Geoffrey Chaucer:* The Canterbury Tales. Cambridge: Cambridge University Press, 1990.